D0927966

THE CAMPUS
AND
THE RACIAL CRISIS

THE CAMPUS
AND
THE RACIAL CRISIS

Edited by DAVID C. NICHOLS *and* OLIVE MILLS

AMERICAN COUNCIL ON EDUCATION   ·   *Washington, D.C.*

© 1970 by American Council on Education
One Dupont Circle
Washington, D.C. 20036

Library of Congress Catalog Card No. 78-118851
SBN 8268-1217-1

Printed in the United States of America

Contributors

MORRIS B. ABRAM
President, Brandeis University

CHERYL D. ADAMS
Black Students Union, The George Washington University

JAMES E. ALLEN, JR.
Assistant Secretary for Education, U.S. Department of Health, Education, and Welfare; U.S. Commissioner of Education

ALEXANDER W. ASTIN
Director, Office of Research, American Council on Education

JULIAN BOND
Member, Georgia State Senate

DAVID G. BROWN
Provost and Vice-President for Academic Administration, Drake University

JOHN J. BUDDS
Chairman, Board of Trustees, University of Connecticut

JOSEPH P. COSAND
President, Junior College District of St. Louis

ROBERT D. CROSS
President, Swarthmore College

DOUGLAS F. DOWD
Professor of Economics, Cornell University

THOMAS H. ELIOT
Chancellor, Washington University

HAROLD L. ENARSON
President, Cleveland State University

SANDY ENGLISH
President, Student Bar Association, The American University; Special Assistant to U.S. Senator Mark O. Hatfield

AMITAI ETZIONI
Professor of Sociology, Columbia University

ROBERT H. FINCH
Secretary of Health, Education, and Welfare

Contents

Part Five   From the Federal View

Foreword

IF, AS the eminent black educator and statesman Sir W. Arthur Lewis has asserted, "The trade unions are the black man's greatest enemy," it should be noted also that American higher education is potentially his best friend. Few if any colleges and universities today are deliberately racist, and many of them are making strenuous efforts to offset past neglect and discrimination. This volume shows, however, that the typical campus is caught up in the racial crisis of our society. Some campuses, in fact, have become caldrons where ethnic issues are brought to a boil.

As is pointed out in the introductory section of this book, the purpose of the American Council on Education's 1969 Annual Meeting was to get a better understanding of problems relating to the racial crisis on the campus and to further the kinds of changes needed to effect improvements. The Council's annual meetings provide forums to bring together opinion leaders to discuss and debate the great educational issues of the time, and the theme chosen for 1969 was, and still is, one of deep concern to all Americans.

To provide a background of information and insight, we invited a number of individuals to prepare papers. With several exceptions, all of the commentaries appearing here were written for the meeting that took place last fall in Washington. Almost two thousand persons were there, and we expect that thousands more will read some or all of the observations and views set forth in print in *The Campus and the Racial Crisis*.

It will be noted that the authors include students, faculty members, administrators, trustees, public officials, and others who are concerned with the current crisis. Their vantage points and perceptions differ markedly, but all of them share a sense of involvement and a desire to find constructive solutions. The fact that most of the authors are participants in, as well as observers of, what is happening on campuses all over the nation lends added interest and significance to what they have to say. Personally and for the Council, I want to thank them for their contributions to this volume.

My hope is that their comments will be widely read and that this book will itself be a contribution to the resolution of still unsettled issues in American society and its institutions of higher education.

LOGAN WILSON, *President*
American Council on Education

March 23, 1970

Preface

THE CONTRIBUTIONS to this volume were, with three exceptions, first prepared for the Annual Meeting of the American Council, held in Washington, D.C., in October 1969. The topic for those discussions gives this book its title.

The views expressed range widely, for the vantage points of the contributors also range widely: the immediate constituents of institutions of higher education—faculty, students and recent graduates, trustees, administrators; members of the black community, both on and off the campus; representatives of the Federal government; persons from other sectors of the society with deep concern for the two elements that were conjoined for consideration.

The general sessions of the meeting were addressed by the Honorable Robert H. Finch, Logan Wilson, T. E. McKinney, Jr., the Honorable James E. Allen, Jr., and Julian Bond. Eight papers—by W. Todd Furniss, Samuel D. Proctor, Lincoln Gordon, Thomas H. Eliot, Alexander Astin, David G. Brown, Amitai Etzioni, and Harold L. Enarson—were distributed in paperback form prior to the meeting to serve as background for those planning to attend the sessions. The commentators added critical analyses of the papers and other views of the subjects presented.

Two papers are reprinted here from other sources because of their unusual appropriateness to this volume: Sir Arthur Lewis' contribution is taken from *University: A Princeton Quarterly,* Spring 1969 issue, and the paper by Paul E. Wisdom and Kenneth A. Shaw first appeared in the *Educational Record* for Fall 1969. The paper prepared by the senior editor is intended as an overview and a setting for the discussions.

Both the meeting and this volume owe much to the members of the Council's Board of Directors and its executive staff for their conceptions of the topics and suggestions for formulating the discussions. Special acknowledgment is owed to Harry A. Marmion, then of the Council staff, who conceived the idea and carried forward preparation of the materials.

To all the authors, the Council expresses its gratitude for their contributions to the meeting and to this volume.

D.C.N. and O.M.

PART ONE

PERSPECTIVES

The Coming of Crisis

DAVID C. NICHOLS

THE TOPIC of the 1969 Annual Meeting of the American Council on Education affirmed that there is a racial crisis on the campus and that it has come about as part of the crisis in the larger society. This being so, it is worthwhile and fitting to note, at decade's end, the themes of the other meetings: "Integrity of Educational Purpose," 1960; "The Future Pattern of Higher Education and the Council's Role," 1961; "Higher Education and the Federal Government: Programs and Problems," 1962; "National Commitments and Institutional Responsibilities," 1963; "Autonomy and Interdependence: Emerging Systems in Higher Education," 1964; "The Student in Higher Education," 1965; "Improving College Teaching," 1966; "Whose Goals for American Higher Education?" 1967; and "The Future Academic Community: Continuity and Change," 1968.

While, with one or two exceptions, these are issues of comparable, considerable, and growing magnitude, on rereading the list one gains, I believe, the strong impression that the seeds of the campus crisis were evident in the very beginning, when the 1960 meeting speaks to the protection of educational integrity, and that the crisis grows larger until it erupts finally before our eyes and is given its name late in the decade. I am not implying any blindness to what was taking place; rather, I would stress the apparent inevitability of the crisis, given the exclusive traditions of higher education, on the one hand, and its increasing importance to individuals and society, on the other. Furthermore, it seems certain that the campus crisis would have occurred sooner or later, without any reference to racial issues. The demands of black people, beyond their intrinsic merit, gave focus to widespread frustrations and served as one of the principal thrusts against established order.

The racial crisis is part of a greater and more basic crisis of values and ideologies gathering momentum in American society and bringing turbulence to the college campus. Because of the pervasive nature of the conflicts within the society at large, in retrospect it is astonishing that the coming of crisis was but dimly perceived. On their part the universities, hit early

3

by organized protest, responded quickly to limited demands, but those demands that called for basic structural change in the universities were received with considerable dismay. Although the university is at least as responsive to change as other social institutions, this time the university was particularly vulnerable because it was specifically being attacked for doing efficiently and well those things that previous generations had insisted it do. Ironically, some of the university's great strengths had become great weaknesses in the eyes of its new critics.

Clark Kerr was by no means alone when, in 1963, he gave a basically optimistic report on the condition of the great American university, that accretion of the best models of the Western world brought to unprecedented heights. In *The Uses of the University,* Kerr's own institution was the prototype, the very model of a modern multiversity, and college administrators almost everywhere strove mightily to emulate it. Virtually all of them had argued repeatedly and successfully before their legislators or benefactors that since the university had become a central factor in the nation's economic and social development, it deserved a much larger share of public and private aid to keep the "knowledge industry" growing. Few among the public at that time doubted the validity of a message that promised more and better education for the children of Americans who had themselves learned how very much education means to success in life.

John F. Kennedy, championing the cause of education in the public investment sense, had resolved to make massive Federal aid available to education. He had also resolved to do something about poverty in a direct and immediate way, through other massive forms of social welfare legislation, but education too was to be part of the strategy for increasing national growth and reducing the number of the poor. With combined attacks on the two fronts of ignorance and poverty, most of America's ills would be cured; so it was said, heard, hoped, and sometimes believed. America was rich enough to do it. To all but a handful of Americans, Vietnam was then a little-known speck ten thousand miles around the globe. For Establishment liberals, these were happy times; it was Camelot. The universities were heartened: they would not only have a variety of aids to support ongoing responsibilities, but many could also join the crusade against poverty. The university—the key agent in the knowledge industry—seemed destined to become the organizing point for a New Frontier, a fourth branch of government, a research and development center for the good of the entire society.

The first and staggering blow to this design came in the fall of 1963.

The tragedy in Dallas shocked and saddened a populace which, partly out of memorial tribute, gladly supported Lyndon Johnson's unprecedented legislative achievements in education. More than fifty education bills were enacted in the next four years, beginning with the massive Elementary and Secondary Education Act and concluding with the Higher Education Amendments of 1968. Despite this prodigious effort, which pumped billions of new dollars into America's educational system and more billions into antipoverty programs, a malaise grew which seemed beyond the reach of money.

Beginning in the South, strategies of nonviolent protest for civil rights provoked violence which in turn brought about a polarization of public opinion. The crisis mounted with the escalation of an increasingly unpopular war, with unrest in the cities which turned to widespread rioting, and with the assassinations of two more men who best commanded the respect of the black, the young, and the poor. In the face of the growing demands for equal opportunity, justice, jobs, housing, and an end to the war, the legislative largess for education, which in more stable times would have seemed to the public a windfall, more nearly resembled an extravagance; some even perceived this legislative beneficence to be a diversionary tactic spearheaded by the Establishment to prevent radical social change.

The focal point of domestic revolt remained in the central cities. But once the surface outrage of urban blacks had been spent in burning and looting, it became clear that the price of the violence was exacted of black people themselves, with only minimal social change produced. Constricted by limited job and housing opportunities, the urban low-income blacks had nowhere to go but back into a burned-out ghetto. A massive rebuilding of the cities would have to await a public will to proceed; so long as the war consumed the tax dollar and the silent majority remained unmoved in the absence of leadership, such talk was futile political rhetoric. And so action shifted to the campus.

Revolt on the campus was part of the same phenomenon, triggered by the issues of free speech and fair process, but motivated by the civil rights movement, which gave it nobler calling. If student rebels began to think of themselves as the "niggers of higher education," it was not without cause on many campuses where the hegemony of faculty-administration was complete and to rebel against it might lead to expulsion, which in turn carried a further risk as the draft calls escalated and nine out of ten drafted were sent to the infantry in Vietnam. But on another symbolic level there was a growing existential motivation among students, rooted in the silent generation's Beats who had taken in Sartre and Camus. In the sixties, it occurred to many that the fate of Sisyphus had been visited most harshly upon black people. Richard Wright had pointed the way a few years before when he wrote that "Negro life is [all] life lifted to the heights of pain and pathos, drama and tragedy. The history of the Negro in America is the history of America written in vivid and bloody terms; it is the history of Western man writ small. . . . The Negro is America's metaphor." [1]

The rediscovery of the Negro by student rebels led to their sometime identification with black people as the existential archetype in a hostile civilization. To many students it seemed that America had become an evil presence in the world, a nation projecting a foreign policy with a decidedly pro-white, pro-Western bias. Talk of genocide became loose and virulent. With these students, a small but vocal minority, morally certain about demonstrable uncertainties, how was the university—whose faculties too infrequently could make the dictates of reason more compelling to students than their emotions—to cope? The universities seemingly had been out-maneuvered by students in the field of social criticism, a belief of many students which was reinforced when some of the university teachers most sympathetic to their cause confessed that they had little of value to teach about righting social wrongs. At the same time, empirical evidence was gathered which demonstrated that too little is known about how students learn or whether the curriculum makes very much difference in how much they learn. Three hundred years of experience seemed to have produced disappointingly few certainties about some basic things in which the universities were thought to have particular expertise.

As the decade grew older, colleges increasingly adopted reforms. Institutions began to admit more of the so-called disadvantaged, having acquired new Federal aid for the purpose. Remedial, compensatory, pre-paratory—by whatever euphemism—special programs were provided for students who needed them. Black students were sought through Talent Search and Upward Bound programs, black studies were studied by whites as well as blacks, and equal opportunity among the races for higher education leaped further in one decade than it had come in a century. If the context of the times had not been such as to impose the utmost skepticism upon every attempt at reordering the university, these would have been more widely recognized for what they are: truly historic shifts in higher education. But as the essays and commentaries in this book point out, there is scant satisfaction with those changes that have taken place. Some

[1] Wright, *White Man, Listen!* (New York: Doubleday & Co., 1957), pp. 108–9.

fear that change has devalued the quality of higher education, while others urge its further transformation; almost no one seems content with things as they are.

Though there is recognition that crisis is upon the university and the society, there appears to be little agreement about how far the universities should change in response to it. In these pages the gap between generations and between ideologies, and between the traditionalists and the revolutionaries, is at least as visible as any conflict between the races. If there is one thing to which most would seem to agree, it is that something has gone wrong with the external relationship between the university and society and the internal relationship among students, teachers, and administrative processes. Samuel Proctor notes this point of consensus:

> Today's students, despite some uncalled-for tactics, may be saving universities from becoming a barren colony of sycophants who would soon become the object of contempt for everyone, quoting each other to each other and becoming more and more parasitic on private philanthropy and the tax dollar. Something has really gone wrong when both the blacks, poor and not so poor, and the affluent whites have all decided at the same time that a new relevance must be found on campus.

Of what does this relevance consist? Julian Bond suggests that it does not include the accepted techniques used by the multiversity to impart knowledge when he asks, "What is there beyond four years of compressing all the world's knowledge from lecture notes to the little blue book?" He then affirms that "It must be . . . the development, not just of curriculum, but an ideology suited to extricate man from himself." Others point out that this existential quest for relevance comes at a high price both for institutions and individuals if it means that the best and most gifted among them are forced to expend their resources and energies in mediating the conflicts of interest that inevitably arise when one tries to become all things to all people. Logan Wilson urges that some form of postsecondary education should be available for virtually everybody, but also argues that it would be disastrous to assume that traditional higher education is the model for educating those who are less-gifted academically: "Under the growing pressure on institutions to become all things to all kinds of students and other constituencies, many are in a dilemma that could push them onto a collision course. The collision would occur when the demands of meritocracy and of equalitarianism become irreconcilable." If the papers assembled here are indicative, that collision would appear to be upon us.

In his essay, David G. Brown reminds us of the hard economic realities facing college administrators as they choose among the various strategies of accommodating racial and equalitarian pressures. As the decade ended, increases in the cost of education consumed available resources, and many institutions faced the grim necessity of slashing their budgets and services; none enjoyed a prospect for more than token increases in financial resources. Under budget pressure, how were all the new demands to be met? Few administrators any longer seemed convinced that the end of the war would bring massive amounts of aid to the support of higher education, or, indeed, that massive aid would turn higher education from its collision course. For as the universities seemingly increase their influence over social and occupational upward mobility through their credentialing function, and as Americans begin to perceive higher education as a right and not a privilege, equal educational opportunity has come to mean more than simply admission to higher education. Not only do people demand the opportunity to enter, but they increasingly expect, also, their efforts to be encouraged and rewarded with some measure of success. In a putative equalitarian society, pressures on institutions to guarantee some success for all comers may become relentless.

It is to help assure more equity and success for minority students that the proposals of Alexander W. Astin, Amitai Etzioni, and W. Todd Furniss are set forth. Astin would substitute "potential for change" for academic aptitude as the principal criterion in college admissions. Etzioni would provide more "bridging" education to help compensate for inadequate preparation. Furniss argues that black studies, if designed to relate the rigors of abstraction and the application of theory to real problems, might form a model for the reform of all studies. There is general agreement that much larger numbers of blacks should be enrolled in colleges and universities and that special programs should be provided for any of them, if necessary, to help assure higher levels of achievement. Other contributors document the very real problems universities confront in the face of revolutionary social pressures.

Most of the contributors share, sometimes explicitly, an uneasiness about the future. If there are few optimists here, however, neither are there prophets of doom. Several ask whether the university as we have known it can or should any longer exist, or, more dramatically, whether American civilization as we have known it can survive. But there is respect, throughout, for the liberating qualities of university education and a basic and implicit assumption that present difficulties will be overcome. In a time of neo-romanticism, when most institutions are under fire, there is tacit acknowledgment that despite its faults, the university is at least as relevant and important to the society as it has ever been in the past.

There are few indications that most universities will be radically changed in the immediate future, except as incremental reforms may add up to it. As the authors imply, there obviously will be some change in the balances of power within universities. Students are being compared with consumers who have rights deserving protection; they will be heard. Black studies, in one form or another, will be found in the curriculum. Colleges of liberal arts will, perhaps more than before, help their students to ask teleological questions. Perhaps teaching will gain more importance in the careers of professors. Universities will take more seriously their community responsibilities as neighbor, employer, as a presence in the city; and they will be more circumspect in their participation in defense-related activities, including research. Although no one knows whether the storm is past, it would seem that the university has emerged so far with certain losses, to be sure, but also with certain gains of a self-evaluative nature. Perhaps with qualitative and attitudinal change in the direction of more individualization and democratization, and more mutual respect among its constituents, the idea of the multiversity remains as viable as ever in a society demanding higher and higher education for more and more people.

As before, those students who want to very likely will educate themselves, with help from their friends and professors. Students who want the credentials will gain them through the schools that hold the keys to professional entry. Black and white students alike will sort it all out, despite the system laid out for them, and do their own thing with it for a time, and then do the system's thing as they grow older and perhaps discover the sobering truism that reforming the system is better than destroying it when there are no better alternatives in sight. Some will drop out of the system and learn the art of writing about or painting about experience; they always have. Many will stay in the educational system—the professors and the administrators—and try to change it for the better. To promote constructive change is the purpose of this book.

We Hold These Truths

JULIAN BOND

THE CRISIS in race that exists on the college campus is, of course, only a reflection of a larger, more serious crisis in the country, and indeed throughout the world. The roots of the crisis are as old as the world itself; they involve the continuing failure of the white minority of peoples of this world to share power and wealth with the nonwhite majority. That struggle has been in the streets of every city in this country, both violently and nonviolently. It is a part of the struggle that inspired Fidel Castro to overthrow a dictator in Cuba, and it is the same struggle that is inspiring the patriots of Vietnam to continue—successfully, it seems—their twenty-year-old struggle to resist foreign domination of the homeland.

That it should come to the college campus is not at all unusual; here, after all, are the people who have been told since the day they graduated from high school that the earth is theirs for taking, that they are the inheritors of tomorrow. Who is to blame if they believe it? That it is spreading downward into high schools and even elementary schools is not surprising either. It ought not to be surprising that young people who learned how to organize the poor and powerless in the Mississippi Delta would transfer their expertise to the powerless at Berkeley and Cornell. And it ought not be surprising that race has played a large part in the continuing struggle of man against man.

To tie today's on-campus unrest only to yesterday's off-campus protests is unreal, however. There is a great deal more at stake than that.

Dilemmas of Educational Choice

A great deal has been made by some scholars and pollsters of the difference in the demands of black and white student activists. The whites want revolution, the experts say, while all the blacks want, despite their revolutionary rhetoric, is reform, a chance to bend the established system to their own ends, which are as safe and as ordinary as those shared by the rest of middle-class America.

Therein lies, I think, the conflict present in the black mind on the American campus. The black student is torn between the need for a regular, formal education, part of the socialization process that we are told everyone needs in order to seek an acceptable role in society, and his need to carve out a new education experience, one that is meaningful to him as a black person.

A young girl, a student at Tougaloo College in Mississippi, summed up this feeling when she wrote of her reaction to learning that Tougaloo and Brown University had entered into an educational compact, with Brown acting as Big Brother.

> We argued [she wrote] that Tougaloo could do better, that we did not have to pattern ourselves after Brown or any of the Ivy League schools, that we had a unique opportunity to make Tougaloo a revolutionary institute of learning. We questioned the notion that places like Brown offered a superior education; we felt in fact that they dealt in mis-education. We felt that if schools like Brown had been truly educating their students, then the state of the country and the world would be a lot different.[1]

The dilemma of whether to change the Tougaloos of the world or to get what can be got from the Browns is the continuing one among young blacks. The demand for a black dorm or an Afro-American center is a part of this dilemma. The unscholarly attacks on black educational institutions by scholars who should know better are a part of that dilemma. So the current and future course for those blacks interested in solving—or rather eliminating—the crisis of race is unclear.

The World of Educated and Civilized Man

One has to realize that it is educated and civilized man who has put us where we are today. The rape of Vietnam was not begun by high school dropouts, but by liberally educated men. The pollution of the air and water is not carried out by fools and idiots, but by men educated at the best scientific and technical centers. The ability to shape a society that spends nearly one hundred billions on conquering space and dominating the globe militarily comes from men of genius, not from men whose minds are limited.

Civilized man, or educated man, is supposed to solve his problems in a civilized manner.

But the problems of the twentieth century are so vast that many have quite properly been urged to seek uncivilized solutions to them. These problems include the poisoning of the air and water; the rape of the land; the new colonialization of peoples, both here and abroad; the new impe-

[1] Arverna Adams, in *Wilson Library Bulletin,* September 1968.

rialism practiced by Western democracy, and the continuing struggle of those who have not against those who have.

With the birth, two hundred years ago, of the colossus called the United States, rational and educated men began to believe that civilization stretched to its highest order had begun. Building on a heritage of revolution, expressing a belief in the equality of most, if not all men, this new democracy was to be the highest elevation of man's relations, one to the other, and a new beginning of decency between nations. Civilization, as it was then defined, included imposing limitations on war between nations, encouraging the spread of industrialization, the civilizing of so-called heathen elements, the harnessing of nature for the benefit and pleasure of man. It was believed generally that man's better nature would triumph over his base desire to conquer and rule and make war, and that intellect, reason, and logic would share equally with morality in deciding man's fate.

Of course it has not been so. Man still makes war. He still insists that one group subordinate its wishes and desires to that of another. He still insists on gathering material wealth at the expense of his fellows and his environment. Men and nations have grown arrogant, and the struggle of the twentieth century has continued.

And while the struggle has continued, the university has remained aloof, a center for the study of why man behaves as he does, but never a center for the study of how to make man behave in a civilized manner. Robert M. Hutchins, former chancellor of the University of Chicago, describes the present-day university:

> [It was hoped] it would lead the way to national power and prosperity . . . become the central factory of the knowledge industry, the foundation of our future. [But it became] . . . the national screening device through which individuals were to be put in the proper productive relationship to the national program of power and prosperity.
>   . . . [but] the world has moved too fast for the university. The leaders of the younger generation see that the problem is not to get wealth and power; [nations] have enough of those already. The problem is justice, or what to do with wealth and power. An institution that evidently has little interest in this question cannot command the allegiance of the young.

The Unintended Education

That the allegiance of some of the young is not with the university but with the oppressed and downtrodden is evident. Every continent has seen its young rise up against the evils the university is supposed to teach them how to destroy, and many have risen up against the university itself.

Despite its goal of producing individuals who know their societal relationship to be as managers of the new industrial and technological society, the university has—fortunately but probably against its desires—produced a new crop of people, a group of activists whose current demands on the university will, we may hope, be expanded to include assaults on the foundations of a society which has perverted education to reinforce inequity.

So then it is the entire fabric of education that is being attacked—its purposes, its ends. All that black students have done is allow their demands to be colored by their race.

Why should we not demand amnesty, the young ask, when you have allowed yourselves amnesty for over three hundred years. Why should we negotiate, they ask, when you have received it since you came to power. Why should we not use weapons, when you have used them time and time again against us? Why should we be accused of tearing down the university and having nothing to put in its place, when you have torn down Vietnam and left the ghetto standing?

Why should we not have a black house on campus, the blacks ask, when the Methodists, Episcopalians, Jews, and Catholics often have theirs. Why shouldn't we take over a building and evict the deans; isn't every big city university, in connivance with urban renewal, doing the same thing to entire families on a permanent basis every day? Why should we not learn about ourselves, the blacks ask. Haven't we been made to learn more than we ever wanted to know about you? Why shouldn't any and every black high school graduate be admitted freely to this college, the blacks ask. Aren't they being taught by your graduates, and therefore shouldn't they have learned what it takes to fit in here? Why should Dow Chemical or ROTC be on campus, the students ask. We are not here to learn to make napalm or to learn how to be soldiers. This is not a vocational school for *any* employer, or at least it should not be.

A New Politics for Higher Education

This ought to be, the students say, a center for the shaping of civilized man; a center for the study of, not just why man behaves as he does, but also a center for the study of how to make him behave better.

To do this, the university must rid itself of several old notions. First of all, higher education can no longer be regarded as a privilege for a few, but must be seen as a right for the many. None of the rhetoric of the past several years about an education for everyone really approaches this aim; higher education is still an elitist and largely white preserve in America today. In an age when education itself is being questioned, to permit or even to require that everyone receive a piece of parchment which will establish that he knows what millions of people already know with little profit to mankind will not suffice; it is simply not enough and simply will not do.

What is it then that is lacking? What is there beyond four years of compressing all the world's knowledge from lecture notes to the little blue book? For the blacks, it must be more than Swahili lessons and Afro-American centers, although these have their place. For white universities, it must be more than raiding Southern black schools and taking their most talented faculty and students. For the black school, it must be more than pride in blackness. It must be, for all of these, the development, not just of curriculum, but an ideology suited to extricate man from himself.

A writer in the *Center Magazine* described the schools' failing function:

> Students are encouraged to relinquish their own wills, their freedom of volition; they are taught that value and culture reside outside oneself, and must be acquired from the institutions, and almost everything in their education is designed to discourage them from activity, from the wedding of idea and act. It is almost as if we hoped to discourage them from thought itself, by making ideas so lifeless, so hopeless, that their despair would be enough to make them manipulable and obedient.[2]

While the university may have bred despair, it has not bred obedience. Violence occurs where there is no politics. While there is no politics of race, or rather while there is no antiracist politics, on the university campus, violence—physical and intellectual—will flourish.

Until the university develops a politics or, in better terms perhaps for this gathering, a curriculum and a discipline that stifles war and poverty and racism, until then, the university will be in doubt.

If education is a socializing process, in our society it has prepared white people to continue enjoying privileged traditions and positions, while black people, through it, have been programed for social and economic oblivion. Today's black and white students see this. They see the university nurturing war and directing counterrevolution; they see their professors employed in the Pentagon; they see their presidents serving on commission after commission investigating and recommending last year's solution to the last century's problems; they see the university recruit ghetto students with substandard backgrounds and then submit these students to standards of white middle-class America. They believe, as does the Tougaloo student I quoted from earlier, that

2 Peter Marin, in *Center Magazine,* September 1969.

the task for black students and black Americans is much greater than trying to change white institutions and their white counterparts in the South. The task is to create revolutionary institutes of learning. The act of trying to be a better person, or trying to imagine and create humane institutions is formidable, but we have no other alternative. We must have a prototype from which to build a good society. The point which I make is an old one: that revolution is not only the seizure of power, but is also the building of a society that is qualitatively better than the one we presently live in.[3]

But perhaps what the university's response ought to be in sentiments like that is best expressed in the words of the late Dr. W. E. B. Du Bois, words written almost fifty years ago:

> . . . we believe that the vocation of man in a modern, civilized land includes not only the technique of his actual work but intelligent comprehension of his elementary duties as a father, citizen, maker of public opinion . . . a conservor of the public health, an intelligent follower of moral customs, and one who can appreciate if not partake something of the higher spiritual life of the world. We do not pretend that this can be taught to each individual in school, but it can be put into his social environment, and the more that environment is restricted and curtailed the more emphatic is the demand that . . . [man] shall be trained and trained thoroughly in these matters of human development if he is to share the surrounding civilisation.

Or indeed, if there is to be any civilization at all.

[3] Arverna Adams, op. cit.

Black Power and the American University

W. ARTHUR LEWIS

WHEN A FRIEND suggested that since I had spent all my adult life in black power movements and in universities, I might make some comments on the highly topical subject of black power in the American university, it did not at first seem to be a good idea. Now that I have come to grips with it, I am even more conscious of my folly in tackling so difficult and controversial a subject.

I am also very conscious that my credentials are inadequate, since the black power movements in the countries with which I am familiar differ fundamentally from black power in the United States. My stamping grounds are the West Indies, where I was born, and Africa, where I have worked. But in both those places blacks are the great majority of the people—97 percent in Jamaica, 99 percent in Nigeria. The objective of the political movements was therefore to capture the central legislature and the executive and judicial powers. In the United States, in contrast, blacks are only 11 percent of the population and have neither claim to nor prospect of capturing the Congress, the executive branch, or the Supreme Court for themselves alone. The objectives have to be different, and the strategy must also be different. Comparison between the colonial situation and the position of blacks in America is bound to mislead if it is suggested as a basis for deciding political strategy.

The struggle of the blacks in America is a unique experience, with no parallel in Africa. And since it is unique, the appropriate strategies are likely to be forged only by trial and error. We are all finding the process a great trial, and since our leaders are going off in all directions at once, a great deal of error is also inevitable. I myself, in venturing onto this ground, claim the protection of the First Amendment, but do not aspire to wear the cloak of Papal infallibility.

A reprint, with minor changes, of an article by the same title which appeared in *University: A Princeton Quarterly,* Spring 1969, pp. 8–12. Used with permission. Copyright 1969 by Princeton University.

The goals and tactics of black power in America have to be adjusted to the reality of America. Take the issue of segregation. Everywhere in the black world, except among a small minority of American blacks, the fight against segregation has been in the foreground of black power movements. This goes without saying in countries where blacks are the great majority; yet there are situations where a minority may strengthen itself by temporary self-segregation of a limited kind.

All American minorities have passed through a stage of temporary self-segregation: not just the Afro-Americans. Foreigners speak of the United States as a "melting pot" and it may one day be that; but for the present America is really not a melting pot but a welding shop. It is a country in which many different groups of people live and work together side by side, without coalescing. There are Poles, and Irish, and Chinese, and Jews, and Germans, and many other ethnic groups. And their way of living together is set by the clock; there is integration between seven o'clock in the morning and five o'clock at night, when all mingle and work together in the center of the city, in the banks and factories, department stores and universities. But after five o'clock each ethnic group returns to its own neighborhood. There it has its own separate social life. There Poles do not marry Italians, even though they are both white Catholics. The neighborhood has its own schools, its own little shops, its own doctors, and its own celebrations. Integration by day is accompanied by segregation by night.

It is important to note that this self-segregation is voluntary and not imposed by law. An Italian *can* buy a house in an Irish neighborhood if he wishes to do so, *can* marry an Irish girl, and *can* go to an Irish Catholic church. Many people also insist that this voluntary segregation is only a temporary phase in the acculturation of ethnic groups. They live together until they have found their feet on the American way of life, after which they disperse. The immigrants from Germany and Scandinavia have for the most part already moved out of segregated neighborhoods. The Irish and the Jews are just in the process, and sooner or later the Poles, the Chinese, and even the Afro-Americans may have dispersed. But in the meantime this voluntary self-segregation shelters those who are not yet ready to lose themselves completely in the American mainstream. Other people believe that there will always be cultural pluralism in America, and that this may even be a source of strength. Whether or not they are right about the long run, there is no disputing that voluntary social self-segregation is the current norm.

The black power movement is therefore fully in the American tradition in recognizing that certain neighborhoods are essentially black neighborhoods, where the black politician, the black doctor, the black teacher, the black grocer, and the black clergyman are going to be able to play roles which are not open to them, de facto, in other neighborhoods. Many Southern Negroes claim vigorously that blacks are better off in the South than in the North precisely because the Southern white philosophy has reserved a place for a black middle class in the black neighborhoods—for the black preacher or doctor or grocer.

Essentially, what black power is now saying in the North is that the North too should recognize that the middle-class occupations in the black neighborhoods belong to blacks, who are not permitted to hold such jobs in Italian, Polish, or other ethnic neighborhoods. The issue is phrased in terms of community power—that is to say, of giving to each neighborhood control over its own institutions—but this is tied inextricably to the distribution of middle-class jobs inside the neighborhood. It is unquestionably part of the American tradition that members of each ethnic group should be trained for the middle-class occupations in their neighborhoods, and that, given the training, they should have preference in employment in their own neighborhoods.

This kind of voluntary self-segregation has nothing in common with the compulsory segregation of other countries. An American neighborhood is not a ghetto. A ghetto is an area where members of an ethnic group are forced by law to live, and from which it is a criminal offense to emerge without the license of the oppressing power. This is what apartheid means in the Union of South Africa. An American neighborhood is not a place where members of an ethnic group are required by law to live; they may in the first instance have been forced to live there by circumstances, but it is soon transmuted, ideally, into a place where members of the group *choose* to live, and from which, ideally, anybody can emerge at any time that he wishes to do so. To confuse this neighborhood concept with apartheid is an egregious error.

The fundamental difference between apartheid and the American neighborhood comes out most clearly when one turns from what happens after five P.M. to what happens during the daytime. A neighborhood is a work place for less than half the community. The teachers, the doctors, the police, the grocers—these work where they live. But these people are supported by the labors of those who work in the factories and in other basic occupations outside the neighborhood. Some 50–60 percent of the labor force moves out of the neighborhood every morning to work in the country's basic industries. So a black strategy which concentrated exclusively on building up the black neighborhoods would be dealing with less than half the black man's economic problems. The neighborhood itself will not flourish unless the man who goes out of it in the morning brings back into it from the outside world an income adequate to support its institutions.

I said earlier that the American pattern is segregation in *social* life after five P.M. but integration in the *economic* life of the country during the day. American economic life is dominated by a few large corporations which do the greater part of the country's business; indeed, in manufacturing, half the assets of the entire country are owned by just 100 corporations. The world of these big corporations is an integrated world. There will be black grocery shops in black neighborhoods, but in your lifetime and mine there isn't going to be a black General Motors, a black Union Carbide, a black Penn-Central Railway, or a black Standard Oil Company. These great corporations serve all ethnic groups and employ all ethnic groups. American economic life is inconceivable except on an integrated basis.

The majority of Afro-Americans work not in their neighborhoods but for one of the nonneighborhood corporations or employers, and so it shall be for as far ahead as we can see. The black problem is that while we are 11 percent of the population, we have only 2 percent of the jobs at the top, 4 percent of the jobs in the middle, and are forced into 16 percent of the jobs at the bottom—indeed into as much as 40 percent of some of the jobs at the very bottom. Clearly our minimum objective must be to capture 11 percent of the jobs in the middle, and 11 percent of the jobs at the top. Or, for those of us who have a pride in ourselves, it could even be an objective to have 15 percent of the jobs at the top and in the middle, and only 8 percent of those at the bottom, leaving the very bottom to less ambitious ethnic groups.

Not all our leaders understand that our central economic problem is not in the neighborhoods, but is in the fact that outside the neighborhoods, where most of us have to work, we are concentrated in the bottom jobs. For if they understood this they could not be as hostile as they are toward the black middle and upper classes. The measure of whether we are winning our battle is in how many of us rise to the middle and the top. When a so-called militant abuses a successful Afro-American for having, by virtue of extreme hard work and immense self-discipline, managed to get to the top in the outside world, instead of devoting his energies to being—in the neighborhood—a social worker, or a night school teacher, or a semipoliti-cian, such a critic is merely being absurd. Rising from the bottom to the middle or the top, in the face of stiff white competition, prejudice, and arbi-trary barriers, takes everything that a man can give to it. It is our militants who should month-by-month chalk up the score of those who have broken through the barriers, should glory in their achievement, and should hold it up before our young to show them what black men can achieve.

Now at last I reach my central topic, which is the black man and the university. The road to the top in the great American corporations and other institutions is through higher education. Scientists, research workers, engi-neers, accountants, lawyers, financial administrators, presidential advisers —all these people are recruited from the university. And indeed nearly all of the top people are taken from a very small number of colleges—from not more than some 50 or 60 of the 2,000 degree-granting institutions in the United States. The Afro-American could not make it to the top so long as he was effectively excluded from this small number of select institutions. The breakthrough of the Afro-American into these colleges is therefore absolutely fundamental to the larger economic strategy of black power.

I do not mean to suggest that the most important black strategy is to get more blacks into the best colleges. Probably the greatest contribution to black advancement would be to break the trade union barriers which keep our people out of apprenticeships in the building and printing trades, and prevent our upgrading or promotion in other industries. The trade unions are the black man's greatest enemy in the United States. The number of people who would be at the top, if we had our numerical share of the top, would be small. Our greatest task, in terms of numbers, is to conquer the middle—getting into skilled posts, foremen's posts, supervisory and white collar jobs—through better use of apprenticeships, of the high schools, and of technical colleges. I am going to talk about the universities not because this is numerically important, but partly because it has become so controver-sial, and partly because if we did conquer the top it would make much easier the conquering of the middle—both in our own minds, and in other people's minds, by altering our young people's image of themselves and of what they can achieve.

What can the good white college do for its black students that Howard or Lincoln or Fisk cannot do? It can open the road into the top jobs. It can do this because the aura of these colleges is specially sought by people filling top jobs. To put it in unpopular language, it can train them to become top members of the Establishment.

If it is wrong for young blacks to be trained for the top jobs in the big corporations, for top jobs in the government service, for ambassadorships, for the editorial staff of the *New York Times,* and so on, then there is little point in sending them to the best white colleges. On the contrary, if what one wants is people trained to live and work in black neighborhoods, they will do much better to go to the black colleges, of which there are, after all, over 100, which know much better than Yale or Princeton or Dartmouth what the problems of black neighborhoods are, and how people should be trained to handle them. The point about the best white colleges is that they are a part, not of the neighborhood side of American life, but of the integrated part of American life, training people to run the economy and the administration in the integrated part of the day before five P.M.

But how can it be wrong for young Afro-Americans to be trained to hold superior positions in the integrated working world outside the neighborhood when in fact the neighborhood cannot provide work for even a half of its people? Whether we like it or not, most Afro-Americans *have* to work in the integrated world, and if we do not train for superior positions there, all that will happen is what happens now—that we shall be crowded into the worst paid jobs.

If one grasps this point, that these 50 colleges are the gateway to the superior jobs, then the current attitudes of some of our black leaders to these colleges is not a little bewildering. In its most extreme form what is asked is that the college should set aside a special part of itself which is to be the black part. There will be a separate building for black studies, and separate dormitories and living accommodations for blacks. There will be separate teachers, all black, teaching classes open only to blacks. The teachers are to be chosen by the students, and will for the most part be men whom no African or Indian or Chinese university would recognize as scholars or be willing to hire as teachers.

Doubtless some colleges under militant pressure will give in to this, but I do not see what Afro-Americans will gain thereby. Employers will not hire the students who emerge from this process, and their usefulness even in black neighborhoods will be minimal.

I yield to none in thinking that every respectable university should give courses on African life and on Afro-American life, which are of course two entirely different subjects, and I am very anxious to see such courses developed in our universities. It is, however, my hope that they will be attended mostly by white students, and that the majority of the black students will find more important uses for their time—that they may attend one or two such courses, but will reject any suggestion that black studies must be the major focus of their programs.

The principal argument for forcing black students to spend a great deal of their time in college studying African and Afro-American anthropology, history, languages, and literature is that they need such studies to overcome their racial inferiority complex. I am not impressed by this argument. The youngster discovers that he is black around the age of six or seven; from then on the whites he meets, the books he reads, and the situation of the Negro in America all combine to persuade him that he is an inferior species of homo sapiens. By the time he is fourteen or fifteen, he has made up his mind on this one way or the other. Nothing that the college can do, after he reaches 18 or 19, is going to have much effect on his basic personality. To expect the colleges to eradicate the inferiority complexes of young black adults is to ask the impossible. And to expect this to come about by segregating black students in black studies under inferior teachers suggests some deficiency of thought.

Perhaps I am wrong about this. The proposition is essentially that the young black has been brainwashed into thinking himself inferior, so now he must spend four years in some place where he will be re-brainwashed into thinking himself equal. But the prospect that the 50 best colleges in the United States can be forced to take on this re-brainwashing operation is an idle dream. Those who are now putting all their energies into working for this are doomed to disappointment.

We are knocking our heads against the wrong wall. Every black student should learn some Afro-American history, and study various aspects of his people's culture, but the place for him to do this compulsorily is in the high school, and the best age to start this seriously is even earlier, perhaps around the age of ten. By the time the student gets to a first-rate college he should be ready for business—for the business of acquiring the skills which he is going to be able to use, whether in his neighborhood or in the integrated economy. Let the clever young black go to a university to study engineering, medicine, chemistry, economics, law, agriculture, and other subjects which are going to be of value to him and his people. And let the clever whites go to college to read black novels, to learn Swahili, and to record the exploits of Negro heroes of the past: they are the ones to whom this will come as an eye-opener.

This incidentally is very much what happens in African universities. Most of these have well-equipped departments of African studies, which are popular with visiting whites, but very few African students waste their time (as they see it) on such studies, when there is so much to be learned for the jobs they will have to do. The attitude of Africans to their past conforms to the historian's observation that only decadent peoples, on the way down, feel an urgent need to mythologize and live in their past. A vigorous people, on the way up, has visions of its future, and cares next to nothing about its past.

It will be obvious to some of you that my attitude to the role of black studies in the education of college blacks derives not only from an unconventional view of what is to be gained therefrom, but also from an unconventional view of the purpose of going to college. The United States is the only country in the world which thinks that the purpose of going to college is to be educated. Everywhere else one goes to high school to be educated, but goes to college to be trained for one's life work. In the United States serious training does not begin until one reaches graduate school at the age of twenty-two. Before that one spends four years in college being educated —that is to say spending twelve weeks getting some tidbits on religion, twelve weeks learning French, twelve weeks seeing whether the history professor is stimulating, twelve weeks seeking entertainment from the economics professor, twelve weeks confirming that one is not going to be able to master calculus, and so on.

If the purpose of going to college is to be educated, and serious study will not begin until one is twenty-two, one might just as well perhaps spend the four years reading black novels, studying black history, and learning to speak Fanti. But I do not think that American blacks can afford this luxury. I think our young people ought to get down to the business of serious preparation for their life work as soon after eighteen as they can.

And I also note, incidentally, that many of the more intelligent white students are now in revolt against the way so many colleges fritter away their precious years in meaningless peregrination from subject to subject between the ages of eighteen and twenty-two.

Let me make my position clear. Any Afro-American who wishes to become a specialist in black studies, or to spend some of his time on such work, should be absolutely free to do so. But I hope that, of those students who get the opportunity to attend the 50 best colleges, the proportion who want to specialize in black studies may, in their interest and that of the black community, turn out to be rather small, in comparison with our scientists, or engineers, accountants, economists, or doctors.

Another attitude which puzzles me is that which requires black students in the better white colleges to mix only with each other; to have a dormitory to themselves; to eat at separate tables in the refectory, and so on. I have pointed out that these colleges are the gateway to leadership positions in the integrated part of the economy, and that what they can best do for young blacks is to prepare them to capture our 11 percent share of the best jobs at the top—one of every nine ambassadorships, one of every nine vice-presidencies of General Motors, one of every nine senior directors of engineering laboratories, and so on. Now I am told that the reason black students stick together is that they are uncomfortable in white company. But how is one to be Ambassador to Finland or Luxembourg—jobs which American Negroes have already held with distinction—if one is uncomfortable in white company? Anybody who occupies a supervisory post, from foreman upwards, is going to have white people working under him, who will expect him to be friendly and fair; is this going to be possible, after four years spent in boycotting white company?

Nowadays in business and in government most decisions are made in committees. Top Afro-Americans cannot hope to be more than one in nine; they will always be greatly outnumbered by white people at their level. But how can one survive as the only black vice-president sitting on the executive committee of a large corporation if one is not so familiar with the ways and thoughts of other vice-presidents that one can even anticipate how they are going to think? Blacks in America are inevitably and perpetually a minority. This means that in all administrative and leadership positions we are going to be outnumbered by white folks, and will have to compete with them not on our terms but on theirs. The only way to win this game is to know them so thoroughly that we can outpace them. Being in one of the best white colleges, where they are molded, gives us this opportunity. For us to turn our backs on this opportunity, by insisting on mingling only with other black students in college, is folly of the highest order.

This kind of social self-segregation is encouraged by two myths about the possibilities for black economic progress in the United States which need to be nailed. One is the Nixon myth, and the other, its opposite, is the revolutionary myth.

The first postulates that the solution is black capitalism—to help as many blacks as possible to become big businessmen. To be sure, it is feasible to have more successful small businesses operating inside the protection of the neighborhood—more grocers and drug stores and lunch counters; but I have emphasized that the members of every ethnic group mostly work outside their neighborhood in the integrated economy, buying from and selling to all ethnic groups. In this part of the economy the prospects for small business are bleak.

No doubt a few Negroes, born with the special talents which success in a highly competitive business world demands, will succeed in establishing sizable and highly competitive concerns. But the great majority who start on this road, whether white or black, go bankrupt in a short time. Indeed, about half of the new white businesses go bankrupt within the first three years. To tell the blacks that this is the direction in which they must move is almost a form of cruelty. To pretend that black America is going to be saved by the emergence of black capitalism, competing in the integrated economy with white capitalism, is little more than a hoax.

Neither is black America going to be saved by a Marxist revolution. Revolution takes power from one set of persons and gives it to another, but it does not change the hierarchical structure of the economy. Any kind of America that you can visualize, whether capitalist, communist, fascist, or any other kind of ist, is going to consist of large institutions like General Motors under one name or another. It will have people at the top, people in the middle, and people at the bottom. Its leading engineers, doctors, scientists, and administrators—leaving out a few top professional politicians—are going to be recruited from a small number of highly select colleges. The problem of the black will essentially be the same—that problem being whether he is going to be mostly in the bottom jobs, or whether he will also get his 11 percent share of the top and the middle. And his chance at the top is going to depend on his getting into those select schools and getting the same kind of technical training that the whites are getting— not some segregated schooling specially adapted for him, but the same kind that the whites get as their gateway to the top. Those black leaders who wish us to concentrate our efforts on working for revolution in America are living on a myth, for our problems and needed strategies are going to be exactly the same whether there is a revolution or not. In the integrated part of the American economy our essential strategy has to be to use all the normal channels of advancement—the high schools, the colleges, apprentice-ships, night schools: it is only by climbing this ladder that the black man is going to escape from his concentration in the bottom jobs of the economy.

This progress is not, of course, simply a matter of schooling. The bar-riers of prejudice which keep us off the ladder still have to be broken down: the task of the civil rights movement is still not completed, and we need all the liberal help, black and white, that we can get to help to keep the ladder clear. We need also to raise our own sights; to recognize that there are now more opportunities than there were, and to take every opportunity that offers. Here our record is good. For as the barriers came down in sports and entertainment, our young people moved swiftly to the top in baseball, foot-ball, the theater, or wherever else the road was cleared. We will do exactly the same in other spheres, given the opportunity.

The secret is to inspire our young people with confidence in their poten-tial achievement. And psychologists tell us that the background to this is a warm and secure family life. The most successful minorities in America, the Chinese, the Japanese, and the Jews, are distinguished by their close and highly disciplined family, which is the exact opposite of what has now become the stereotype of the white American family, with its undisci-plined and uncontrollable children reared on what are alleged to be the principles of Dr. Spock. African families are warm, highly disciplined structures just like Jewish or Chinese families. If black Americans are look-ing to Africa for aspects of culture which will distinguish them from white Americans, let them turn their back on Spockism, and rear their children on African principles, for this is the way to the middle and the top. Given a disciplined family life and open doors to opportunity, I have no doubt that American blacks will capture one field after another, as fast as bar-riers come down.

The point which I have been trying to make is that the choice some of our leaders offer us between segregation and integration is false in the American context. America is integrated in the day and segregates itself at night. Some of our leaders who have just discovered the potential strength of neighborhood self-segregation have got drunk on it to the point of advo-cating segregation for all spheres of Afro-American life. But the struggle for community power in the neighborhood is not an alternative to the strug-gle for a better share of the integrated world outside the neighborhood, in which inevitably most of our people must earn their living. The way to a better share of this integrated economy is through the integrated colleges; but they can help us only if we take from them the same things that they give to our white competitors.

If we enter them merely to segregate ourselves in blackness, we shall lose the opportunity of our lives. Render homage unto segregated community power in the neighborhoods where it belongs, but do not let it mess up our chance of capturing our share of the economic world outside the neighborhood, where segregation weakens our power to compete. This is what I wanted to say.

Merit and Equality in Higher Education

LOGAN WILSON

THE CURRENT RACIAL CRISIS on many campuses is a reminder of responsibilities thrust upon educational institutions to transform American society from a caste to an open-class system. Civil rights legislation formally removed many of the impediments to this transformation, to be sure, but the common expectation seems to be that education must do the main job. Since an individual's life chances are admittedly influenced more by his own educational attainments than by the nation's laws, this expectation should not surprise us. In an era of rising egalitarianism, moreover, we can expect nonwhites as well as whites to demand more equality of opportunity. Whether, without vastly increased public understanding and support, educational institutions can meet the demands placed upon them is open to question. About the growing aspirations of the American people, however, there can be no question.

Some of these circumstances are by no means new. As was noted a quarter of a century ago in the Harvard Report *General Education in a Free Society,*[1] American higher education has long had a dual obligation to further the Jacksonian principle of elevating the people at large and to advance the Jeffersonian principle of drawing upon all strata in training a natural aristocracy of leaders. More successfully than any other nation in the world, we have indeed reconciled the demands for quantity and quality in higher education.

In light of this accomplishment, there would seem to be no basis for posing a fundamental antithesis between quantity and quality in our educational enterprise. Although disadvantaged members of our society have not received their fair share of educational opportunities, the consensus is that this nation is headed toward universal postsecondary education. Furthermore, the quality of opportunity has steadily improved, and will doubtless continue to do so.

Forward movement in higher education has always been fraught with uncertainties, however, and in my judgment some of the uncertainties now

[1] Cambridge, Mass.: Harvard University Press, 1945.

28

confronting us may prove to be particularly hazardous. Elsewhere I have commented on the perils of overextended institutional involvements without concomitant increases in resources. The problem on which I wish to focus here concerns a growing contradiction of guiding principles behind educational endeavor.

This emerging contradiction or paradox stems in the main, I believe, from a general reluctance to acknowledge that in organized educational activity, the principles of merit and of equality often appear to be irreconcilable. Since the American system of higher education as we know it today is essentially meritocratic in function and structure, impulsive responses to modify it to accommodate egalitarian pressures are necessarily producing confusion and conflict. Of these, I shall have more to say, but first I shall review briefly the meaning and significance of "merit" as it applies in and to colleges and universities.

The Meaning of Meritocracy

The functional underpinning for a meritocratic structuring of the higher learning derives logically from the fact that nobody becomes educated by inheritance, gift, or decree. Even when provided with unrestricted opportunity, every person is limited by his own will, desires, and capabilities. The main virtue of the merit principle when applied to educational processes, however, is that it couples individual advancement with ability and effort. Thus it was no accident of history that led the founders of our nation to recognize the importance of universal and free education in maintaining the viability of a democratic society. This recognition began with the common schools, extended to high school, and is now moving rapidly upward to include advanced levels of education. In short, higher education, once regarded as a luxury for those who could afford it, is coming under meritocracy to be viewed as a right for the many rather than a privilege for the few.

In terms of numbers at the various learning levels, our educational system still resembles a pyramid. Correspondingly, the sustaining ideology—at least in the past—has included the concept that the system should sift and sort as well as retain and advance the millions of individuals it encompasses. Impacts of the educational process are judged most immediately, of course, by fairly standardized procedures of testing, grading, and certifying. Although these routinized tests of human worth have long been criticized, it has been generally conceded that in an open society evaluation of individuals based primarily on what they know and can do is more equitable and certainly more functional than assigning status according to "who they are." In sum, whatever its defects, the meritocratic principle in higher education does have the virtue of emphasizing *achieved* rather than *ascribed* status.

In a society as complex as ours, higher education has to be a serious enterprise, and a significant proportion of the student population must be prepared in institutions that place a premium on cognitive efficiency, intellectual competence, and specialized knowledge. The competitive rewards for brains and effort are attended by deprivations for dullness and laziness, of course, and the consequent frustrations admittedly produce stresses and strains within the educational system.

You may recall that Michael Young's book *The Rise of the Meritocracy,*[2] a satire intended to describe what happened to English education between the years 1870 and 2033, sets forth the presumed consequences of an educational system that eventually succeeded in sorting and training all members of that society to the point that the dullest were at the bottom and the brightest at the top. The final outcome was no longer an open society with high levels of native ability born into all social strata, but in effect a closed society where everybody was objectively evaluated on his contributions to social productivity and then placed accordingly.

Even in the perfect meritocracy, however, popular demand for a classless society based upon the denial that one man is in any fundamental way superior to another finally asserted itself in what Young identified as the "Chelsea Manifesto." The "Manifesto" states:

> The classless society would be one which both possessed and acted upon plural values. Were we to evaluate people, not only according to their intelligence and their education, their occupation, and their power, but according to their kindliness and their courage, their imagination and sensitivity, their sympathy and generosity, there could be no classes. Who would be able to say that the scientist was superior to the porter with admirable qualities as a father, the civil servant with unusual skill at gaining prizes superior to the lorry-driver with unusual skill at growing roses? The classless society would also be the tolerant society, in which individual differences were actively encouraged as well as passively tolerated, in which full meaning was at last given to the dignity of man. Every human being would then have equal opportunity, not to rise up in the world in the light of any mathematical measure, but to develop his own special capacities for leading a rich life. [P. 169]

The problem of equality and merit in American life and education was dealt with eloquently by John W. Gardner in his widely discussed book

[2] Baltimore, Md.: Penguin Books, 1961.

Excellence.[3] In general, he gave an affirmative answer to the question, Can we be equal and excellent too? The author acknowledged, nonetheless, that there are no easy and ready-made solutions to such problems as: Does our devotion to equality condemn us to a pervasive mediocrity? How can one honestly explain or justify the slovenliness that is so often accepted as normal in our schools, in trade unions, in industry, in government—in short, everywhere in our society?

Aspects of Egalitarianism

Turning now to the meaning and significance of the equality principle, we can hark back to the preamble of the American Declaration of Independence, which asserted almost two hundred years ago that "all men are created equal." Despite the irony that some of the signers were slave owners, they were in the main egalitarians rather than elitists in their views about the kind of nation they wanted the United States to become.[4]

Because of the inherent impracticality of radical egalitarianism as a working principle of social organization, however, no major American leader has ever seriously advocated it. And, among the others, few would argue that differences in ability, effort, occupation, and civic service can or should be ignored in the social status accorded to individuals. Not many would contend that problem-makers and problem-solvers should share equally in the fruits of human productivity. Even so, radical egalitarians do hold that social inequalities—whether political, legal, or economic—can be changed and should be eliminated.

Other kinds of egalitarians differentiate between justifiable and unjustifiable inequalities. Their varying conceptions give rise to such maxims of distributive justice as: "To each according to his merit," "To each according to his work," "To each according to his need." They hold that where nature or society imposes individual or group handicaps, the state has a moral obligation to attempt to compensate for the impediments, as in the instances of the physically handicapped, the culturally deprived, and the economically disadvantaged. Moreover, the majority of our citizens support a system of taxation that is in part a mechanism for taking money from the less needy and turning it over to the more needy in the form of cash, goods, or services.

Although some of these conceptions of equality find little acceptance

[3] New York: Harper & Bros., 1961.
[4] Some of my comments on the equality principle are derived from contributors to *Equality,* ed. J. Roland Pennock and John W. Chapman (New York: Atherton Press, 1967).

today, most Americans accept the idea of what they regard as equality of opportunity. Without implying that everybody can or will succeed, the principle is assumed to give a fair chance for all to try. Nearly all parents want to gain special advantages for their own children, to be sure, and not many would be willing for the sake of complete equality of opportunity to have all children reared in orphanages. Nevertheless, we give at least lip service to the Federal government's program to equalize educational opportunities by region, race, class, and other differentials that now relate to discrepancies in learning opportunities. In most colleges and universities, scholarship programs have for many years made special financial concessions for deserving but impecunious students.

Yet, as one writer has pointed out, the usual formulation of equality of opportunity can be misleading; the runner with weak ankles has little chance against a Roger Bannister. Our society, like every other, admires and rewards some abilities more than others and encourages those pursuits it values. Nobody gets paid for "doing his own thing" unless it also happens to be the thing other persons want to buy.[5] The formal system of education is thus more likely to be geared to the pursuit of success than to the pursuit of happiness; and, with schools and colleges for the most part heavily subsidized, there is also an understandable public reluctance to invest in persons or endeavors that offer scant "pay off" prospects.

Some critics of equality of opportunity as a guiding principle in society and in education further point out that it heightens social competition rather than cooperation, stimulates too many individuals beyond their real potentials, and results in countless frustrations. One man's gain is too often another man's loss, with success taken to be proof of personal worth and with human relations turned into a kind of contest for superiority.

If excellence, or excelling others, is the common goal in education, then by definition the vast majority must necessarily fall short of that objective. It seems important, therefore, to emphasize that equality of opportunity need not mean identity of opportunities. Education for competence or adequacy in a wide variety of undertakings is also an essential purpose in our system of higher education, and we can offset the sense of failure for large numbers of young people by adjusting opportunities to fit their capabilities.

By confusing equality of opportunity with identity of opportunities, we can mistakenly homogenize the rich diversity of American higher education.

[5] A colleague of mine has pointed out that some tenured professors are obvious exceptions to this rule.

Sir Eric Ashby has noted with approval that Great Britain is now pursuing the American example in colleges and universities of setting up the educational equivalents of assembly lines to produce Fords as well as Lincolns. With the pluralism of the American system, a wide variety of educational opportunities is available—from the very selective institutions to the open-door junior colleges. In view of the range of human talents and socioeconomic needs, together with rising egalitarianism, one might logically conclude that, taken as a whole, our colleges and universities are admirably suited to the new demands placed upon them.

The Enlarging Dialectic

However this may be, under the growing pressure on institutions to become all things to all kinds of students and other constituencies, many are in a dilemma that could push them onto a collision course. The collision would occur when the demands of meritocracy and of egalitarianism become irreconcilable. Taking some liberties with the Hegelian dialectic as it might be applied to current trends in higher education, I think that meritocracy might be regarded as the established thesis and egalitarianism as the rising antithesis. The outcome or synthesis, of course, is as yet unknown.

Although historical evidence of how and why meritocracy came to be the dominant motif in American higher education is abundant, there also are now at hand ample data to support the view that the antithetical forces are gaining ascendancy. Egalitarians are attacking admissions policies, testing and grading practices, standardized curricular requirements, long-accepted modes of certification, and many hierarchical arrangements, particularly in some of the more elitist institutions. The policies and practices are variously criticized as being anachronistic, elitist, undemocratic, irrelevant, and even dysfunctional.

As Jencks and Riesman have pointed out, for both social and economic reasons a college diploma has become a virtual union card for membership in the middle and upper social classes, but opportunities to acquire the card have been severely restricted for lower-class young people, and especially so for Negroes. Rising costs and rising standards, coupled with long-standing discrimination against blacks, have overall diminished their chances. Even though almost half of all high school graduates now go on to some form of advanced education, in contrast to one in every six in 1940, Negroes and other minorities have lost ground proportionately while gaining in numbers.

According to one study[6] "From elementary school on, the meritocratic system tests, measures, grades and culls, to the progressive advantage of affluent whites." Institutions created for Negroes have assumed most of the burden for educating blacks, and the opportunities for them in white institutions have been minuscule. Within the last two or three years, to be sure, "high risk" and Upward Bound programs, financial aid packages, and special recruitment have constituted serious efforts to improve the picture.

This same study of state universities blames faculties for their reluctance to make changes in the composition of the student body, the nature of the curriculum, or "the prestige level of their own ranks." Faculty members, the survey asserts, more often talk of "strict nondiscrimination, merit, quality, and color-blindness" than of compensatory measures to offset past discrimination. It asserts further that black demands for entrée, relevance, recognition, and dignity coincide with the need to cure such common institutional ills as "the equating of excellence and prestige with elitism and exclusiveness," "bureaucratic impersonality," "the feudalism and fragmentation of academic departments, the arbitrariness of certification and credentialing systems," "high student attrition," "the protection of incompetence by tenure and academic freedom," "ivory-tower detachment from the surrounding society," and so on. Thus, many of the things regarded as wrong about American higher education are presumed to relate to its meritocratic elements.

In their zeal for changing the status quo in higher education, egalitarians apparently forget that historically it was the rise of meritocracy that enabled democracy to supplant elitism. The merit principle, for example, led to the disappearance of the *numerus clausus,* or quota, system that set admissions ceilings for various ethnic minorities. Laws in a number of states and the Civil Rights Act of 1964 added a legal requirement to the trend toward institutional "color blindness." Ironically, a contorted racialism is now demanding that some institutions restore quota systems, but with quotas *for* rather than *against* particular groups. (The consequences of such a policy, as Moynihan and others have noted, can result in serious repercussions, not only among the WASPs but also, in some of our most prestigious colleges and universities, among Jewish, Japanese, and Chinese Americans.)

Another merit principle in admissions has been the use of uniform criteria, with no favors granted to any applicants because of their social status. Of late, however, a double standard of entry is being used overtly or covertly

[6] John Egerton, *State Universities and Black Americans* (Atlanta, Ga.: Southern Education Reporting Service, May 1969), pp. 93–96.

by some institutions to admit larger numbers of disadvantaged students. Although this change has been quietly effected in most instances, the 1969 experience of City College in New York illustrates the furor that can occur when the issue becomes publicized and politicized.

Pressures for open enrollment are being accompanied by attacks on standardized tests. Even though nobody has yet demonstrated how such tests are less meaningfully predictive of *academic performance* for the disadvantaged than for middle- and upper-class students, they are increasingly regarded as unfair to the culturally deprived. The real target, I suspect, is the meritocratic model of sorting and grading human talent.

In an unpublished paper, William W. Turnbull, vice-president of the Educational Testing Service, has pointed out three competing views about the roles of educational institutions and the rights and privileges of individuals in society. First, he notes that the conception of graded abilities to perform is quite foreign to some fields of endeavor. In some labor unions, for example, a standard of output is set for all members, with a presumed dichotomy only between the qualified and the unqualified. Second, the "remote criterion" concept aims simply to maximize the supply of trained persons in some posteducation category—as more black lawyers or more male elementary school teachers. Under this view, the educational objective is purely instrumental. Third, the "student-centered" view adjusts educational programs to suit student needs or wishes rather than fitting students to resources and programs. Even though the third view is not entirely new, according to Turnbull, "what is new is the proposition that each college, and therefore all colleges, including the most selective, should adopt this philosophy."

Revolutionary and radical reformist attitudes toward traditional values in American higher education are also evidenced in efforts to abolish letter grading, grade-point averages, and class standings. Although few, if any, institutions have responded by eliminating all performance comparisons, in some, pass-fail ratings are being adopted. A recent survey conducted for CBS News has shown that whereas 89 percent of all parents and 80 percent of all youth believe that "competition encourages excellence," only 31 percent of youthful revolutionaries and 66 percent of radical reformers have similar attitudes. The influence of these minority dissenters on institutional policies is thus quite apparent.

Another evidence of the rising egalitarianism among the young, as expressed in views on participatory democracy, was brought out recently in a nationwide survey conducted by the Gallup poll. In reply to the question

"Do you think college students should or should not have a greater say in the running of colleges?", the "Yes, should" response was 81 percent for all students, 92 percent for student demonstrators, and only 25 percent for the general public. Similarly, in answering the question "Do you think college students should or should not have a greater say concerning the academic side of colleges—that is, the courses, examinations and so forth?", the "Yes, should" response was 75 percent for all students, 86 percent for the demonstrators, and 33 percent for the general public.

One academic commentator on the egalitarian push sees it as a collision of objective judgments and subjective demands, with the amateur (as contrasted with the professional) "exalted as a kind of democratic culture hero, subject to no standards or restrictions." He wonders what has happened to the conception of the campus as a place where those who know communicate with those who do not, and why the faculty is willing to abandon its authoritative position in order to placate the young. The advancement of knowledge and learning, he fears, is becoming "less important than self-expression." [7]

Lest it be thought that egalitarianism in academe is confined largely to students, however, one should also observe indications here and there of faculty movements away from meritocracy, as signified by professionalism, and toward a leveling down as well as up in the system of recognitions and rewards. Although the threat of collective bargaining is still remote on most campuses, unionization is already a reality in a considerable number of community colleges and urban institutions. With unionization, seniority rather than merit tends to become the main criterion for individual advancement, and teacher welfare rather than professional improvement the goal of the collective enterprise. In matters of governance, the one-man one-vote basis of decision making displaces earned competence as the dominant mode of participation.

Still another kind of opposition to meritocracy in higher education is illustrated in a recent article, "Diplomaism: How We Zone People." [8] Brushing aside the widely accepted idea that a certificate, diploma, or degree is a useful symbol attesting individual achievement, the author asserts, "We are well on our way to repealing the American dream of individual accomplishment and replacing it with a system in which the diploma is the measure of a man; a diploma which usually bears no relation to perfor-

---

[7] See Robert Brustein, "The Case for Professionalism," *New Republic,* April 26, 1969, pp. 16–18.

[8] David Hapgood in *Washington Monthly,* May 1969, pp. 2–8.

mance." He goes on to charge our system with being a credentialing rather than a humanizing agency, and with fostering a diploma aristocracy.

Institutional and Governmental Reactions

The gamut of strictures I have summarized, ranging from criticism of a particular aspect of meritocracy in higher education to rejection of its basic rationale, exemplifies what is at best a competition and at worst a conflict between meritocratic and egalitarian principles as determinants of policy. An individual institution that has traditionally selected students to fit its resources and programs, for instance, may feel strongly impelled to take a more widely representative group of young people and adjust its programs to fit their professed needs and wishes. As the college honestly desires to maintain its autonomy and distinctiveness while also seeking to extend its usefulness to society, it may be caught in a real dilemma. Where the institutional status quo is highly resistant to change and the push of opposing forces is strong, the campus can become an arena.

Insofar as the whole system of higher education is concerned, the nation's twenty-three hundred or so campuses afford enough diversity of opportunity to be able to accommodate almost any variety of needs and wishes, and thus to offset the prospect of wholesale conflict—or, at least, so it would seem. On both the state and national levels, nonetheless, public resources are not unlimited and hard choices must be made in determining allocations. State legislatures and state boards or commissions of higher education often try to simplify their tasks by resorting to formula methods of allocating funds to competing claimants. Comparable programs tend to be given common denominators of student credit hours as measures of dollars to be provided without regard to qualitative differences among institutions. This approach, of course, implies egalitarianism rather than meritocracy.

Although some institutional stratification of individual opportunity in public higher education is evidenced everywhere, California is thus far the only state having a planned system based explicitly upon the meritocracy principle. Originally looked upon by many educational authorities as a model for other states, the California plan is being widely criticized within that state for the alleged inequities in the distribution of educational resources it is said to perpetuate. Thus, an already unresolved issue rises afresh: whether master planning or the marketplace is the better mechanism for promoting equity and excellence in higher education.

On the Federal level also, a consensus is lacking about guiding principles and priorities of effort. Federal aid to higher education, until recent years, was quite limited in amount and selective in emphasis. Public reactions to Sputnik and the resulting questions about this nation's capabilities in science and technology led Congress to make unprecedented funds available for specialized manpower training and research. Although the initial thrust was meritocratic in its mode of allocating support, in the course of time Federal aid to higher education has become progressively more egalitarian. Partly in response to widespread criticism of the concentration of Federal support for particular types of programs, for selected kinds of institutions, and for certain geographic regions where the more prestigious institutions are clustered, the congressional response has been to correct "imbalances." The Federal government has gone even further by underwriting programs intended specifically for needy students and for underdeveloped institutions. Federal aid is in the main still selective, to be sure, but there is no mistaking the recent movement toward egalitarianism.

Touching upon this matter in a recent speech at the Rockefeller University, Julius Stratton warned, "As one watches the actions of Congress, I cannot help but fear that the status of institutional *equality* has become more important than the concept of *quality* itself. We seek the highest mean level in the world, but we must never forget that the pace of progress is set not by the mean but by the best." Dr. Stratton also expressed the judgment that too few institutions are distinctive today, and too many show marks of a common mold.[9]

In an era of rising egalitarianism, highly selective colleges and universities do indeed find themselves increasingly on the defensive. Although nobody has as yet proposed open admissions for all of them or advocated dividing up the Harvard and California faculties and libraries to spread around the country, many persons seem to believe that pluralism in American higher education is yielding to uniformity. Other observers maintain, however, that the financial circumstances of private institutions will orient them even more in the future than in the past toward middle- and upper-class clienteles and objectives.

It is of interest to note that in Great Britain as well as in the United States, concern is being expressed in some quarters about alleged erosions of quality in higher education. The novelist Kingsley Amis, for example, has asserted that there the major cause of campus unrest is "the presence in our universities of an academically unfit majority, or large minority." Lord Snow has charged that England is in danger of neglecting her most

---

[9] "The Importance of Being Different," Oct. 9, 1968 (Ford Foundation Reprint).

gifted children because of an obsession with egalitarianism during the last twenty years and a lessened regard for academic excellence.

On the other hand, egalitarians argue that the modern economies of abundance flourish through maximum development of the abilities of all their members. In affluent societies, with potential plenty for everybody, the widest development of individual capabilities adds to national wealth while raising the general cultural and social level. The egalitarians also contend that modern technology's expansion of wealth encourages the have-nots to demand their share by force and violence if necessary, and thus governmental promotion of equality of educational opportunity serves as a countermeasure to revolution by furthering social mobility and serving as a solvent of rigid stratification.

The growing competition and conflict over priorities in American higher education is certainly one manifestation of the unstable equilibrium of contemporary society. On individual campuses and throughout the educational system debate spreads about what the mix of people and purposes should be within and among institutions. The meritocratic thesis and the egalitarian antithesis, under whatever guises, become more sharply opposed, and in most places, the synthesis is not yet in sight. Meritorians are charged with being mere elitists; egalitarians are charged with being anti-intellectuals. Ignoring the hard realities of resource allocation, optimists try to comfort everyone with the easy assurance that somehow we shall arrive at the best possible education of the gifted while simultaneously achieving the highest possible level of the great number.

In a rapidly changing and free society, nobody can predict a certain outcome or impose a common resolution of the issues we now confront in higher education; the synthesis that will emerge in our historic dialectic is thus anybody's guess. It seems to me, nonetheless, that educational leaders have an obligation to bring their informed judgments to bear as much as they can in shaping the course of events. Our main job, I believe, is to see that our society gets what it needs rather than what some of its more vocal members may want at the moment.

To clarify means and ends, it might be useful to conceptualize our complex situation in terms of game analogies. The name of the game is formal education; in a competitive world all nations must play it, and the desired outcome is survival and well-being. Although every nation has its own system for training citizen participants, among them the United States has the largest proportion of its population engaged in higher education. Many foreigners regard our scheme as being wasteful of resources, but our justification is that every individual—rich or poor, black or white, gifted or not —benefits society as well as himself through the maximum feasible use of educational opportunity.

Game strategies also differ markedly from one nation to another. In totalitarian states, for example, the purposes of higher education and the participants in it are centrally determined. Our system, in principle, allows considerable latitude in both respects. Unlike athletic team coaches, at least insofar as the whole system is concerned, American educators cannot focus effort solely on the most adept. Demands for universal postsecondary education are such that, by virtue of their sheer numbers, the less and the least adept get more time and attention in the aggregate than the most adept. The rationale is that advanced opportunity is a right rather than a privilege. And who is to say that it does not also have functional justifications.

Every society consists of all its members, not just some of them. Using the game analogy, all of their contributions—good, bad, and indifferent— count in the total effort of the collectivity. If cultural deprivations and economic disadvantages permit educational inadequacies among ethnic minorities and other groups, the whole society also pays a price for the neglect. If the talents of the gifted and creative are slighted—whatever their race or creed—the nation's progress is handicapped. The moral imperatives of egalitarianism and the functional imperatives of meritocracy thus coincide in justifying the most effective possible system of higher education.

As we go about modifying our system to meet changed needs and to build a better society for all, it would be, in my judgment, a serious error to undermine its pluralism and diversity in the belief that this would further the purposes of a democratic society. On the contrary, I believe that we should make more postsecondary options available—including those of a notably vocational emphasis—to the growing number and variety of students. Moreover, I believe that the division of labor among institutions should be made much more explicit than it now is, with no college or university undertaking functions it cannot effectively perform. Some form of postsecondary education should be available for everybody, but it is time to emphasize what traditional higher education can and cannot do for the society that supports it. With these qualifications in mind, I am convinced, we can resolve our differences about merit and equality and have in this nation a system of higher education that not only serves the best interests of our own people but also of all mankind.

PART TWO

RACIAL PRESSURES
ON EDUCATIONAL INSTITUTIONS

Racial Pressures on Urban Institutions

SAMUEL D. PROCTOR

EDUCATION is the corridor through which America's minorities move from rejection, deprivation, and isolation to acceptance, economic sufficiency, and inclusion. Other dynamic social forces do indeed dissolve class rigidities, but that process is preliminary to the critical one—the movement of minority members from the pockets of poverty to the mainstream of full participation in the political and economic arenas of the nation.

Until the most recent influx of black and Puerto Rican students onto the major campuses of America, the university community was the preserve mainly of the white middle class. Admission standards, the campus atmosphere, the costs, and the general social expectancy factor conspired to protect the population of the major universities from invasions of minority students. Programs such as the Equal Opportunity Grants, NDEA loans, Upward Bound, and the Intensive Summer Studies Program at Yale, Harvard, and Columbia opened the eyes of the universities to new vistas of service. But these, even combined, could not be expected to raise the minority percentage on campuses more than a few points above the prevailing 1 percent.

For many years, the black population has heralded those few among their number who had negotiated degrees at the name campuses. Indeed, the names of John Hope, Montague Cobb, William Hastie, Robert Weaver, Paul Robeson, Jerome Holland, Saunders Redding, Hollis Price, William Carter, Felton Clark, Arthur Davis, George Gore, and Willa Player will only trigger the recollection of countless others who a generation ago—and longer—braved the chill and the challenge of white campuses and succeeded. Colby College, Park College, Amherst College, Oberlin College, Bowdoin College, Dartmouth, Brown, Rutgers, Yale, Princeton, Cornell, and Columbia have in their alumni archives the names of black "greats" who made it before the flood. Most educated blacks over thirty in their undergraduate years had black Ivy League alumni to teach them.

The full assessment of the influence of such persons has not been made and, possibly, cannot be made. Today, among the black leadership class

43

are thousands who formed conclusions about their innate capacities and their intrinsic human worth as a consequence of what they saw among that elite who held prestige degrees. While this self-assurance must not be taken as a sole solution to any pressing problem, the influence of this distinguished group was immeasurable in killing the rumor about the subhuman status of the Negro.

More can be said to establish the nature of the black educated class prior to the return of the GI and the Kennedy-Johnson programs toward expanded opportunity in higher education. In the twenties, the thirties, and the early forties it was common to find a sizable town—for example, Fredericksburg, Virginia—without a public high school for blacks. Often there was a public subsidy of some kind for a church-related school but it was a paltry one. The blacks were expected to find their way to a county school several miles distant.

Obviously, under such a "system" few blacks survived the earliest years of grade school. High school graduation was a rare attainment among Negroes in the lowest economic class. Then, college was another matter. For those who did make it, there was a faint replication of New England liberal arts training circumscribed by religious interests. It can be fairly stated that up to 1945, the college-bound black had been taught by public school teachers who were also Sunday School teachers and church officers, reared in the tradition of Puritanism, disciplined to be passive in conflict or controversial situations, given to peace and harmony, congenial toward friendly whites, and in hot pursuit of the "standard brand culture" embraced by the majority culture.

The World War II GIs saw the whole world. They left their buddies buried in North Africa, England, Burma, and the islands of the sea. They witnessed the bold postwar drive for independence on the part of colonial subjects in Africa, Asia, and the Caribbean. Roosevelt and Truman brought freedom and equality for blacks a whiff closer and its fragrance was impelling. These factors, added to the steady, relentless work of the NAACP and the National Urban League, along with the less sensational contributions of the American Friends, the Southern Regional Council, and intermittent activities often generated in New York City that had national impact, these combined to create an intellectual appetite for racial inclusiveness. And, whereas freedom, equality, opportunity could not be implemented in the life of the GI himself, his children, who ate at his table and were nurtured by him, these children are now the new blacks on the large, urban campuses.

The New Mood of the Young Black

Administrators over forty-five who recall their few black schoolmates and their black friends from years past see no trace of those gentle spirits in today's self-directed, brittle, angry, alienated blacks in the student population. The corridor that was narrow indeed a generation ago and which saw a slow thin line of polite blacks moving through is now widening, and the young black of today wants it to widen faster and move many more blacks through—on their terms.

In order to cope with the new mood of the young black, one must remember the difference between his outlook and that of his father. His father grew up with a tacit acceptance of the slow pace of change, change at the pleasure and convenience of the white majority. The young black on campus is furious at such a thought. The word *tolerance* is not in his vocabulary. Next, his father—before World War II—had a world view shaped by *National Geographic* and *Reader's Digest*. He had not scrutinized white colonialism and he knew only remotely about the colonies of the big powers on a map. Thus, he did not see his status as a black man in America in the context of the total color issue in the world. His son does. Third, his father saw no protection for himself, his wife, or his children if he should fling himself against the wall of monumental customs, mores, and entrenched power. He held his peace.

In the light of this generation gap, we see a paradox in this whole issue. The generation that went off to World War II left behind them segregated hotels, schools, bus stations, restaurants—and came back to them. It was ten years before a real confrontation took place. The delay came not out of cowardice or fear; it was the result of a practical assessment of police power, fire power, political power, and the apathy of most people, black and white. Yet when King's Montgomery Improvement Association moved out and broke the inertia, and both President Kennedy and President Johnson began to respond, it did *not* bring hope and encouragement. Instead, it caused the young black to pass a harsher judgment on his country; it exposed the totality of racism; it created an awareness and a consciousness of the color factor that has now enveloped the nation.

There are two other considerations that educators must not overlook in trying to understand the mood of the young black. The first concerns his view of the American culture and the second, his view of the Judaeo-Christian ethical tradition. His views are best understood by comparing the present generation, again, with their parents.

The American culture is indeed an amalgam of Judaistic moralism, European humanism, Christian soteriology, and capitalistic acquisitiveness. The blend has nurtured this young nation from a virgin wilderness to the most powerful and affluent society ever known. The young black is a witness of this power and he takes many of America's benefits for granted without a thought. But he has learned how to probe and examine things and ideas. He is not carried away with the glitter and shimmer of shiny things, blind to their relationship to the total social process.

The Grand Incongruities

His appreciation for the general standard of living enjoyed by most Americans and his appreciation for the favorable comparative comforts available to Americans are both dulled by his awareness of the plight of Africans, Asians, and Latins and, at home, the high visibility of the black, Indian, and Mexican poor. Therefore, he is not enthusiastic about America's economic supremacy. He associates it with the exploitation of the weak and the helpless. And, to whatever extent education seeks, in however subtle a form, to induct him into the cult of "Western man," to that same extent he will be resistant. Granted, there is something inevitable about the young black being compelled to effect some kind of rapprochement with the culture as he approaches careerism and family responsibility, but that point he wants to defer until it becomes relevant. Now, he is a student with all of the rights, privileges, and immunities appertaining thereto.

His condemnation of this society and its goals is something fierce. That which seems to spell success to others is to him nothing but vulgar compromise and self-destruction. He has put his finger on all of the contradictions, the ironies, and the hypocrisies of America and he has put it to music. Of course, America's vulnerability is patent because of her big promises made to her citizens. She starts out promising her people that they are going to have the rights of life, liberty, and the pursuit of happiness. She has a structure of justice that brings pauper and privileged before the same bar without distinction before the law. Implicit in these doctrines is inherent human worth that defies racism and poverty.

The previous generation of blacks was not as aware of America's promise or her forfeiture. The big picture was seen by an intellectual elite, but the masses were far less knowledgeable. Since SNCC and SCLC on the one hand and urban revolt on the other—plus television—the black students stay close to the facts, closer than breathing and nearer than hands and feet.

The culture, then, embraced by the majority is rejected by the young black as a home for his soul. He will appropriate its beneficences but to embrace it would be regarded as a sellout. He finds his peace by living in contempt of "the good old American way of life." The demands for separate facilities on some campuses and the withdrawal of black students from fraternity with white students is a manifestation of this rejection of the whole culture. The new hair styles, "Afro" mode in dress, and so on are, likewise, manifestations of contempt for the majority culture; they are far more profound than merely reverting to the psychological nest of segregation. It is a rejection of the culture of the white majority or, at least, a symbol of that rejection.

It may be concluded that the young black recognizes the necessity of "making it" in this society and the ideals of this democracy he endorses. But he feels that its protections and benefits have not extended far enough to include his parents or himself. He feels that the physical brutalizing of the slave was just a more intense form of the continual brutalizing of the psyche and the ego of the contemporary black youth.

The schools and colleges of our country derive their value hierarchy from the Judaeo-Christian tradition. This tradition treasures two important concepts. One is that the world of nature is superintended by an Intelligence that is also the moral monitor of the world of human values. The corollary to this notion is that the world—history—is a "veil of soul making." The supreme achievement of nature and history is, therefore, a human being whose true beauty and perfection are found in his rectitude and his charity. The other notion is that man's harmony with this purposiveness is not found in the "abundance of things that he possesseth" but in his loving relationship with his neighbor. When all of the chanting and liturgies are done and when the architects and building campaigns are thrown in, the above is what it should be all about.

The parents of the young blacks have bought this package. They have emulated the "white" churches and have gone through the same motions. But the young black is not following. He is less and less a believer. He gazes on the grand incongruities, the distance between profession and performance, and he has stepped aside. This is serious. It is utterly serious because, in spite of its own failures, society has no other basis for judging itself or the conduct of the young black. In other words, when the deans and trustees meet with the black for understanding, the former start the conversation in the context of moral norms that the blacks feel they have no right to use. These same norms, the blacks feel, have already indicted the leadership and rendered them morally counterfeit.

The foregoing constitute the *real* pressures on the urban universities. The rallies, the fires, the lock-ups, sit-ins, and disruptions are merely the blisters. The fever is a deeper pathology. The colleges and universities are not dealing with spoiled, lawless hoodlums who are simply demanding special favors. Rather, they are dealing with very determined young men and women who bear the marks of America's racism and who are hurt over the slow pace of change and angry over the pervasiveness of racism through every crevice of the society.

Because the urban university is the specific habitation of young adults between ages eighteen and twenty-two, and because these Gothic arches stand guard over the treasured traditions of the culture, and because the university is the distribution center for the refinement and diffusion of those traditions from one generation to the next, it is where trouble breaks out.

The colleges, in their innocence and with the best of intentions, began recently to open their doors to more black students. They meant well. When the blacks arrived on the campuses in larger numbers in 1966, 1967, and 1968, they found several assumptions operative. One assumption was that they should be grateful for this big break; two, they should be ready to prove their capacity and should, if need be, sacrifice to compete successfully; three, they should emulate "white" standards of social decorum; four, their success would pave the way for others and for the enlargement of programs for the "disadvantaged"; five, the best thing for blacks to do is to learn to maneuver the "system," get the skills, join the five-figure suburbanites, and become a role model for young blacks in the ghetto. These assumptions were radiated to blacks, not in a manual, but in the unspoken words that one reads in smiles, handshakes, announcements, committee appointments, and all the rest. They got the message.

Let's face it, this generation of college administrators really cannot be held accountable for the sins of 1619, 1896, or 1956. It is now their turn and they have tried to be responsive by opening new opportunities for young blacks. But just as the young black stands at the end of a long chain of events that delivered him to this moment, and just as he finds the historical antecedents to his present situation determinative in his life, so, likewise, the young, innocent dean must live with his moral legacy too and he cannot escape. This is not a principle of corporate guilt; it is the principle of the moral continuum in man's life. Since Adam bit the apple, we have not been privileged to wipe the scoreboard clean and start a new game. It is an unbroken, ceaseless continuum. So, neither the young black nor the administrator is in a position to exempt himself, and it is from full awareness of this inevitability that great good may come out of what appears to be a motley mess.

The Conventional University and Black Students

Now, we should examine the university and its commitments and see how these gibe or fail to gibe with the aspirations and assumptions of the new black thrust for rapid change.

First, any university catalog and its menu of courses will reveal a bias in favor of the understanding and appreciation of the Western European, Anglo-Saxon, Germanic, French, and Mediterranean cultures. The gentle winds of truth blow softly over the Aegean Sea, the Rubicon, the Rhine, and the Thames. The promulgation of this theme intoxicates a black student with a sense of worthlessness. Courses that speak approvingly of other cultures often are "special" and offered in "alternate years." But the main diet is Western Civilization. This would not be so bad if Western Civilization laid itself bare, but the implicit aggrandizement without the concomitant revelation of failures is discomforting to a black student whose status as a person was fixed long ago by an instrumentality of this "Civilization." Man, total man, all men and their strivings toward the good, the beautiful, the true, and the ultimate should be paraded before students in honesty and fairness. Now, with the imbalance so long in the other direction, immediate correctives are in order.

Second, the governance of the university is in the hands of an appointed (by the governor) or a self-perpetuating board of trustees. The personnel of the boards reflect the business, professional, and industrial life of the school's locus. The black community has had occasional—and sometimes adequate—representation on such boards, but in the main they have been expected to render such service on boards of all-Negro institutions. The pattern has indeed reflected the patterns in the country generally. But, for this reason exactly, the black students have made universities—and churches—their targets. These have been the prestige institutions, the cradles of culture, and the cells of perpetuity.

A handful of selected blacks have been frazzled by overwork on boards and committees. This use of an elite has not been mistaken by the students as a move toward inclusion but is recognized as a token signifying more general exclusion. Moreover, the blacks so chosen have been comfortable, "adjusted" blacks in whose minds those tough questions asked by the poor and the dispossessed would occur only in moments of intense introspection. Never in the genteel atmosphere of pre-meeting martinis. And, never in the perfunctory atmosphere of reports, motions, and secondings to the motions. The entire system has been, until very recently, designed without the interests of the minority population in mind. Not one black man—at this moment—is head of a single one of over two thousand four-year colleges except black schools.[1] Charitably, the skewness is understandable if not excusable. But it must all change if the confidence and the support of blacks is to be earned.

Third, the facilities, the costs, the calendar, and the organization of the school year (four long recesses and four round-trip tickets), the periods when food service is shut down, and so on, all suggest that one should have a fairly substantial home base of support. Every dean of students dealing with considerable numbers of foreign students knows this issue all too well. At Thanksgiving, Christmas, Easter, spring break, and in the summer he has had to go to the missionary societies to arrange for Sunday dinners on a very demeaning basis. These students were sent wherever food and hospitality were and could not choose to go where they wanted to be. In a sense, black students have been as helpless as the foreign students. Through no fault of their own, born black and poor, heirs of the slave legacy, they have had to adjust their lives to the punishing expense of the school year, arranged to conform to the social tastes of the affluent. Poor whites have suffered the same lot, only they have known that their condition was temporary and that relief was close in sight.

Colleges and universities that offer tuition and room and board, often with Potomac largesse, still cannot imagine the hurt, the humiliation, the agony undergone on the part of poor whites, blacks, Mexicans, Puerto Ricans, et al., in trying to cope with the costs that accompany college life on country club style. The clothing, hairdos, tickets, joining fees, transportation, and all the rest amount to one huge embarrassment for the poor. The mortification stems from the atmosphere in America's schools. They are responsive to the class structures in the society. Their doors are open to the lower classes but, in lieu of money, insult must be endured.

Fourth, the procedures for making the hurdles toward success and "honors" rest heavily on the early accumulation of facts and a healthy memory. The testing (elimination!) procedure is unfavorable to a late entrant in the academic procession. The implication is that in order to finish

[1] Clifton Wharton, Jr., a Negro, was appointed president of Michigan State University in December 1969.—Ed.

near the top, no matter how smart, one must be near the top from the earliest of his days.

At best the examinations are asking students, "What do you know?" They are not asking how well one thinks, how eager one is to learn or what one would do with knowledge when acquired. They are probes into the memory chambers of the mind. Now, if one happened to be born poor—and black—and suffered the disadvantages of the kind of education and intellectual stimulation reserved for poor blacks in America, there simply is not that much to be found in the memory chambers to present him in a competitive position.

There must be standards, but there must also be some assurance that tax-supported and tax-exempt institutions are not the minions of a process that continues to distribute favors to the already favored and cause those who have been victimized by the evils of a slave heritage and a racist society to lose ground endlessly in a highly competitive world. The money that needs to be spent does not compare with the subsidies that we provide for the rich or the support that we provide for those who are the real losers. It would be a fair and a prudent expense to provide the funds necessary to enable the universities to hold their standards but bring larger numbers of blacks within reach of those standards.

Fifth, a quick walk through the campus will show that the university, with all of its pretensions at freedom, will almost invariably follow slavishly the mores of the community at its worst. Blacks are always found in the kitchen, behind the steam table, on the north end of the mops and brooms, and riding the mowers; there are exceptions, but they are rare. Cashiers, registration clerks, lab supervisors, plant engineers, librarians, and the whole range of auxiliary personnel—bookstore managers, greenhouse managers, and the like—are usually white. In other words: What the community does to its minorities, the sign given to young blacks by the general employment pattern, the discouraging message sent forth by the businesses and industries regarding equal employment opportunity, the same is done, given, and sent by the campuses. No hard effort has been made to demonstrate to white students how they should act as future employers or show blacks what the society could look like. A lazy and thoughtless imitation of the same tired patterns of employment can be found on most campuses. Against this students are revolting. They demand more of the university community.

The foregoing, a picture of the new young black and a brief characterization of the life style of the modern, urban university, may be familiar but it bears repeating as we move toward the search for answers to our present dilemmas. We cannot settle for perennial violent confrontations or even the arbitrary suppression of revolts by police as an answer. The issue itself must be dealt with.

Cynical observers will reject this whole discussion as another blurry-eyed cry for "socialistic" egalitarianism. If a way could be found to give blacks an equal footing without these hortatory essays and cajolings, blacks would find that way far more acceptable and self-respecting. But no one can measure the deficit that a ghetto black inherited as compared, let us say, with a second-generation Balkan migrant. Who knows what a white face is worth in smoothing one's path from rejection, poverty, and ignorance to acceptance, sufficiency, and enlightenment. So, even if someone wanted to "buy up" this noise and forget it, what would the price be and who is wise enough to quantify the stifling of millions of minds and the inhibiting of millions of souls from soaring the heights of human aspiration for three hundred and fifty years?

The Issue Must Be Dealt With

The universities are undergoing a thorough, searching self-examination. It is unfortunate that it has been brought on by student revolts, that the students identified the universities as the enemies—not the friends—of those noble social ends extolled in the classrooms. In order to bring about change, the policies in admission, financial aid, employment, and tenure should be re-examined.

Let us consider admission. Most schools have altered their approaches, but some of the actions have only aggravated the problem. Many students have been brought in who meet the poverty criterion but bring little else. These admissions are a poor use of precious chairs in college classrooms. There must be some way found of judging who wants to go to school and who does not, and a way must be found to bring in many more of those whose aspirations are serious. If we bring 200 poor blacks into a population of 20,000 whites, of whom a few are inconspicuously poor, it is rough on the pride and the self-image of the 200 blacks. They simply cannot thrive on charity, condescension, and tutoring. If 200 poor blacks are found, then 200 blacks who can cope in every way should be lured to the campus also. A school that adopts a method of artificial insemination must choose its semen, and all poor blacks is not a wise choice. It reinforces the whites' stereotype and the blacks' feelings of defeat and futility.

Forty percent of the black population falls below the poverty line. There is a critical mass in the next 40 percent that is also neglected in the sparse enrollment of blacks in the top schools. These are the sons and daughters of home owners, civil servants, and others—not rich but not on welfare. Thus, a revised admissions policy will consider more than the factor of poverty, eligibility for Federal grants for the poor; it will recognize as well the more subtle factors of ghetto existence. Poverty is more than the shortage of dollars. It is the absence of encouragement, of confidence, of aspiration, and of achievement. Segregated living and, hence, segregated schools lump blacks both above and below the poverty line in one category in terms of college readiness. The policy of exempting financially only the very poor from the normal college admissions is a denial to others who have been victimized in other ways by ghetto living, by other forms of poverty. In order for blacks to feel wanted on the campuses, their enrollment must approach 6–8 percent. A bolder challenge would seek out 10–12 percent.

The University Community Redefined

The essence is that the urban university must declare what kind of community it intends to be. Christianity began as a new religious community, obliterating all other requirements for membership except love of God and love of one's fellowman. It transcended the lines between bond and free, Jewish ancestry and non-Jewish ancestry, male and female, Greek and barbarian, learned and unlearned, rich and poor. A moral commitment was the nexus of community. Universities in the modern world need to decide who they are. If they regard themselves as merely agential in passing a cultural package from one generation to the next, they may continue as they are. If they are the discoverers and distributors of truth, and their community is based upon this function, it does no violation to this principle to find a way to induct those into this process who have heretofore been shut out. Christianity lost its uniqueness by acceding to class and political allegiances. Early in its history one had to read Latin to serve the Church or to read its Scriptures. It had changed the nexus of community. The earliest universities were for the clergy. That changed as theology lost its pre-eminence as the queen of the sciences. Later the Morrill Act extended the mission of higher education. The boundaries extended beyond the liberal arts to include the mechanic arts, homemaking, and farming. Another shift in boundaries is now in order. We need now to include those who would like to enrich their lives, change their economic status, improve on the legacy that they were bequeathed before passing it on to their posterity.

Changes in admission should be accompanied by changes in employment patterns—the nonteaching staff has been discussed. It is also just as urgent to reward with tenure those who prove that they can make the search for truth appetizing to the intellectually disadvantaged, as we now reward those who discover new truth, publish, and gain recognition but who too often look with contempt upon the fundamental task of teaching those who have not been taught. What passes for "professionalism" is often no more than academic snobbishness—the absence of humility and a disdain for those who need to be taught. In this sense, new ranking standards would compel teachers to quit bragging about how few students they have to "contact" but rather look to how many they have led to drink deep from the Pierian spring.

Universities need to measure themselves by how effectively they can launch successive generations of students on their search for selfhood and the expansion of knowledge. If this is the new criterion, then the laurels should go to those who can initiate this process among those persons and among those social classes that have heretofore been excluded.

A revitalized purpose constitutes no pressure, really. It is opportunity. Today's students, despite some uncalled-for tactics, may be saving universities from becoming a barren colony of sycophants who would soon become the object of contempt for everyone, quoting each other to each other and becoming more and more parasitic on private philanthropy and the tax dollar. Something has really gone wrong when both the blacks, poor and not so poor, and the affluent and not so affluent whites have all decided at the same time that a new relevance must be found on campus.

There may be some specialized universities who should justifiably cater to an intellectual elite for very advanced work in critical fields. These would be few. But the urban university is called upon to do for the commonwealth, in the humanizing of life, in the refinement of democracy and the establishment of peace and justice, what the land-grant universities have done for cattle breeding, hybrid corn, synthetic fertilizers, and butterfat. The changes wrought on America's farms need now to be brought about in America's decaying cities. Since a main function of a university is instruction, perhaps we should look into this area first, both for the cause of so much unhappiness and for the promise of something better

Re-viewing Teaching and Learning

For many years the large salaries and the power have been associated with administration. Therefore, the best brains have been spent on budgets, new campus layouts, legislative hearings, and football deficits. Every time a new presidency became vacant, another great teacher left the classroom, either by direct ascent or by musical chairs. That game is changing. Not as many great teachers can get their physician's permission to take on the field generalship of the modern campus. How fortunate for teaching and students. More and more presidencies will have to settle for less than the sharpest teachers.

Revision of purpose should bring a great day for creative teaching, especially in the urban universities. First we need to exploit the talent "in town" as allies to creative teachers. Many schools have dropped the traditional Ph.D. membership card as a requirement for teaching privileges. This is good. Many cities have so much talent in town, working on tough assignments, that it would be criminal to limit students to the textbook-recitation ritual as a substitute for real learning. A new concept of teaching does not mean that every firebrand is sane enough to teach anybody, but there are people in the cities now about whom textbooks will be written ten years from now. They have their hands in the stuff of the reality that is today's city. Let the students live with this reality now! Again, this is not a pressure but an opportunity. We wrote textbooks because the experience itself was out of reach.

Next, we need to exploit the laboratory that surrounds us. Student teachers, for example, can start from the first day of the freshman year getting acquainted with the center city, its schools, its problems, its opportunities. Fledgling doctors can volunteer in undermanned hospitals. Every human problem groans for solution. Every human condition is laid bare. Accountants can learn by helping a poverty agency keep its records. Computer science students can find opportunities in any large agency. In other words, there need not be any third-hand simulation of experience projected by an uninitiated teacher. The teacher needs to provide the guidance and the evaluation, and move over so students can learn.

Granted, both teachers and students need some preparation and orientation to the new teaching-learning environment. But the city today is a laboratory for almost any discipline, and it should be used. The sharp line between student and worker, or student and professional, was tolerable before cities became so deeply troubled and when life was simpler. Now, one must graduate already experienced, landing on the job on the run, rehearsed and briefed, and—only incidentally—degreed.

We need to examine some of the cultures that have been left unattended by the scholars. More is made over black studies and Puerto Rican studies than need be. They are legitimate, and whoever teaches them should know them, black or white. That they have been neglected is not debatable.

More important than the individual courses is the approach made by the social sciences to the subjects that affect the blacks and Puerto Ricans, Mexicans, and Indians. Classical approaches to sociology, economics, government, and history will never get to the issues. There must be a vertical fathoming of deep questions that will cut through all of these disciplines. Students need that exercise. How do we get rid of rural poverty? What can a big city mayor do? Who runs the Republican party? Who finances the radical Right, the radical Left? What should a modern defense system look like? Who is killing the U.N., and why? Has socialism failed in Africa? Whither Latin America? How can such questions be dealt with on a narrow, one-discipline basis?

The same is true of the sciences. A city child watches the Apollo 11 shot. That is his world. Commentators speak freely of the associated problems of gravity, of blood circulation, of food preservation, weightlessness, re-entry, sinus infections, and all the rest. All are related to space exploration. And the student lives vicariously through it all. How can he go to school and suffer the real world to be fragmented, subject by subject, without being bored with the unreality?

Television has packaged experience, selected its modules of excitement and interest, and invited us—not to study and cogitate—to live through them in existential intensity. This presence has changed the classroom for everyone. The child of limited book victories—the poor—sees no reason to repeat that experience. He wants to jump on a moving experience.

To Be an Urban Institution and Relevant

Not only do racial pressures require that the style of operation and the program of instruction in an urban university change, but that the involvement in the community also be different. Deprived people now know that it is not merely luck or brains that control status in this society. It is not simply that one person was too stupid at birth and others born very bright that determines the make-up of an urban student body. They know that the quality of early education was different, the stimuli in the environments varied widely, and the forces impelling toward careerism and success were dissimilar in quantity and in quality.

No one institution can redress all social wrong. The urban university, especially, does not have the money or the political muscle. But every institution bears some kind of social witness. By what it does, it chooses to alter the social wrongs or to conform to their perpetual and fecund nature.

The latter is most frightening. Unless one or another segment of the society does something, things compound and reproduce their kind. That is the nature of social wrong; there is no way to check its fallout. We take the wrong for granted for so long that it begins to look right and its manifestations multiply. Black children and uncollected garbage are seen together so much that they seem like inseparable entities. Then, all that goes along with uncollected garbage seems permissible as part of the black child's environment.

Moreover, it is awfully difficult to assess guilt or to invent an adequate grievance mechanism. In a big city bureaucracy, it is well-nigh impossible for the poor to get through the labyrinths of city hall. So they take to the streets. The problem of guilt is not simply that good men do nothing but that the wrong done does not seem to have been deliberately perpetrated. It is hard to find the *deliberate* transgressor. The evil is embroidered in contracts, leases, laws, franchises, precedents, nominating committees, and unanimous voting.

But a university is a *deliberating* organ in society. It *deliberately* contracts to serve medicine, industry, or the Pentagon. It does indeed create new concepts and new things. Both the A-bomb and polio vaccine came out of universities. This institution can choose to involve itself and become a creator of new social and educational mutations that will start a new thrust in the society, breaking the deadly continuum of the old and initiating the vibrantly new. Deliberately, therefore, the urban universities must point their schools of medicine, social work, education, business, architecture, and law toward that natural laboratory that surrounds them. One thing should be clear: middle-class whites and blacks are not going to experience any peace as they traverse a city slum to get to air-conditioned libraries and classes to indulge in an escape into antiquity. Antiquity is important, but it will have to find a place on the priority scale in relation to other pressing claims.

There is no justification for universities' changing merely because of riots and disorders. If that were all there was to it, the answer would be the call for matching or superior fire power. There is more to it. Bountiful America can do better by its poor and its blacks. And universities cannot, however unwittingly, remain partners to a social system that responds sluggishly and only under pressure to the call to justice.

On Petit Jean Mountain, in Arkansas, there is a beautiful state park bearing that name. It is one of our country's most restful spots. The eye easily follows the neat contours of the well-spaced, shimmering lakes, spread generously at the feet of tapered mountain peaks. This sight awaits the traveler as he winds his way up Highway 10 to a new Arkansas, created largely by the philanthropy and ideas of Governor Rockefeller. Suddenly, the dusty dungarees, the worn-out tractors, and the parched white flesh of Ozark poverty give way to the movement of clean, green trucks, handsome thoroughbred bulls and horses by the thousands, and the impeccable landscaping that somehow follows money. One feels guilty after the first hour, leaving behind so much confusion and incoherence as he sits on a rock and lets nature unspoiled speak to him.

Along the roadside, a few hundred yards from the Lodge, however, there is a tall pine tree that tells its story too. When it was a young, wet sprig, some hunter, some highway cement finisher, some grass-cutter, or just a boy with a dog mindlessly tied a knot in that sprig. How long ago? Who knows? But there she stands today, her top level with the rest. But midway her trunk is a loop, a tied knot that was supposed to cut her life short as a young thing. That tree outgrew that knot. She sent her roots drilling into the mountain soil in search of nurture. She waited for the rains; she stretched her pores to absorb the sun's radiation. She let her environment serve her, and because that environment served so well, she grew, in spite of that mischievous knot tied to choke her lifeline.

While the majestic mountains speak of wars and trailblazers and things aboriginal, when the world was young, this deformed tree standing nobly with the rest tells that when the environment is supportive, when help is unbegrudging, and when creation is in harmony with its Grand Original, the follies of man can be overcome, his mischief can be canceled out, and his high potential can be realized. The black student is asking the universities to be that environment. He will respond and reach his height treetop tall, with only an appearance a little bit different.

Commentaries on

Racial Pressures on Urban Institutions

WILLIAM REA KEAST, GWENDOLYN PATTON WOODS
CHARLES D. GELATT, NORVEL L. SMITH

A National Effort for Educational Justice

WILLIAM REA KEAST

ALTHOUGH I have some reservations about details in the history and analysis Professor Proctor presents as background, I am in complete agreement with him that universities must promptly carry out a thoroughgoing redefinition of their responsibilities to an urban society in which the black and the poor are denied full status. I share the view recently expressed by Hubert Locke:

> I am convinced [that] higher education can make an immense, perhaps pivotal contribution to the twin problems of the racial and urban revolutions in American society. If it cannot or will not, then the nation, which is for all practical purposes urban, may not have a future and indeed may not deserve one.

The time for rhetoric and recriminations is past. What we need most is thought, planning, resources, and action. I shall comment only on a few aspects of the broad problem of our racial crisis as it affects and is affected by education, especially in urban settings, that require careful attention.

I want to underline Professor Proctor's point that we must stop describing the claims of black students and of our abused cities for educational opportunity and for university assistance as "pressures." That language suggests a continuous atmosphere of crisis, prompts primarily ad hoc solutions, and implies that if only "something" is done—often in a token way, as a safety-valve—to relieve or reduce the pressure, the problem will go away. This is wrong, and it accounts in part for the continuation of our difficulties. We are really concerned with permanent changes in our society and in our universities. The so-called pressures, as Mr. Proctor rightly says, are in fact opportunities. Unless we see pressures in that light and not as temporary disturbances or short-term crises, we will never use them to the full for institutional and social renovation.

Nothing less than a fundamental and permanent realignment of the universities in relation to *the whole* of our society will preserve our universities and our society. If this is so, we must do a number of things we are not now doing at all or are not doing to any noticeable effect.

1. We must decide which of the new opportunities the universities and colleges are best qualified to deal with. Our problems are so numerous and so acute that every institution finds itself called upon to move in hundreds of directions. Not all of them are directions in which the special talents and energies of educational institutions—even if reformed in major ways—can be best exerted. There must be a more systematic sharing of responsibility between universities and the other institutions of our society. Otherwise, our universities and colleges will do nothing well, and our other institutions will continue to decay. Since our universities have never been distinguished for the clarity of their purposes, this is a large order, and the pressures to which they are now exposed make this kind of self-awareness especially difficult. But I am convinced we will make little progress if definition is much longer delayed.

2. If we must think hard about the best roles of universities and colleges *in general,* each *individual* institution must decide what, in view of its own history, tradition, resources, and abilities it can do best. It is obvious enough that every institution should reform its curriculum to reduce the present bias toward white, Western civilization. It is equally obvious that every institution must increase its enrollment of black and other minority group students, although clearly they should not all proceed or be expected to proceed at the same rate or toward the same target numbers or under the same guidelines. Homogenization has always been a failing of American higher education, as in American society generally. This ingrained leveling impulse is today reinforced by the national dimensions of the racial crisis, by the effects of Federal programs, and by the desire of all well-intentioned faculties and administrations to do something. But permanent solutions will come only if we conserve our institutional strengths, which lie largely in the unique capabilities of our colleges and universities, working out diversified but equally responsible ways of rising to their opportunities.

3. If such solutions are to come about, then we must make new and unprecedented arrangements for interinstitutional collaboration, among

schools in our major cities, and on state, regional, and national bases; and we must plan the development of our institutions in relation to state and Federal programs and to the efforts of the foundations. I am convinced that we cannot cope with our opportunities on the present catch-as-catch-can basis.

Nothing less will do, in my opinion, than a clear and firm set of national goals for higher education, with a specific timetable for their achievement. The national goals should provide the rationale for all Federal programs in support of higher education. Congress and the executive branch should agree to put them beyond politics. The national goals should be in turn translated into state plans, using present coordinating arrangements or inventing new ones, in which each existing institution and each institution to be created over the next few years will have a distinct role and a unique commitment. Federal and state assistance to higher education should be geared to the execution of these plans and should be contingent on institutional performance.

The heart of the undertaking should be a national commitment to ensure —perhaps by 1976—that blacks and other minority groups are in fact attending programs of their choice at all levels of higher education, from community colleges to schools of medicine and law, in a proportion of their numbers in the population that is not less than the proportion of the white population in attendance. Any objective less than this is unacceptable. To achieve it, we must have a national commitment and a national plan in which each of us can have a definite responsibility. We are far from that point today.

Such a national and institutional commitment is the only basis I can see for coming to an accurate estimate of the resources we will need if we are to equalize educational opportunity in this country. At the moment no one knows what it would take to do the job because we haven't a clear notion of what the job is or when we should complete it. Until we have an estimate and a timetable, we will continue to temporize and compromise. Federal and state programs will continue to be inadequately financed, and they will continue to be fragmented and uncoordinated. Some institutions will do too little and a few may do too much. In such complex fields as medicine, law, pharmacy, engineering, and the graduate disciplines—where black enrollment today lags far behind even our pitiful performance at the undergraduate level—we are likely to fall even further behind.

Without such a commitment and plan, I do not see how we will be able to command the widespread public support that we must have if the resources needed for this great task are to be provided. Large additional expenditures for facilities, programs, and people will be needed, beginning at a time when neither Congress nor most state governments seem eager to increase spending for higher education. We must mobilize the support of all our people for a truly national effort, beyond rhetoric and politics, for educational justice and national survival. It would be a worthy goal for 1976.

Pro-Black, Not Anti-White

GWENDOLYN PATTON WOODS

I FIND the background paper by Dr. Samuel Proctor one of the most honest papers written about black students at the predominantly white institutions. His assessment of the problem in many instances is correct and at the same time he has a positive approach to how to remedy the situation. It does not smack of liberalism, nor is it condescending.

The National Association of Black Students has raised many of the issues presented by Dr. Proctor. We have ideas for a test and measurement for black students at all age levels to determine motivation, attitudes, and intelligence. Our only criterion will be the black experience in America.

Dr. Proctor in many words supports black studies that will move beyond black history and black culture. However, there must be at the same time a complete overhaul of the white educational experience with a built-in program for white students' emotional needs so that they will not "freak out," seeking another form of unreality.

Black students many times are fighting racist attitudes of other ethnic groups. Ethnic groups use this strategy and then run for cover under the all-white racist attitude so that they will not be singled out. At the same time they are building a fortress against the black students (Jews at C.C.N.Y., Irish at Notre Dame). When black students point to the particular group, they become "anti-Semitic" or "intolerant of religious beliefs." These ascriptions distort the issues of admission, black studies, and other major innovations and reforms that black students are pressing.

Dr. Proctor talks about rejection of Western values by young black students. This is not totally true. Black people have always been about finding an identity which is comfortable for them—thus, casual clothing and other forms of a life style that have been sanctioned by black people and co-opted by white people as "hip, cool, groovy, soul," etc. Natural hair and African attire are only extensions and a continuation of finding a comfortable life style. For many, a life style is the only form of freedom they have in this country. Furthermore, it is an assertion on the part of black people that they do, indeed have a historical culture and that this culture is latent in most black people, particularly those who have not wholly assimilated Western values. This trend is a positive attitude toward self-worth and dignity, not necessarily a rejection of white values. We must view this as pro-black in lieu of anti-white.

Black students for the past nine years have approached administrations and the society at large with positive programs. At this stage students are altruistic and idealistic. The students' major thrust has been to open the doors for more black young people. The more recent thrust is for black studies programs because we all know that students learn better when they have a knowledge of themselves and of their people. The university and society have rejected these positive programs. And because of this "rejection" all hell breaks loose and black students through some weird turn of events become the negative ones, the ones who are rejecting positive programs and approaches. Dr. Proctor must give this some consideration.

More than a Culture Gap, More than a Generation Gap

CHARLES D. GELATT

DR. PROCTOR has vividly detailed the differences in background, viewpoint, and especially forward thrust of the black student now compared with those of his parents. He has then shown how the present university fails to accommodate itself to the needs and ambitions of the new black. And finally, he suggests changes whereby the university can effectively, and I quote, "launch successive generations of students on their search for selfhood and the expansion of knowledge."

I come to comment on his paper as a white American, from a city of 50,000 population, more than one hundred and twenty-five miles from any urban center. My mother was a Norwegian emigrant, my father's forebears came to this country in the mid-eighteenth century. My father was forced for economic reasons to drop out of Kansas City High School in 1893. My mother worked as a servant and then became a trained nurse, and such training meant two years of seven-day-a-week, twelve-hour days. She died when I was three. I graduated from the University of Wisconsin in 1939 and have been in business ever since. I have been a regent of the University of Wisconsin since 1947 and have been enrolled as a graduate student in economics at Madison since 1967.

I agree with Dr. Proctor's analysis of the pressure on the urban university. If I read him correctly, it is more a culture gap than a generation gap. The young black does not accept the norms of the university, nor of those who have built and governed it over the past two hundred years. The university, with its standards, finds that to meet the demands of the black requires compromise or change of the kind which goes to the heart of the purpose of the American university. The resulting friction is great. I do disagree with Dr. Proctor about the causes of the new black. And although the new black is different in many ways from the white militant and the apparent majority of young students who enjoy, enlarge, and exploit the generation gap, they have much in common. It starts in many cases from the wider perceptions of the world that TV has given this generation. They see and feel and absorb. They are more aware of the problems of the world. They are better informed of the crises of the world. But they have not had the time nor the patience nor the training to read history or literature, nor have they related today's events and today's problems to similar ones of the past. They are not so well educated as earlier generations. And they are not as civilized.

The younger generation is also the product of rapid and often uneconomic urbanization. The welfare system, which is under considerable attack, has expanded the numbers of people who have moved to the city for no other reason apparently than to better themselves on a cash income basis, while leaving behind areas where opportunities for productive improvement are increasing. It is ironic, somewhat incomprehensible, and aggravating to a businessman today to be searching for employees at the same time that welfare rolls increase so rapidly. The cities have created a culture of their own, particularly the core of the city. I cannot speak from any firsthand knowledge or even firsthand observation, but Dr. Proctor has pointed out the culture gap and I accept it as a real one. We have on one hand the mainstream of American culture, the white, Western European culture, transplanted to America, changed by conditions here, developing through the ideals of America. And on the other hand we have the culture of the black who unhappily did not partake of that great era of American public education when it was dedicated to being the melting pot for the various nationalities from Europe.

Universities have expanded too rapidly over the past ten or fifteen years. They are in great danger of becoming so massive that they will suffer the same fate as the high schools when high school education became so nearly universal sixty years ago. A university a generation and more ago was a very special place. It achieved widespread reputation because the selection process made sure that only the gifted intellectually and the favored economically attended. Thus those who came out of college were almost assured of career success in life. Those less favored by earlier education or family position, but still sharing the common culture of America, inferred that the college education itself produced the result that, rather, was predictable from the selection of the student. The university having a selected student body could go about its major concerns of scholarship, professional standards, and the search for truth. In its intellectual rigor the university made demands on young people for self-discipline. It fought off urgings by legislatures and business to become more relevant to current problems. Its response was to establish colleges of agriculture and schools of business and law, but the university maintained always its own autonomy; the university set the standards of performance and the standards of employment within those fields, and it concentrated its greatest efforts on pure research and scholarship in the sciences and humanities.

Demands are now being made on universities to become relevant to today's problems, to look at the immediate rather than to seek for the permanent, to establish standards of performance based on the individual's background rather than on the ideal within a specific subject field. Universities have changed with the great influx of students. Performance standards are more lax. Subject matter is more "relevant." Young professors are more political in their viewpoint. They seek of the university a commitment for social revolution.

Should they succeed in politicizing the university, intellectual freedom and attainment will be forced to find another home. The university cannot enter the battleground of politics and escape that battle without wounds which will be mortal to its objectivity and prestige.

I agree with Dr. Proctor that no good will come from selecting and helping only poor blacks to a college education. He urges a ratio of at least 50-50 between poor blacks and blacks who can "cope in every way." I would prefer a ratio of 1 to 2. I further concur that for new academic subjects, the Ph.D. should not be a prerequisite to a teaching position. In the past it has not been a prerequisite for universities starting new programs or for emerging universities either.

A re-examination of the balance between teaching load and subsidized research load can be beneficial. Reread Willa Cather's *The Professor's House* to recapture the sense of dedication to teaching and the sacrifices to research that were made two generations ago in an academic community.

I would be wary of using as a laboratory the community that surrounds us. Cities offer endless opportunities to practice while learning, but I can not agree that universities should experiment on the populace. Elected representatives of the people are the ones who have the responsibility and the authority to make changes in society—that is if one believes in democracy. If, however, one believes in an oligarchy of intelligence, then the universities might well claim the right so to experiment, to change civilization in accordance with their judgment rather than on the basis of a plebiscite.

The cures, of course, lie well beyond the university alone. They start with elementary and secondary schooling. They start with black people themselves and with white people. They start with job opportunities and willingness to sacrifice present pleasure for one's future and for one's children's future. The so-called materialism of America has been the long look. It has been investment in people, an investment in ideas, an investment in machinery. It has even been an investment in change. The universities can indeed add this much to the solution of the problem: to find in American culture, in the mainstream of American culture, those threads and those elements that are not only worthy of emulation by all of its citizens but also are necessary for the survival of any complex, integrated, open-end society. And certainly these include the long look, the sense of responsibility for one's own act, the sense of responsibility for one's own children, the sense of relating one's self, not just to today or even tomorrow, but also to centuries preceding and centuries ahead. Colleges and universities can emphasize more than they recently have the positive element in all aspects of American society, while at the same time criticizing, as they should, the shortcomings and aberrations. Let us again raise the standard to which the wise and honest may repair.

Institutions Must Change

NORVEL L. SMITH

DR. PROCTOR'S ANALYSIS of the historical background of the present crisis on campus is outstanding and I cannot add significantly to his perceptions. A number of observations concerning the current situation, however, seem to me to be appropriate.

We need to be concerned about the paternalistic Educational Opportunity programs that, in many ways, are being used as excuses for not allowing good, average black students to enter the colleges through normal admission procedures or without being "superniggers."

We must recognize that adequate programs of supportive services (tutoring, financial aid, counseling, part-time jobs) are essential to the survival of black students in the institutions. Otherwise, we play a numbers game in admissions, and we further accentuate the frustrations and the alienation of black and other disadvantaged students. It has been estimated by admissions experts that 90 percent of the black students aspiring to higher education need some kind of financial assistance and that the majority of them need *full* financial assistance.

I think we must be sensitive to the peculiarities of certain "national" institutions, such as the University of California, Berkeley, which has chosen to be a national (international?) resource, instead of serving the needs of its public constituency as a state university. There are other examples, I am sure, of such institutions that should take a hard look at their out-of-state student and foreign student quotas as they attempt to identify resources to serve the needs of their indigenous populations. Whereas approximately 30 percent of the total college population is attending public institutions of higher learning, only 2 percent of the black college population is found in those institutions.

As to separate ethnic studies programs, I feel they are justified to the extent that traditional academic programs are not relevant to the needs of minority students, particularly in the social sciences, and for so long as the racial and ethnic composition of the faculties continues to be disproportionate to that of the student bodies and total populations being served.

Pressure must be applied on universities and colleges to integrate their faculties and to do so immediately, even if it means having college administrators challenge the tyranny of faculties in wanting to remain inbred. This would also expose the sham of the minority group "shadow faculties" which now proliferate on our major campuses as nontenured assistants and visiting professors.

And we are going to have to reward faculty members who can deal with the disadvantaged as highly as we reward those who only have skills in traditional research techniques and production. We have not begun to tap the talent pool in the overall community to supplement the limited skills of talented academics.

In summary, we must try to step up the pace of institutional change to keep up with the aspirations growing out of the civil rights revolution. The character of the institutions must change, not just the personality and the performance of the black and disadvantaged students.

Racial Minorities and Curriculum Change

W. TODD FURNISS

Most academics would agree that colleges and universities in the United States have not met their obligations to all students who need advanced education and particularly to those of minority racial groups. Meeting these obligations in a time of campus calm would be difficult enough in view of the many unknowns that only experimentation can illuminate. Meeting them in a time of revolutionary crisis such as some of our campuses are now experiencing calls for all the intelligence and good-will that can be mustered. Nevertheless, the effort must be made.

What follows is an attempt to analyze the needs, examine the assumptions lying behind proposed solutions, and suggest positions that may be both progressive and acceptable to those involved. The discussion focuses almost exclusively on black studies, yet most of it is also applicable to the situation of other racial minorities which are experiencing largely the same disadvantages as blacks even though they did not come to the United States as slaves.

Recommendations or demands for black studies programs presented in the winter and spring of 1969 have been motivated by several considerations, including the following:

Correcting American history by a more adequate recognition of the past and present experience of 25 million black citizens.

Hastening integration by improving the understanding of blacks by nonblacks.

Hastening integration by preparing black students to take part in American society with pride and self-confidence.

Preparing black students to understand and work for a black community.

Providing black students with a sense of "power."

The programs for achieving these ends are known as "black studies" or "Afro-American studies." Their proponents ordinarily justify them by assertions, and institutions contemplating the establishment of some form of black studies often find themselves adjudicating conflicting assertions.

Going behind the assertions to their underlying assumptions, we may find enough areas of agreement to indicate those decisions most likely to produce desirable results. As a framework, I use the five considerations above, understanding that the interrelationships among them are complex and that some concerns defy neat categorization.

Historical Rehabilitation and Black Historiography

> We are dealing with 25 million of our own people with a special history, culture, and range of problems. It can hardly be doubted that the study of black men in America is a legitimate and urgent academic endeavor.[1]

Quite apart from the question of whether some of the 25 million want their history, culture, and range of problems studied, the above statement of a Harvard committee asserts that such academic study is legitimate and urgent, just as not many years ago the Congress agreed upon the national urgency of the study of foreign history, culture, and other problems.

What is the state of black history today? Professor Richard Long of Atlanta University, in an address in January 1969, said,

> Up until yesterday, everything about the black man in America that has been studied, both by black men and white men alike, has been studied uniquely from the Euro-American point of view. Naturally, such a procedure can only reveal Euro-American traits. The residual matter has been either ignored or described as independent, but local variation. This particular denial of the black American's cultural heritage is only a special case of the rejection of the black man from world history by European and American scholars alike.[2]

Many analyses of published histories and recent accounts of the status of the black in our society make the same charges.

But agreement that the account of the black experience in America shall be rewritten and incorporated into general accounts of American society still leaves some disagreement about what kind of revised history is needed. Is it to be what William Golding calls "academic, or if you like, campus history . . . that objective yet devoted stare with which humanity observes its own past; and in that stare, that attempt to see how things have become what they are, where they went wrong, and where right"? It is in such a history "that our only hope lies of having some control over

---

[1] *Report of the Faculty Committee on African and Afro-American Studies,* Harvard University, Jan. 20, 1969, p. 14.

[2] "Africa and America: Race and Scholarship" (Keynote address at Conference on Southern Africa, Shaw University, Jan. 10, 1969), mimeo., p. 6.

our own future." Golding contrasts campus history with the "history felt in the blood and bones. Sometimes it is dignified by a pretty name, but I am not sure in my own mind that it is ever anything but pernicious." [3] He refers, of course, to the kind of history that grows out of politics, religion, and other stimuli to prejudgment, the literal equivalent of prejudice.

The issue of black historiography is faced squarely by Louis R. Harlan in a recent article:

> History is more than a matter of recreating the past in a mechanical, value-free way. The historical perspective is worth something, hard to measure but significant, for policy making, because history is actually an extension of human memory and experience. But if you try to make history jump through hoops it was not meant to jump through, it may bite! Particularly if it is bad history to begin with.

He condemns both the historians who accuse all black leaders of the past of race betrayal and those who

> change the tortured odyssey of the black man along Freedom Road into a succession of sugar-coated success stories, designed to give black children a more favorable and hopeful self-concept but dangerous because they are bad history.[4]

The Harvard committee and Harlan both consider "academic history," in Golding's term, to be essential to the health of America. Nevertheless, the rewriting of black history is not waiting for the academics. Courses in black history are being taught, books are being published, the memory of black notables is being revived, and black history is being cited to back up political positions from moderate to extreme.

Colleges seeking assistance in locating up-to-date materials on black history may refer to several new bibliographies.[5] Some caution should be exercised in selecting items from these and other bibliographies now available. The College Language Association in a "Statement on Publishers," approved in April 1969, asserts, "Many books now appearing have been

---

[3] "Fable," *The Hot Gates and Other Occasional Pieces* (New York: Pocket Books ed., 1967), pp. 89–90.

[4] "Tell It Like It Was: Suggestions on Black History," *Social Education*, April 1969, p. 391.

[5] For example, *Social Education*, April 1969, pp. 447–94; "The Heritage of the Negro" (Berea, Ohio: Humanities Institute, Baldwin Wallace College); bibliographies in several fields prepared by Focus: Black America, Rm. 223, Woodburn Hall, Indiana University, Bloomington, Ind. 47401.

prepared by 'instant' experts and have apparently been seen only by such experts before they reach publication." Faculty research and publication sponsored by colleges, foundations, the National Endowment for the Humanities, and professional associations could improve the output of accurate histories. Participation by knowledgeable black students and faculty in the selection of texts can help curriculum planners avoid the work of instant experts.

Although I have used the term *history,* I am not speaking only of the distant past. In fact, the history of today as it becomes yesterday will be the hardest to write, and its authors, however objective, will inevitably be subject to attacks from those whose prejudices are not supported by the facts. The only defense against such attacks will be the best and most careful job that historians can produce. Those who support the work of the historians and those charged with translating history into the curriculum will do well then to eschew the support and transmission of anything but the best "academic history," regardless of the pressures to do otherwise.

I have dwelt at some length on what may be obvious because an accurate knowledge of what has happened and is happening in the American community is fundamental to every other aspect of black studies. To the extent that we lack knowledge or are misinformed, we will grope from ignorance to myth and our remedies will be unicorns' horns.

Nonblacks and Integration

The integration of black and nonblack citizens of the United States was made national policy some years ago. The means for integration are of two sorts. Breaking down legal barriers that foster unequal treatment on the basis of race is one; the other is the harder one of changing attitudes. The principal instrument for the second is education, especially formal education in schools and colleges.

Two assumptions underlie the use of educational institutions to bring about change in attitude. The first is noncurricular. Its argument runs that regular proximity of dissimilar people produces understanding which in turn produces tolerant attitudes. Further, it is contended, small children are color-blind and tolerant; bringing them together in school will reinforce their openness and prevent the development of intolerance; and even those who may have brought intolerant attitudes from family or neighborhood will lose them in school. The second main argument is curricular: the content of the curriculum and the methods of teaching that content will change attitudes, in this case, from intolerance to tolerance.

Proximity, the curriculum, and behavior models

Even if these devices can actually produce the purported changes, are they the best ones or only poor ones? Will other factors wholly negate the effects desired? Can it be imagined that proximity in college might under certain circumstances have an effect opposite to that hoped for? For example, what will this white Wesleyan University senior carry with him from a college deliberately designed to provide both proximity and curricular stimuli to integration?

> I'm not prejudiced or racist, and I'm tired of their accusations. I know that my ancestors mistreated their ancestors, but I'll be damned if I'll feel guilty about it now. But the fact that I don't want to be identified saying this does, I guess, indicate some insecurity about it all. Nevertheless, racial discrimination of any kind is wrong, and what I've seen at Wesleyan is reverse discrimination. The Afro-Am house is segregation, and Etherington's administration seems completely preoccupied with Negroes.[6]

For another example, there is the black girl who had attended predominantly white schools until she went to Spelman College:

> I just don't like the idea of black people being on display. I was on display all through high school. Being at an all-black school is like a rebirth. I don't have to prove anything here. I'm accepted for what I am.[7]

For these two, proximity had not yet, at least, had the effect it was supposed to have.

These two examples prove nothing, of course, about the desirability of proximity in college as a device to reduce intolerance. But I also suspect that the very rapid recent changes in the role of blacks, particularly in some formerly all-white colleges, may to an extent invalidate the findings of earlier studies showing success. The argument that proximity in college is one of the best devices for guaranteeing tolerance in white students must be tested by systematic longitudinal studies. Until these are done, we must in honesty consider the possibility that some forms of separatism should not be rejected out of hand on the grounds that we "know" that required proximity in college is desirable.

The curriculum argument may possibly also have some flaws. It contends that the white student, learning about blacks, will understand them better and thus will become less intolerant. The argument assumes that he

[6] *New York Times*, Jan. 31, 1969, p. 42.
[7] *Newsweek*, Feb. 10, 1969, p. 55.

enters college intolerant, that what he learns will tempt him to be more tolerant, and that in fact he will become more tolerant. Other possibilities are seldom considered. For example, he may enter tolerant, learn things about blacks that put him off, and exit with more knowledge and less tolerance. Or he may find the instruction beneficial (it seems to have reinforced the Wesleyan student's notion that all discrimination is wrong), but the milieu—the noncurricular side of his life—offsets the good effects of the curriculum.

Discussions of changing attitudes in college seldom refer to the influence of behavior models. Elementary and secondary teachers seem to be far more conscious than college teachers of the effects of their own attitudes on their students, and of the models one student sets for another. College teachers and administrators are conscious of the influence of parental models on students, but seldom do they consider themselves as models and almost never do they consider institutional policy as providing a model for students. In institutions where faculty are workmen in the disciplines, administrators are deft managers, trustees are defenders of the status quo, and the institutions—by definition—not human, are they therefore not required to act humanely? Does any significant part of such academic communities provide a pervasive model of humane tolerance? If not, then curricular and physically integrative devices may be nearly useless.

Differences and similarities

Thus far, I have referred to white and black students as if they were discrete categories and alike within each category, an assumption common to black studies proposals. Granted that the real differences go beyond color to culture and that in a pair of students, one black and one white, it is more likely than not that some differences will be found to grow out of the racial distinction. But it is also appropriate to ask whether other differences and similarities can be discerned that will have greater bearing educationally on the nature of black studies programs. For example, each racial group may display wide differences in academic performance in school, and some of the poor performances in both racial groups will be attributable to cultural deprivation, some to physical factors, some to lack of motivation, broken homes, and so on. If a college is to admit and try to help these high-risk students, much that it does will be based on factors other than race. Perhaps cultural deprivation of a black student can be "cured" more readily by the personal attention of a concerned teacher of whatever color than by a stiff dose of "black awareness."

A recent survey of 12,300 black and 230,582 nonblack freshmen entering college in the fall of 1968 indicates far more similarities than differences between the racial groups in the characteristics that educational institutions deal with academically: attitudes, goals, activities, and achievements.[8] The greater differences tend to lie in their backgrounds: where they lived, family income, education of parents, and the like. For the whole sample, the black student is more likely than the white to have higher academic aspirations, "to assign personal importance to being an authority in his field, obtaining recognition from his peers, being well-off financially, helping others in difficulty, and becoming a community leader" (page 19). Another recent study, one of black students at eight selective girls colleges, detects significant differences between *their* black and white students (the white students at these colleges have, however, already been specially selected from the total white student population). Yet the differences in the aspirations of these black girls are the same as those observed in the whole black student population: their aims are more instrumental (preparing for jobs) than those of the whites (to become "a well-rounded person").[9] To the extent that the black students differ significantly from whites on a particular campus, that campus may have to modify its conventional programs or create new ones.

However, the differences that educational institutions most often need to cope with programmatically—particularly institutions admitting a less selected student body—are shared by blacks and whites in nearly equal proportions. For example, in the past year the most apparent differences among students have perhaps been political differences as expressed by militant and conservative factions. Although the SDS and Black Student Union on a single campus may for other reasons not wish to associate, they may join on a fairly large group of issues in which they see "repression by the Establishment." At the same time a seemingly large percentage of both racial groups want to avoid political activities as they prepare themselves for productive and lucrative work in business and the professions.

Thus, institutions may recognize that some black students have special problems that the institutions themselves may appropriately try to solve. Before they set up special programs, however, they need to be sure that the

---

[8] Alan E. Bayer and Robert F. Boruch, *The Black Student in American Colleges* (Washington: Office of Research, American Council on Education, 1969).
[9] Kenneth M. Wilson, *Black Students Entering CRC Colleges: Their Characteristics and Their First-Year Academic Performance*, College Research Center Research Memorandum 69-1 (Poughkeepsie, N.Y.: Vassar College, 1969).

problems are not exactly the same as those of white students and amenable to solution by the same methods.

Black Pride, Self-confidence, and Success

It is axiomatic that success contributes to the establishment of pride and self-confidence and that failure does not. A correlative assumption is that integration will not come about if blacks are doomed to failure even before they start on the road to success. Thus colleges have a part in helping their students succeed in their goals and therefore will have an indirect part in achieving eventual racial integration.

The Bayer and Boruch study suggests that most—not all—students, black and white, already know what their goals are and have the academic ability to achieve them in existing programs. For these, probably the best that institutions can do is to get out of their way and let them reach their goals with the classes and facilities at hand.

Preventing failure

Students who do not succeed in their college careers are not limited to the high-risk group. And not all are dropouts: they may graduate but be wholly discontent. Among reasons for dropping out, we find the following: financial troubles, marriage, the transfer of parents from the locality, the draft, academic failure, and a discovery that the college's program is not "relevant." Let us take the last two as factors that a black studies program might affect.

A stereotype is implied in some (though not all) black studies proposals: the black student from the ghetto, whose academic preparation has not been good, arrives on the predominantly white campus where his white classmates at best ignore him and at worst harass him. In his classes, he must face white teachers who talk a language he has difficulty understanding, whose outlook is so different from his own that he cannot comprehend it, and who express no sympathy with his plight. To complicate matters, he has constantly to justify to his own community his presence in this alien world: he must do well and he must return from his sojourn with useful knowledge to be put at the service of his community. He is fearful, lacks confidence, and may be doomed to failure.

The stereotype has been used to justify certain kinds of special treatment for black students. The argument runs: Black studies courses in history, literature, and the arts will add to his sense of pride; courses in the sociology of the black family, economics of the ghetto, and the politics of repression will give him a basic understanding of his own subculture and its relation to other subcultures in our society. To reduce the pressures of constantly living behind a mask in the white world, to increase the communication in the classroom, and thus to increase his capacity to learn academic material, the teachers of these courses must be black. Besides black teachers, he will have black counselors to help him with his academic, social, and personal problems, black because he will be so uncomfortable with white counselors that only misunderstanding or conflict can result. And finally, he will have a black social center or dormitory where he can take off his mask and be himself among his own.

Before looking at the propriety of the proposed solutions to these difficulties, we may remind ourselves that the same kind of image can be constructed of many foreign students, particularly those from non-Western cultures and those for whom English is not the native language. And to take the matter a step further, for years in nearly all our colleges, white and black, particularly those drawing from a very diverse economic and social group, we have been much concerned with the academically and socially unprepared student. At our large state universities, we have the lost, fearful, un-self-confident white student, unable to understand his teachers, finding himself excluded or scorned ("Hayseed," "one of those New York types"), unable to find a counselor who understands. Skin color is by no means the only cause of distress and failure, just as it is by no means the only key to success.

The concern of colleges to improve the lot of all their potential failures and their success in doing so vary widely. A recent study by Lewis B. Mayhew reports a very mixed record of achievement among the several kinds of programs that have been tried.[10] The apparently successful programs depend, he finds, primarily on adequate counseling, chiefly academic but carrying over to personal and social areas, and on a heterogeneous— not wholly remedial—academic program allowing for a sense of accomplishment early in the student's career. This finding is confirmed in a recent report on the gratifying success of academically unprepared students at Boston University.[11] Boston's program is centered on teams of five teachers and 100–125 students, a ratio that differs little from that in the ordinary freshman program and therefore calls for no exceptional outlay of funds.

[10] "Programs for the Disadvantaged Student" (MS of research supported by the College Entrance Examination Board).
[11] Gene M. Smith, "The Two-Year Compensatory Program of the College of Basic Studies: Implications of a Successful Model," to be published in a book edited by Frederick Mosteller and Daniel P. Moynihan.

Mayhew's study and the Boston experience suggest that some of the assertions about ways to save the unprepared black student from initial academic failure are based on very shaky foundations. But they also suggest that some kinds of programs for high-risk students can succeed and might well be included under the rubric of black studies. Care should be taken, however, in their selection. For example, students with difficulties in reading, writing, and speaking Standard English may be flunked out or they may have the misfortune to be put into a remedial program based on a philosophy of stamping out ghetto dialect. Linguistic evidence and experience with ghetto students as well as with other dialect-using students, such as those in Hawaii using pidgin, show that far more successful programs can be set up if Standard English is taught as virtually a second language.[12]

Relevance

If ways can be devised to prevent immediate demise of the academically disadvantaged student, a long step toward success will have been taken. Subsequent academic failure will then probably depend more on his view of the value of upperclass studies than on his inability to handle them. Several factors may affect the attitude of the student who is pursuing a standard liberal arts or preprofessional curriculum in the expectation of making his career in the community at large.

Black students do not stand alone in questioning the relevance of the standard curriculum; white students are some years ahead of them. The liberal arts curriculum described in our catalog, with its stress on abstraction in history, philosophy, and the arts, and on theory in the sciences and social sciences, fails to turn on many of our students and particularly the increasing numbers whose background includes little reading and less conversation in abstract and theoretical terms. Pragmatic and instrumentally oriented, these students see such liberal education as a waste of time. And by the same token, those whose bent is toward liberal studies look upon professional studies as forcing them into patterns that are distasteful and bind them to an economic and social system they see as hypocritical.

To the extent that a college's curriculum has neglected or distorted the role of blacks in America, it should certainly be modified, and some of the modifications may be listed in the catalog as black studies. The larger and far more difficult questions of "relevance" will be solved only as faculties re-examine the balances between tradition and contemporaneity, theory

[12] Stephen S. and Joan C. Baratz, "Negro Ghetto Children and Urban Education: A Cultural Solution," *Social Education*, April 1969, pp. 401–4.

and application, ivory tower and marketplace, professional preparation and liberal learning. It is possible to design curricula in which many students now discontent could discover a satisfying relationship between the rigors of abstraction and the application of theory to real problems.[13] Curricula of this kind would be applicable to all students. If adopted first for black students, they might well be labeled black studies and form a model for the reform of all studies.

"Soul courses"

Remedial work and relevant programs, if they form the basis for a black studies program, should go a long way toward assuring academic success for black students and thus, presumably, toward building identity and self-confidence. They should also satisfy the doubts of blacks like W. Arthur Lewis, who speaks disparagingly of segregated black studies programs, saying, "Employers will not hire students who emerge from this process, and their usefulness even in black neighborhoods will be minimal," [14] or of Bayard Rustin, recently reported to have said, "What the hell are soul courses worth in the real world? In the real world no one gives a damn if you've taken soul courses. They want to know if you can do mathematics and write a correct sentence." [15]

Examples of what Rustin calls "soul courses" are, in fact, hard to discover. The rhetoric that sometimes accompanies demands for black studies courses suggests that the real desire is for classwork that makes no intellectual demand on the students, simple "gut courses" designed to give them passing grades while creating myths about an imaginary "black nation"; courses taught in ghetto dialects to give the students a cozy feeling of oneness with a group; courses taught by unqualified instructors chosen only because they are black; and similar aberrations of traditional academic standards.

It seems unlikely that such courses, even if instituted, will last long. If the student's goals are self-confidence with self-awareness and pride with skill, he will not attain them with cheap academic programs. His own motivation and self-interest will require the maintenance of adequate standards.

Lewis sees success in academia as only a first step toward the legitimate goal of full participation of blacks in the American community and thus

---

[13] An example of such a curriculum may be found in Joseph H. Schwab, *College Curriculum and Student Protest* (Chicago: University of Chicago Press, 1969).

[14] "Black Power and the American University," *University: A Princeton Quarterly,* Spring 1969, p. 10. [The article is here reprinted, pp. 16–27.—Ed.]

[15] *Chicago Tribune,* April 28, 1969.

questions the value of a segregated academic program, whether segregated by intention or by the nature of the student body. Is segregation desirable if the goal is working in the black community alone? Will it make even skilled students unfit to help the black community? Are there jobs enough in the black community to absorb the graduates? Will special training for work in the black community in fact serve the black community?

The Black Student and the Black Community

Black studies programs, it is contended, will prepare black students to work effectively in and for the black community, by which is usually meant the large urban and rural communities which have suffered most from lack of opportunity, although some programs conceive the community as extending to Africa, the Caribbean, and Latin America. (It is assumed, of course, that such work is designed to help, not further exploit, the communities in question.)

Until fairly recently, those graduates of predominantly white colleges whose work was to help black communities were for the most part white. The image of the social worker as white is standard. It is alleged that trained black workers stand a far better chance of being helpful and I see no reason to doubt this. The questions here are curricular: Do black students need a special, separate training in order to be effective? If so, how much must the curriculum be modified to prepare such people?

Requirements

One kind of modification has already been dealt with under the heading of "historical rehabilitation"—the worker will need to understand the community as it is, and to do so he will need to know its antecedents. I include here not only the history of events but also contemporary sociological, economic, medical, and psychological information.

A second requirement for the worker is skill in the techniques he is going to apply, in law, nursing, or banking. The curricula now used to prepare white lawyers, nurses, or bankers are not necessarily inappropriate for black students. Of course, for those blacks planning to work in the black community, the curricula could be supplemented to focus on such work, but such modifications would not preclude students of any color benefiting. The essential point is: *whoever* works in the ghetto needs to be skilled.

A third requirement of some programs, however, is a commitment to "the black nation." Without such a commitment, it is claimed, the work in the community will be in the end detrimental. Thus, a prelude to all the work is a curricular attempt to "decolonize the mind" of the student by special courses. The assumptions here appear to be that all blacks have been brainwashed in the United States to an extent that they cannot work effectively with their brothers until they have been rebrainwashed, and the appropriate method for vitalization is curricular. If we get rid of the terms "decolonize" and "brainwash" and use the one we began with—attitude change—we may be free to agree that an ingeniously constructed curriculum, reinforced by extracurricular activities, may be a means of changing attitudes. In fact, the catalog of every liberal arts college in the country proclaims this purpose for its college. It may also be true that certain kinds of attitudes will be beneficial in working in the black community and that they need to be cultivated, just as schools of law, nursing, and banking try to instill special attitudes in their students. It may also be true that the attitudes of black students are now inappropriate for work in the black community.

Attitudes

We are then faced with the question of what attitudes are or would be appropriate for such work? Here, great care is needed before an answer is given. The direction given to the question by the terms "decolonize" and "brainwash" suggests that the answer must inevitably be given in racial terms: all white attitudes must be rejected and black attitudes substituted. "White attitudes" in this context can mean either "all attitudes toward anything that may be held by white people," or it can and more properly does mean "all attitudes of white people that are based on racial prejudice. . . ." "Black attitudes" may be defined analogously.

If we step back from the racial terms, the distinctions become clearer. The appropriate attitudes for one working in the black community, attitudes that should be fostered, may be defined as: concern for the welfare of those to be helped, for justice, and for freedom, and opposition to oppression, neglect, and exploitation. It seems fruitless to label these by color. Such attitudes are to be fostered in the white community as well.

Why then a special black studies program to develop such attitudes? The answer appears to be twofold and based on the past experience of blacks with whites. First, it is claimed, the black student in the white college suffers from prejudicial white attitudes which nothing will change and therefore he must be isolated if he is to learn; second, the unisolated black student in a white college will be subtly corrupted so that he, like the whites, will neglect, exploit, or oppress his black brothers rather than help them. Therefore, segregated programs will produce the most concerned and just people in our society, and society as a whole will benefit.

Although I have not seen a parallel cited by proponents of black studies, there may be one in the establishment of some religious colleges with similar ends in view. In both the black studies and the religious approach there is a trade-off: ultimately, a working integration and service are the goals, but they cannot be achieved by instant integration. There must be a period of isolation while attitudes are fixed which will carry throughout one's working life. Without pressing the parallel too hard, it is worth noting that religious institutions have tended in recent decades to reduce the isolation they once had in recognition that most of the members of their persuasion would have to deal with the community at large *in* its terms if not always *on* its terms, and that there would have to be at least a working integration (from 9:00 A.M. to 5:00 P.M.) if the workers were to benefit the religious community.

Arthur Lewis contends that isolation of blacks from the white world is self-defeating, just as he feels that working integration is an immediate and achievable goal. He would not, I think, object at all to the additional goal of fostering in black people attitudes of concern and justice, but would still maintain that segregation in the academic program is not the proper means.

Some white colleges have gone far to accommodate the desires of black students for a measure of isolation, and it is too early to know how attitude development will be affected. Other predominantly white institutions have hesitated or refused to support more than a few courses about the black experience. A consideration of the reasons forms the next section.

Power, Authority, Freedom

In the current crisis on our campuses, two definitions of power are operating. The first involves the authority of the agents of society: on campus—administrators, trustees, and faculty; off campus—executives, legislators, and police. The second involves freedom: the power of the individual to make his own choices among options with a minimum of constraint. The American Dream espouses the maximum freedom for all citizens provided only that its exercise does not harm others. People will accept limitations on their freedom if they feel that the authority imposing the limits is legitimate. The sense of legitimacy may be derived from rational considerations, from tradition, from an understanding of shared self-interest, from love or loyalty, or even a common enemy. In a recent article, Edgar Z. Friedenberg says,

Legitimacy is the chief lubricant of the social mechanism: it prevents friction by inducing collaboration among its several parts even in situations in which conflict of interest is apparent.[16]

Individuals may achieve freedom of choice in a number of ways. Inherited wealth may confer it; it may be acquired by bribery, force, or threat. But the socially legitimate way is through ability as refined by education, and thus educational institutions have a central role in the achievement of freedom.

Challenges to authority

The legitimacy of the authority of colleges and universities to admit students, prescribe their curricula and social arrangements, judge them, and invoke discipline has long been assumed to rest on agreement about the central purpose of the institution: fostering individual freedom through a structured college experience. Although campus authority was originally centralized, increasingly it has been shared. In some well-established institutions, faculty have long had a part in governance. But in the past decade the range of institutions has widened and the pace of change has quickened. Through challenges to campus rules and long-standing customs, first the faculty and then the students asserted their rights to more of the "action"— a greater freedom in the areas affecting their own lives. The challenges came first in committee rooms, then in student newspapers, and then in picket lines and sit-ins. Each of these beyond the committee room was in turn met by a reaction from some of the community who interpreted it as, at best, inappropriate for a campus and, at worst, the application of force. Yet each device has been judged finally to be legal, constitutionally protected, and therefore legitimate. The results have in many cases altered the structures of authority while recognizing its continuing legitimacy.

Something over a year ago, however, both the threat of force and its use to support demands for change became common. Physically obstructive sit-ins, deliberate damage to property, and the manhandling of people occurred on campus simultaneously with civil riots in some cities. A few campuses responded by calling police, with varying results: at Wisconsin, Columbia, and more recently Harvard, students and police were hurt. At Purdue and Hawaii, there were no injuries. The step from the tactics mentioned to the use of lethal or potentially lethal weapons—bombs, knives, and guns—has already been taken. As this is written, the guns have been

[16] "The Revolt Against Democracy," *Change in Higher Education,* May–June 1969, p. 11.

used chiefly as symbols. In our society, guns in the hands of protestors of social causes constitute the most threatening of all symbols.

The shift in tactics probably represents what Friedenberg calls "a widespread conviction among dissenting youth today that they are oppressed by a fundamentally illegitimate authority."

> For the younger members of a gerontocracy like ours to regard the authority of the older generation as oppressive is a rational act; that such authority should be logically regarded as oppressive is implicit in the fact that it occasions revolt. But for authority to be regarded likewise as illegitimate is something new. It makes conflict far more disruptive. It is, in fact, the characteristic that most clearly distinguishes today's intergenerational conflict from that which commonly occurs between successive generations.

Challenging the legitimacy of authority has centered on national issues like the draft, the Vietnam war, and civil rights in the cities, as well as on issues that involve the college's authority directly: in loco parentis, recruiting by Dow Chemical or the military, ROTC, tenure cases, student participation in governance, and the like.

Black studies and campus governance

Demands for black studies have coincided with challenges to legitimacy. If one looks at black studies as an attempt to provide black people with a means—education—to freedom, our traditions tell us that black studies should be supported. The question then to be answered is that reviewed above: What will do the job best? The issue of black studies has, however, been introduced in an already tense atmosphere of changing patterns of legitimate authority in institutions, of escalating tactics to bring about reform, and of wholly revolutionary attempts to destroy educational institutions. The issue remains.

Institutions that have not yet resolved the demand for black studies and those on whom the demand is now being made for the first time will find it hard to consider the question dispassionately. The demand for an autonomous program, for example, has some merits. If the purpose of the program is partly to prepare students to exercise freedom of choice, student participation with black faculty in the setting-up, operation, and success or failure of the enterprise is an exercise that could be beneficial. To assume at the outset that neither black students nor black faculty can do the job because of stereotypes that whites may hold about the ability of blacks is perhaps the ultimate example of what the blacks are struggling against. The question of autonomy must be decided on other grounds and must take into account the purposes of the program as well as legal and academic limitations.

But in the present climate, fewer options are available than there were only a few months ago to move the issue of black studies to some satisfactory solution. Refusal to take action on black studies would remove the educational institution from a field in which it has an obligation to take a part. Refusal might also inflame an already dangerous situation on some campuses to the extent that it can be met only with guns.

Summary

In addition to the blacks, there are in the United States a good many other racial minorities, some of whom share the problems of blacks in achieving individual freedom and integration into American society. To the extent that freedom and integration depend on formal education, institutions may be expected to provide appropriate educational programs. This not only implies doing a more effective job with the students they now get; it also requires that they take the lead in increasing the proportion of the neglected minority populations in our total student body.

Most of the issues surrounding ethnic studies are of racial origin—the results of deprivation, exploitation, and neglect. However, the instruments for their solution will often be racially neutral. Despite the current usage of the terms, black studies and ethnic studies are not entities. They are conglomerates of programs, the ultimate aim of which is to equalize the freedom of choice of all parts of our society. The selection of elements in any institution should depend, first, on the needs of its clientele; second, on the determination of the best options available, and, third, on the resources of personnel and funds that can be obtained.

Colleges can contribute to meeting the needs of these students by fostering accurate histories, by offering courses dealing with ethnic minorities, by establishing appropriate compensatory programs, and by supplementing professional programs with work applicable in ethnic communities. Colleges can also undertake consciously to become models of behavior for their students.

Without question, the enterprise that is called for will make enormous demands on an educational system already undersupported and, in some cases, understaffed for the work ahead, even when one recognizes that everything to be done does not require a new or special program. The greatest demand will come in providing for the enrollment of those who today are excluded from the colleges.

Commentaries on

Racial Minorities and Curriculum Change

LAWRENCE C. HOWARD, ROBERT A. MALSON
JOHN U. MONRO

The Validity and Utility of Black Studies

LAWRENCE C. HOWARD

BLACK STUDIES must be studied. Blacks must understand themselves better and be more appreciated by others. Dr. Furniss' paper turns us away from the task of exploring how black studies can find a place within the university and how shedding new light on the black experience can help reform higher education.

The arguments advanced to deny black studies as a discipline, like the opposition to American civilization and urban studies, boil down to the claim that the traditional disciplines are adequate to the task of understanding blacks. This opposition may be overcome because the demand for black studies comes from students and mainly from black students. This reply to Dr. Furniss' paper joins the black students' insistence that black studies have full academic status as a discipline. The movement to define and establish black studies is not so much a request to the academic guilds as it is a challenge to black people in America and the world. Blacks, and those nonblacks who identify with the black experience, must bear the burden of clarifying the validity and utility of black studies for higher education. Dr. Vincent Harding, founder of the Institute of the Black World, said last year in Atlanta, "Black studies is a field being born, a challenge to all American education, a challenge not yet fully understood." [1] There is much merit in that assessment. The signs of birth are apparent. Scores of universities, including prestigious ones like Harvard, Yale, and Wisconsin, are launching new black studies programs. Foundations are beginning to under-

---

[1] Harding, "Negro Colleges Set Black Study," *New York Times,* July 17, 1969.

86

write fellowships, conferences, and pilot projects. Already a National Association of African-American Education has come into existence.[2] Almost all of these are experimental efforts which seem to depend more upon the ingenuity and convictions of the instructional staff than upon accepted parameters for the field. We are at the beginning of a major curricular development. Much remains to be done to spell out just what black studies comprises and what are its possibilities.

Most would agree that black studies is an inquiry into the black experience. Harding has said, "Black studies is the study of the past, present and future of people of African descent."[3] Surely a beginning place is the explication of the life experiences of the average black man's deep and mysterious African roots. Study will pursue in detail the African's experience in America and it will assess the black man's outreach to the peoples of the Third World. But I suspect that the black experience, to be properly understood, will also go beyond the African derivatives. To be black also means to be colored by European and white American influences. It involves interaction with cultural forces, such as class, which are not Afro-American in origin. And, most important, being black is coming to celebrate in the legacy of the black experience.

Creative tension is at the core of the black experience. Being black involves being both European and African and yet also American. Blacks are people whose body coloring is neither black nor white and yet somehow both. Marginality is inherent in blackness. Writing in 1903 in *Souls of Black Folk,* W. E. B. Du Bois pointed to this two-dimensionality. "One feels his two-ness, an American, a Negro; two souls, two thoughts, two unreconciled strivings, two warring ideals in one dark body." Later, Du Bois identified

[2] Especially active in this field are the Southern Association of Colleges and Schools, the National Endowment for the Humanities, the Ford Foundation, and the Danforth Foundation.

[3] Ibid. Note also comments from "Report of the Faculty Committee on African and Afro-American Studies," Harvard University, Jan. 20, 1969, Henry Rosovsky, chairman:

"What the black student wants is an opportunity to study the black experience and to employ the intellectual resources of Harvard in seeking solutions to the problems of the black community—so that he will be better prepared to assist the community in solving these problems" (p. 3).

"In our opinion, the *status quo* with respect to Afro-American Studies is not satisfactory. Quite a number of courses recognize the existence of black men in the development of America; quite a bit of expertise is already available. However, merely recognizing black men as integral segments of certain overall social processes is not good enough. We are dealing with 25 million of our own people with a special history, culture, and range of problems. It can hardly be doubted that the study of black men in America is a legitimate and urgent academic endeavor" (p. 14).

other dimensions: first, profound African roots, and then black links to colored populations oppressed under colonialism. Were he writing today he might have further extended the black experience just as Malcolm in Mecca saw whites as brothers, when their white attitudes were removed.[4] The study of the black experience is more than the reaction of black people to a white culture, as it is more than the isolated study of people with dark pigment. This is not to say that matters of color are unimportant. Du Bois has been shown to be largely right when he wrote in 1903 that color would be the central problem of the twentieth century. But the inclusiveness, that all-embracing character of blackness, the fact that it is at once all colors to the glorification of none, can mean that blackness could be the promise of the twenty-first century.

To understand blackness is the most stimulating aspect of the study of the black experience. Blackness is the quality that Ralph Ellison has pointed out as largely invisible to whites. Blackness, Carmichael has shown, can give Negroes an identity. Blackness bears a deep relation to soul, to being hip, to having rhythm. Black, in the black experience, is a beautiful word precisely because it is both tragedy and the will to overcome tragic consequences. To identify with the black experience also seems to hold promise for whites as it helps neutralize a sense of guilt and often releases in them a sense of their own person. An example of whites coming to see something of the black experience in themselves comes through in a recent comment by C. Vann Woodward, who said,

> I am not about to suggest that the Caucasian is a black man with a white skin, for he is something more and something less than that. I am prepared to maintain, however, that so far as their culture is concerned, all Americans are part Negro.[5]

Such an inquiry into the black experience will strain and stretch higher education. The movement for black studies strains the curriculum as it has been strained in the past when a new discipline emerged, such as economics from moral philosophy. Such strains are inevitable as new questions are asked and answers from the existing disciplines are not satisfying. Nor will current efforts to fill in the gaps suffice. Historians will find Negro Americans who have made noteworthy contributions, but it is questionable whether they will thereby uncover the black experience. Woodward has identified part of the problem.

[4] *The Autobiography of Malcolm X* (New York: Grove Press, 1966), p. 340.

[5] Woodward, "American History (White Man's Version) Needs an Infusion of Soul," *New York Times Magazine,* April 20, 1969, p. 111.

Negro history seems destined to remain the moral storm center of American historiography. . . . . Moral preoccupations shape the character of much that is written about the Negro and race relations by modern white historians, but they are predominantly the preoccupations and problems of the white man . . . however sympathetic they may be, white historians with few exceptions are primarily concerned with the moral, social, political and economic problems of white men and their past.[6]

Comparable problems may also exist in other disciplines and particularly in sociology and anthropology. These disciplines have their own histories and perspectives which may be obstacles to understanding the black experience. The sociologists have long been preoccupied with the Negro's shortcomings and have had an assimilationist bias. The anthropologists have applied their knowledge to firm up colonial structures and have resisted the idea that there were African survivals among American Negroes. It can't be missed that black students have generally rejected white scholars from these disciplines despite their having major reputations for knowing the Negro. The accumulated knowledge about the African and the Negro has not gone much beyond the identifying of Negro Americans who have excelled in white terms.

I suspect that black studies programs will borrow heavily from traditions in university extension, where the boundaries of the university have been extended out to the state; from the continuing education movement, where education is seen as a life-long and community-based process only incidentally aimed at degrees. But black studies, I believe, will remain pre-eminently the work of the university. The best and most original ideas and methods will be needed. The style of study will probably look most like the best in graduate and professional instruction.

De Vere E. Pentony has suggested that the demand for black studies comes less from a desire to update and correct the academy than from the desire to build a black leadership.

The argument is that if there is to be an exodus from the land of physical and psychological bondage, an informed and dedicated leadership is needed to help bring about individual and group pride and a sense of cohesive community. To accomplish this, black people, like all people, need to know that they are not alone. They need to know that their ancestors were not just slaves laboring under the white man's sun but that their lineage can be traced to important kingdoms and significant civilizations. They need to be familiar with the black heroes and the noble deeds of black men. They need

[6] Ibid.

to know that black, too, is beautiful, and that under the African sky people are at proud ease with their blackness. In historical perspective they need to know the whole story of white oppression and of the struggles of some blacks, and some whites too, to overcome that oppression. They need to find sympathetic encouragement to move successfully into the socio-economic areas of American life.[7]

Black studies means using the university to build more truly human communities. In this sense, Daniel Patrick Moynihan touched on a central element in black studies when he recently pointed out the need for an urban policy that would go beyond current urban programs. The first goal of that policy, he said, would be "the transformation of the urban lower class into a stable community based on dependable and adequate income flows, social equality and social mobility." [8] The execution of that task is high on the agenda of black studies.

But all these are only primitive formulations. The probe of the black experience is an exciting undertaking which can have far-reaching implications. The study of the black experience will bring into better focus nonprint areas of knowledge. The black experience will temper our present preoccupation with meritocratic individualism, with organization and efficiency, with private property at the cost of public squalor, with the unreasonableness inherent in unbridled rationality. "What the black experience can bring in the class room," in black schools as well as in white, writes Peter Schrag, "is its own passion, its own humanity, its own technique for survival in a society that threatens increasingly to make every individual invisible." [9] Black studies is fundamentally a liberal art because its aim is to liberate mankind. Soul mixed with the Socratic method will produce a higher education more devoted to man.

Our Aspirations Will Be Pragmatic

ROBERT A. MALSON

OF THE FIVE most frequent reasons given for justifying black studies programs, according to Dr. Furniss, two are primarily concerned with hastening integration. Exactly what is meant by *integration* and its fre-

[7] Pentony, "The Case for Black Studies," *Atlantic*, April 1969, p. 82.
[8] Address at Syracuse University, May 8, 1969.
[9] Schrag, "The New Black Myths," *Harper's Magazine*, May 1969, p. 42.

quent substitute, *desegregation,* becomes more than semantic quibbling, for each is a definite attempt to classify a complex series of attitudes, goals, and values. Integration is frequently differentiated from desegregation on levels of both comprehension and implementation. Although desegregation is often conceived as the destruction of legal and de facto barriers to black participation in jobs, education, and public facilities, integration implies something far more. One easily recalls Barry Goldwater in his 1964 campaign, when he dealt with the matter accurately: you cannot legislate what is in a man's heart. And that is the essence of racial integration—to destroy the psychological and attitudinal barriers that one man manifests toward another of a different race. The questions then become: For whom are black studies designed—whites, blacks, or both? Do black studies programs have clearly defined objectives, or are they intended to be the campus variety of the war on poverty, undefined and the creator of false hopes? Along these lines, two points in the Furniss' paper draw my special attention—black-white aspirations and proximity.

Many educational and psychological studies have tended to show that pragmatic goals tend more frequently to be the aspirations of students of lower and lower-middle social backgrounds. Becoming a "well-rounded person" has been for the most part a trait characteristic of the middle and upper classes. Although I recognize the dangers of transferring a simplistic statement based on class to one based on race, I take the position that as long as black people exist within the United States, our social status will remain secondary to that of the larger white society despite any relative gains in economic levels that may develop. In no sense is this a revolutionary conclusion, but it does create a basis for certain assumptions related to our discussion. Blacks will continue to seek an expanded role in acquiring the educational and professional skills offered in America's universities. Our aspirations will be pragmatic because many of us are talking about change that will ensure survival and self-determination. If the universities are to attempt to correct the results of four hundred years, they must ensure that when we depart, we leave with all the degrees the universities can confer and all the skills they can impart.

In that light, the theories of proximity become a bit thin. I am not so much concerned with the attitude of the white student toward the black as I am about the attitude of the administration toward the black student. I unequivocally agree with Dr. Furniss' comment that "we must not in honesty consider the possibility that some forms of separatism should not be rejected." Care needs to be exercised, however, to ensure that his statement will not be misconstrued to mean a prelude to the revocation of civil rights legislation. If the legal and de facto barriers to jobs, education, and public accommodations are destroyed, then the black graduate can return to the black community and work to resolve the true crisis of proximity, the reinforced antiblack attitude of black people on black people.

Correcting American Historiography— and Other Inequities

JOHN U. MONRO

I HAVE READ Dr. Furniss' paper with a good deal of admiration, now and then irritated that any man could keep so "cool" in a heated arena, but on the whole I am grateful for a thoughtful and just piece of work.

I agree with the emphasis put on the need to prepare black students to devote their energies and talents toward strengthening our black community. In a society like ours, given over to personal, material success and self-indulgence, we should, I agree, be explicit about trying to prepare black students—and I would add, white students too—to devote themselves to the struggle to free our black community from bondage. Therefore, I like his comparison between special kinds of orientation and training that may be expected in a black studies program and what happens in a religious college. There are other analogies—military academies or even, to stretch a point, the great general universities and colleges of our land. Surely Harvard and Yale seek to orient and prepare their young men for service to the great institutions of our national community, as the universities sense that community. We should be doing as well by the black community, but we have not yet sufficiently sensed that community as a legitimate constituency within our nation, as legitimate, say, as big business or the professions.

In Dr. Furniss' treatment of the troubled problem of introducing black studies into our college programs, I like his insistence on involving students in planning and conducting our new black studies programs, for I find impressive the way black students in many colleges have gone to work on the task when given the chance. I feel sure white students will do as well if they are given the chance. More colleges must come to this point of view.

I find some serious faults in his paper, but I think the merits easily balance out the faults; and that perhaps adds up to fairly high praise for any paper, today, on this difficult topic.

My main difficulty with the paper is that I find the case Dr. Furniss makes for black studies is much too "cool," altogether too worried with caveats. Indeed, the case for black studies is not an issue to fret over in a cool way. There is an urgent, imperious necessity that we open up, lay bare, and study hard, the centuries-long, terrible story of racial oppression in our country. Our story of the oppression of black people and the genocide of red people by our proud and pleased and self-satisfied white society is one of the bloodiest and most cruel chapters in the history of mankind. The time is long overdue when the American community must see ourselves as we really are, not as we pretty ourselves up in our textbooks and holiday speeches. The time is long overdue when we must teach our young people the hard, bitter truths of our country's inner history.

The paper makes a plea that, in getting on with black studies, we not go emotional and forego "academic" history, the careful, balanced kind of history with footnotes and bibliography, which our colleges now manufacture so professionally, by the ton. I wonder how much respect we can have for academic history in a day when we discover that, for decade after dangerous decade, as tensions mounted toward revolution in our society, our professional academic historians could not see the importance of Negro history. It is worth remembering that W. E. B. Du Bois took his Ph.D. at Harvard in 1894, and in doing so wrote a fine thesis on the African slave trade that became the first volume of the Harvard Historical Series. Du Bois topped off his professional education in the traditional way at Berlin, but on his return to the United States, he simply was "invisible" to Harvard and the other leading white universities. His first serious recognition and appointment came from a black institution, Atlanta University. I find it hard to plead in cool, dispassionate terms for academic history. Too much of the jam we are now in as a nation grows out of the cool, blind prejudices of our professional historians.

Nowhere in the paper do I find any positive affirmation of the wealth of materials that awaits our scholars when they finally turn their attention to the struggle of black people for freedom these past three centuries—long, terrible centuries of terror and oppression and heroism—and the parallel, successful effort of the white majority in our country to keep the black man in submission and to put him out of mind. That struggle is one of the most awful stories in the history of mankind, but it is also one of the great epics of human existence. The whole world will profit from an exploration of this most prolonged and difficult history of racial confrontation. To put the matter in a different light, we shall be better off as a nation when we try to learn as much about our own awful national epic as we know about the *Iliad*.

This leads me to note that nowhere does the paper suggest that white students have as much to gain from black studies as black students do. White students actually have far more to learn, for the really terrible parts of the black story in our country come from the cruelty and ruthlessness of the white majority. And not only cruelty and ruthlessness in the past, but right here, right now. I do not see how we can have a country worth the name, or worth any man's allegiance, until we start teaching *all* our young people, white and black alike, the hard truth about racism in the United States of America.

I am disturbed by the treatment in the paper of the effects of desegregating our schools and colleges, the effects of bringing our young people together for what he calls "noncurricular" contacts. Dr. Furniss cites two individual cases—a white boy at Wesleyan, and a black girl who attended white schools—to make the point that the racial mixture doesn't always work as we would like, in fact, sometimes puts people off. Dr. Furniss admits that two individual cases do not add up to much of an argument, but then he proceeds to build on the effect created by his two vivid examples, and to conclude that we should go slow in this area and have some "systematic longitudinal studies" of the effects of mixture before going too far, too fast. I must disagree, profoundly, with Dr. Furniss' whole line of argument here, and would urge him to lay aside his cool and his caution. I do not know of a more important, or exciting, or rich, or promising social effort in my time than the effort going on to desegregate our schools and colleges—to desegregate all the other institutions we possibly can in our society, of course, but especially our schools and colleges. Of course, there are going to be difficulties. Of course, our young black men and women, when they find themselves up against the problems of a white college, are going to want to band together and work together for common support, for common goals. Of course, we must recognize that the black community is beginning to see the need to develop its own resources and strength as a separate, self-aware community if black people are ever to gain respect and a proper representation in our national affairs. Indeed, it often occurs to me that the condition of the black community in the United States is not unlike the condition of laboring men in this country some fifty years ago, before labor pulled itself together, got organized, and developed sufficient strength to command respect and representation. Of course, our old ideas about racial "integration" are going to change as the black community finds it had best depend on its own solidarity and strength, and not on any generosity in the white community, as a basis for commanding respect.

But surely we do not need any "systematic longitudinal studies" to tell us we are on the right track. At least not any systematic longitudinal studies conducted by cool academics. In a manner of speaking, the whole new revolution in our colleges *is* an unsystematic, long-range test—a very real test, and not just a study—that will decide whether our society, "or any other society so conceived and so dedicated," can long endure. Our nation is in deep trouble, but never, as I see our history shaping out, have we had as much reason as we do now to hope for a new and fair day to come.

Black Challenge to Higher Education

PAUL E. WISDOM AND KENNETH A. SHAW

Bᴜᴛ I ᴡᴀʟᴋᴇᴅ hand in hand with you in Selma. I was with you in Birmingham, I have backed you all along. Why won't you trust me now?"

How often this question, or a reasonable facsimile, has been asked by conscientious and well-meaning white intellectuals in our colleges and universities over the last several years. What is difficult to realize and even more difficult to accept is that the focus of the civil rights movement has changed. Ten years ago it was integration; today it is separatism. Then the target was the South; today it is the Northern universities. The reasons for the shift are many and both subtle and complex. What has happened, essentially, is that a large and vocal group of young black people has become thoroughly disillusioned with the goal of integration and has adopted a posture of black unity, black awareness, black togetherness—in short, black power.

Without attempting to analyze the reasons for this dramatic change in emphasis, let us review briefly the situation on college and university campuses. Most universities, especially since the 1954 Supreme Court decision, have tried to be "color blind" with respect to academic decisions such as admissions, programing, hiring, and reinstatement. Unfortunately, this color blindness has led to an insidious form of institutional racism which has kept blacks out of the educational mainstream. Charles V. Hamilton and Stokely Carmichael quite accurately pointed out in 1967 that institutional racism is, in effect, a part of the norms of our system, a covert and integral part, and so ingrained that it is almost a reflex action.[1] Many decisions made in higher education over the years, frequently perhaps reflecting unintentional sins of omission, have served to subordinate blacks and to allow society to maintain control over them.

In making admissions decisions, for instance, we have always used such

---

This paper is reprinted from the Fall 1969 issue of the *Educational Record,* published by the American Council on Education.

[1] Carmichael and Hamilton, *Black Power: The Politics of Liberation in America* (New York: Random House, 1967).

traditional indices for predicting academic success as rank in the high school graduating class and college entrance test scores. Consequently, blacks and others have been excluded because of cultural differences that result in poor performances on tests of academic aptitude based on middle-class norms. Yet we have persisted in using these measuring devices despite existing evidence that the traditional indices have tended to measure what students have learned rather than what they can learn.[2]

Another sin of omission has been the assumption, particularly by state colleges and universities, that interested students should come to them and ask to be admitted. Consequently, no group, other than athletes, has been aggressively recruited for fear of committing discrimination in reverse. Again, color blindness has led to blacks coming out on the short end of the academic stick. The few blacks who have requested admission have come for the most part from the middle-class homes with familial aspirations which set a high priority on college attendance, rather than from the more typical lower socioeconomic strata where such motivation is not inwardly generated. A wait-and-see admissions approach produced the expected result: only a few middle-class blacks have attended college.

A third form of institutional racism, the economic barrier, is attributable both to higher education and to national policy. Until the advent of Federal assistance through loans, grants, and work-study programs, there was no effective vehicle for getting blacks to college. Available scholarship money went to the very talented or to athletes. Even as late as 1966, years after the first Federal programs began, few children from poor families had gained entrance to the Halls of Ivy.[3]

In recent years there has been a minor reversal in this trend. Universities and colleges have begun to reach out for blacks, and through effective recruitment and the use of Federal financial aid programs, they have attracted black students in large numbers. It is reasonable to assume that such programs will accelerate in the future, if not because of higher education's commitment to them, then because of pressure applied by the black community. This pressure will intensify until approximately 12 percent of

[2] R. L. Plaut, *Blue Print for Talent Searching* (New York: National Scholarship Service and Fund for Negro Students, 1957); Kenneth B. Clarke and Lawrence Plotkin, *The Negro Student and Integrated Colleges* (New York: National Scholarship Service and Fund for Negro Students, 1963); Robert L. Williams, "What Are We Learning From Current University Programs for Disadvantaged Students?" Unpublished paper presented at a meeting of the National Association of State Universities and Land-Grant Colleges, Washington, D.C., 1968.

[3] *Quality and Equality: New Levels of Federal Responsibility for Higher Education,* Carnegie Commission on Higher Education (New York: McGraw-Hill, 1968).

college students are black. In other words, the black population in higher education will triple: 250,000 will enter each year instead of 70,000 to 100,000.

This rosy prediction should please all truly concerned individuals, but such optimism rarely is felt on campuses these days. Many universities which, in good conscience, have been forerunners in the attempt to recruit and provide support services for blacks have discovered to their dismay that recruitment and financial aid are but a small part of the needed institutional commitment. Ultimately, higher education will discover that success in these programs must become a prime commitment if the colleges and universities are to survive. Tokenism will be a deadly mistake. Black demands have been punctuated with violent and nonviolent confrontations at such "bastions of liberalism" as Brandeis and Swarthmore, as well as at larger state institutions like the Universities of Minnesota and Illinois and San Francisco State. More than a few administrators and faculty have called privately for a return to the "good old days" when all students were treated as "niggers" and tacitly accepted it. However, like it or not, these difficulties will intensify and in some way will affect every college and university in this country as more black students go to college.

The Universities' View

Universities quite honestly have postulated that the basic problem in higher education vis-à-vis black people is simply that the universities need to open the door to more black students through more flexible admissions policies, increased financial aid, and more active recruiting in the ghettos. The basic assumption is almost always that blacks must be provided more opportunity to participate in the university experience, that is, to enjoy the same rights as any white student. What the universities have failed to realize in almost every case is that the American educational experience is a *white* experience, an experience based on white history, white tradition, white culture, white customs, and white thinking, an education designed primarily to produce a culturally sophisticated, middle-class, white American. What is required, consequently, of any black who comes through the system is that he become white, that he be assimilated.

The faculty is no small part of this problem. Ignoring that portion of the faculty which fundamentally is opposed to any kind of program for the benefit of blacks, we find that the great mass of faculty members, the so-called white liberals who have been philosophically committed to the civil rights movement for years, have unresolved hang-ups about the black happening. For the most part they are egalitarians who became committed to the principles of integration and color blindness years ago and see no good reason to change now. They want to treat everyone alike. They want to hire black faculty members if they are available and are qualified. They want to teach their black students in exactly the same way they teach their white students, and they intend to evaluate them by the same criteria. It not only does not occur to them (they say) that there is any difference between white and black students, but also they will deny it if someone suggests such a thing, and for the most part they will fight determinedly any attempt by anyone to establish different policies for blacks.

Since the faculty is or should be the university, universities try to act in a similar color-blind manner. It does not occur to them, and they cannot be easily convinced, that what they are asking these students to do, in effect, is to become white black men. All too often the "experts," the black faculty members to whom administrators turn for advice, are themselves products, and successful ones at that, of the educational system which turns its graduates white.

The key word to black students today is the same one most often used by white critics of our universities: *relevance.* The black students quite simply want an educational experience relevant to their needs and aspirations as black people living in a black world. As Hamilton points out, "today they're understanding that they are black, and that as they go into these colleges—both black and white colleges—they are not going to be made into little middle-class black Sambos." [4] Yet when these black students enroll in the universities, especially in the typical, predominantly all-white universities, they are almost immediately confronted with the realization that they are dealing with another white Establishment.

In English the black student will read novels by and about whites and poetry by whites; he will be expected to understand and to write about the literature as if he had had a white background, expressing himself in white language with white idioms. He will study the history of whites written from the white perspective. If he hears a word about blacks, it will be of a shuffling, lazy slave or of Booker T. Washington or Washington Carver— seldom this much, never more. In music he will study Bach, Beethoven, and perhaps even Stephen Foster, but the chances are remote that he will ever hear about Joe Williams or James Brown or, for that matter, any soul singers. He will study a white political and governmental system run by whites

4 "Black Mood on Campus," *Newsweek,* Feb. 10, 1969, p. 53.

for whites. He will study the economics of Wall Street, of stocks and bonds, of high finance. And as he continues with his studies he will seldom, if ever, find anything more relevant to his life and his people than these parts of our typical white curriculum.

Perhaps even more disheartening and psychologically crushing is the white social environment to which the black student is expected to adapt. He will find the dances, the music, the food, the programs, and the entertainers all geared to the social and recreational needs of the white majority. The people are white and everything there is to do in the typical university town is designed for white people.

It does not take a very astute black man to realize after he has been in a typical white university for a few months that he is undergoing a white preparation for a white world. This is especially apparent now as the movement for black consciousness gets under way. Blacks no longer want to become like whites, and they are subjected to virulent castigation and ostracism by their peers if they try.

Black students do not come to the campuses for the purposes of disruption, destruction, or change. They come to prepare themselves meaningfully to deal with the problems they face as black people in a black community. It is only when they arrive on the campus and realize how totally white it is that they become reformists or revolutionaries. The problem is that black students find whites with control over every element of the university to the total exclusion of blacks; the blacks have nothing of their own. The inequity of this system, paired with the irrelevancy to them of the education it offers, sows the seeds for reform or revolution. The result of this combination—the white Establishment, the white curriculum, the white social environment, the white cultural standards, plus the discovery of hostility, apathy, misunderstanding, and ignorance in the alien world in which they find themselves—is dissatisfaction, bitterness, and the determination to change the system.

Black Student Objectives

There are a number of demands made by black students:

1. Basic to their desires, but not always articulated as such, is the elimination of institutional racism. This is the demand most resented by administrators, a charge denied by most, and the change most difficult to enact.

2. Recruitment of more black students probably is, and will continue to be, the most frequently voiced demand. This year, of approximately 6.5 million university students in the United States, only 275,000 are black,

and half of these are in the all-black Southern universities. The demands of the black community are, and will continue to be, that the number of black students enrolled in the universities be proportionate to the number of black students of college age in this country, as compared to the number of white college-age students. In other words, since 11–12 percent of the population is black, a similar percentage of the college enrollment must be black.

3. The demands for faculty are similar to those for students: 11–12 percent of the faculty and administration must be black. Black students are especially impatient in this area and skeptical of the usual excuse that the supply of qualified black faculty members is just not sufficient. They think the supply would be much larger than we realize if our traditional criteria were relaxed a little.

4. Demands for autonomous black studies programs, that is, programs in either African or Afro-American studies or both, are heard now throughout the country and will be voiced more and more frequently and urgently in the next few years.

5. Demands in the area of social separation are usually either for separate housing or social-cultural centers. The most prevalent theme among black college students today is psychological "togetherness," and in their minds the best way to achieve this is to find ways to be socially and, hence, psychologically together.

These demands and more are being made and will continue to be made, often in what the blacks term *nonnegotiable* form. It is perhaps these nonnegotiable demands which are the hardest for white administrators to understand and to cope with. For instance, when one small, Midwestern, private university with a totally white faculty was presented with a nonnegotiable demand that 10 percent of its faculty be black by the next fall, its administration, faculty, and most of the local townspeople were completely flabbergasted.

These demands can be best understood if we recall some of the similarities between the civil rights movement and the labor union movement in the United States. Most of us can remember the misunderstandings and in fact, the virulent hatred between management and the working class who wanted "in." In fact, the repugnance and aversion thousands felt toward a John L. Lewis in the thirties and forties is not dissimilar to the feelings most whites have today about an H. Rap Brown or a Stokely Carmichael. This analogy could be drawn on and on. Let it suffice, however, to say that the labor unions had essentially the same problem then that blacks have today;

they were outside, and they wanted in. It should not be surprising that there is violence again, nor that the tactics used successfully by the labor unions are now used by the blacks. A classic tactic is the presentation of non-negotiable demands. No successful labor union in the midst of contract negotiations has ever begun by asking for as little as it was prepared to accept. This is not to say that universities should attempt to compromise every demand the blacks make; it is to suggest that universities will be foolish to succumb to the temptation to ignore these demands as unrealistic and silly. Blacks know what they are doing.

Universities, composed of people, all too often assume the worst faults of their human components. One of the most difficult things for any of us, universities included, is to admit that we are wrong; and yet if we intend to solve this problem, unquestionably the most significant of our times, we must begin exactly there. We must publicly admit our ignorance and our past errors and then start correcting them. As Charles Hamilton says,

> First of all, you must admit that as an institution you have not been legitimate. You have left out of your thinking, out of your assumptions, out of your premises a whole group of people and a whole range of questions that are relevant to them.[5]

An example of the type of self-analysis and subsequent public confession each university must make if it intends to be relevant is the recent statement drafted by Northwestern University, which began:

> Northwestern University recognizes that throughout its history it has been a university of the white establishment. This is not to gainsay that many members of its administration, its faculty and its student body have engaged themselves in activities directed to the righting of racial wrongs. It is also true that for many years a few blacks have been members of its administration, faculty and student body. But the fact remains that the university in its overwhelming character has been a white institution. This it has had in common with virtually all institutions of higher learning in the United States. Its members have also had in common with the white community in America, in greater or lesser degree, the racist attitudes that have prevailed in this society and which continue to constitute the most important social problem of our times. This university with other institutions must share responsibility for the continuance over many past years of these racist attitudes.[6]

[5] Erwin Knoll, "Colleges: An Imprint Already," *Southern Education Report,* July/August 1968, p. 17.
[6] Ibid.

From such a statement, relevancy to blacks can begin. Specifically, how-ever, universities must take positive and determined steps in four major areas: *recruitment, compensation, curricular reform,* and *awareness.*

Student-Faculty Recruitment

What the universities must do in the area of recruitment is essentially what the students have demanded: build the black student and faculty population on their campuses to approximately the 12 percent mark. To accomplish this feat in the immediate future would be both impossible and unwise, but to reach this goal during the seventies is essential. Let us look at what can and must be done.

Although there is some truth in the contention of college administrators that black faculty are difficult to come by, it is also true that most adminis-trators have not taken the necessary steps to recruit them. Since most of the hiring in individual academic disciplines is done either by the depart-ment chairman or a very small department screening committee, most de-partments have made no special effort to recruit black faculty, because they think that portion of the university's problem is not their concern. If a black comes along with the proper references and credentials, they may hire him, but that is as far as their efforts usually go.

If a university is to be relevant to its black students, however, it must not only find a way to hire more black faculty, but it must, as well, see that they are hired throughout the system, not just in a few isolated departments. A black geology student needs to see a black face to which he can relate on the geology staff just as desperately as the student in history, English, or black studies.

The first thing a university can do, then, is to hire black faculty in each department, realizing that such an idea smacks dangerously of tokenism, but recognizing also that it must not be executed in a token manner. Most universities, through their academic deans, would need to issue instructions to college deans, department heads, or whoever does the faculty hiring, that they are expected to search out black instructors, and that their success in so doing will be considered prominently in their evaluation by university officials.

A second step necessary in hiring more black faculty is to re-examine the selection criteria. As Nathan Hare of San Francisco State points out, most white department chairmen

> would rather have a white moderate professor with a Ph.D. teaching a
> history sequence starkly barren of blackness than a black man without a

degree who has spent long hours in research on the subject. They hold up the white Ph.D.'s publications in learned journals, unmindful of the fact that a black man doing research, for example, on the slavery era in "learned journals" is obliged to footnote slave-master historians acceptable to a society which then condoned black slavery. Second-rate colleges require black persons with functionally white minds, using the Ph.D. as one tested means of policing that policy, yet at the same time, first class universities think nothing of hiring an unschooled Eric Hoffer, who now holds forth at Berkeley.[7]

We must undergo within universities and departments re-evaluations of our traditional requirements of experience and credentials. There is more than one type of learning experience, some forms of extensive learning do not result in a Ph.D., and in many areas experience outside the ivy walls is more valuable than experience within in preparing a relevant teacher. When we expand our thinking in this area, we will find the supply of good black teachers better than we have realized.

Even with a re-evaluation of criteria, however, black faculty will not be sufficient to comprise 12 percent of our college work force. As a third step we must immediately take measures to train our own black faculty—in other words, accelerate our training programs in black studies to provide black teachers to teach them, and significantly increase our recruitment of black students for graduate programs.

To increase the size of our black student bodies to 12 percent, we must continue and accelerate the recruitment programs many universities have initiated in recent years. The best of these programs use black college students as recruiting staff and send them into the ghetto schools to talk to black graduating seniors. These programs are working, and they have increased dramatically the number of black students on many campuses. But these programs are not sufficient. Too many high school seniors have not taken the requisite preparatory courses or have not thought enough about college to comprehend what it really means to be able to go. To reach these students we must not only continue present recruiting efforts with seniors, but also expand our programs downward into the eleventh, tenth, and ninth grades. We should talk to these students about the opportunities offered by the universities and counsel them on their preparation for college life. This counseling, of course, also should be done by the older black students.

Traditional admissions requirements will have to be waived for many of these students because of inferior educational experiences and environments not conducive to academic excellence. These deficiencies will show

[7] "The Case for Separatism: 'Black Perspective,' " *Newsweek*, Feb. 10, 1969, p. 56.

up in our culturally biased entrance examinations and other traditional methods of evaluation.

Compensatory Measures

We also must expand recruiting efforts beyond the school systems into the neighborhoods. In years past we have missed thousands of blacks with college potential. They are now roaming the streets, doing odd jobs, or working in factories. We must identify the most capable of these people and offer them an opportunity for a higher education.

Since most black students will be the products of an inferior educational system and a cultural and economic background which has ill-equipped them for the demands of an essentially alien university, to expect them to compete on an equal basis with their white colleagues is unrealistic. We must admit that many blacks have not had equal preparation, and compensate them in whatever manner we can. There are several ways we can help.

Although they probably should not be compulsory, remedial programs should be available. Programs designed to improve reading habits and skills and provide help in learning efficient study habits are especially beneficial to these students. Other remedial programs in mathematics, writing, and English usually are needed.

Extensive tutoring programs should be established, staffed for the most part by upperclass black students with special interest or knowledge in specific disciplines. Both group meetings and individual sessions should be a part of the tutoring programs with emphasis on the desirability of all incoming students participating until they are established and discover that they do not require further help. Participation in the tutoring program can be made part of an agreement when black students are admitted to the university. Frequently peer pressure from upperclassmen who realize the importance of tutoring can be used to advantage.

Social and psychological adaptation to universities is a major obstacle for incoming black students. Many cannot and do not want to relate to whites, so it is essential to establish a corps of black counselors. These counselors must be young enough in mind and spirit to understand what is happening among the students and to relate to them. Counselors should be readily available and have access to whatever resources of assistance they need. Although some should be professionally trained and probably members of the dean of students staff, others can be upperclass or graduate students who have demonstrated unusual ability to help their younger brothers and sisters.

Since incoming black students will have a number of strikes against them before they start, they must be given as many breaks in the form of course and instructor selection as possible. A major part of their problem will be success: if they prove to themselves in the first semester or two, in spite of all the difficult adjustments, that they can make it in the system, their major obstacle will have been removed. Consequently, they should be advised carefully and steered into courses in which they will have the best chance of succeeding and into course loads they can handle. Most of these students should take a small course load during their first several semesters.

Special efforts also should be made to help these students select instructors. There is no question that black students can succeed with some instructors, say in freshman English or in introductory sociology, more easily than with others, whatever the reasons. The advisory staff counseling black students should be aware of the differences among instructors and advise their students accordingly. In no case should a black student be forced to take a course from a professor who is considered bigoted.

Curricular Reform

The curricular reform needed in universities if they are to become relevant to blacks is twofold. We must initiate and develop full-fledged programs in African or Afro-American studies, and we must restructure the other disciplines so they take into account the forgotten 12 percent of the population.

Although black studies is a new and relatively unexplored field, most proponents would agree with Nathan Hare, who says,

> Black studies should comprise a comprehensive, integrated body of interdisciplinary courses just as in the case of long-established departments of social science and American studies. There is a desperate need for a pragmatic component which focuses on the applied fields of knowledge such as economics.[8]

Although many students who major in black studies will receive essentially a liberal arts education from a black perspective, the program also should be designed to prepare people to teach portions of the black studies curriculum both in the universities and at the high school and junior high levels. There is a great need for scholarly research in this area.

[8] Ibid.

To initiate a black studies program, a university must first reconcile itself to hiring a black administrator for the program and ensuring black control over curriculum and policies. Quite frequently a program can be started by incorporating existing courses into its initial curriculum (that is, if the university in question has a black history course, a black literature course, and so on). In any event the first step is to commit to a competent black administrator the staff and resources to plan his program. From there the field is wide open. Other than to say the program will be multidisciplinary in nature and somewhat pragmatic in direction, our only advice can be to let the program evolve as the nature of the university, the strengths and weaknesses of its faculty, and the needs of its students determine.

Other curriculum changes undoubtedly will be more difficult to accomplish. Yet the need for them is much more crucial. Here again we must admit that the contributions, perspectives, and needs of our black citizens have been ignored in the teaching and study of most disciplines. We are treading on extremely dangerous ground, that of academic freedom, when we attempt to tell a professor what he should teach, and yet a way consistent with traditional academic freedom must be found. The tragedy is not only that black students are being indoctrinated with all-white courses, but that white graduates also leave with one blind eye. It is especially difficult to tell professors that they should be teaching their courses differently, because they are the experts and know their disciplines. Yet they are blind to the fact that they are teaching essentially what they were taught, and they were taught from an exclusively white point of view.

For instance, when we tell a white Ph.D. in American literature that he should include a few black poets or novelists or essayists in his course, he looks at us with disbelief. He knows his field, he knows American writers, and he knows that, with the exception of perhaps a James Baldwin or Ralph Ellison, there are no black literary people to teach. He fails to realize that he is the product of an educational system which has systematically excluded from its anthologies and textbooks all black writers of note. A survey of American literature anthologies and textbooks will reveal that almost never is a black author included; yet the blacks have Richard Wright, Jean Toomer, Sterling Brown, Langston Hughes, Claude McKay, James Weldon Johnson, Paul Laurence Dunbar, and others who are at least as good as many of the white figures always included. But to get an English Ph.D. to admit this is to get him to admit that he does not know his own discipline, and that is difficult indeed. What we have said about American literature is true in other fields; there are gaping holes that must be filled.

Racial Awareness

If we were to succeed in making our faculties aware of the truth of the racial situation in this country, curricular reform could be accomplished easily; in fact, all the changes suggested here would be enacted. Attempts at increasing awareness of faculty, student bodies, and administrators will not be easy, however, and will require the initiative and imagination of us all. We suggest some initial steps.

Faculty members who have visited all-black ghetto schools have become amazingly enlightened almost overnight. There is nothing comparable to finding oneself suddenly immersed in the sea of black hate so typical today in black schools. Perhaps the best way to accomplish these visits is to enlist faculty members as drivers to accompany black students on recruiting trips. They will see the ghetto situation firsthand; they will have the opportunity to talk to black students and learn from their reactions.

Special efforts should be made to encourage faculty and students to read extensively in materials on black problems, especially such relevant works as the Kerner Report and *Black Rage* by William H. Grier and Price M. Cobbs. As important books are published, perhaps academic deans can impress their significance on their faculties.

There is a growing number of speakers, informed and knowledgeable about the racial situation in this country, who can perform a valuable sensitizing service. Every university should schedule several off-campus speakers each year and encourage its community to hear them. If faculty members can be persuaded to make class assignments in connection with these speakers, their impact can be increased dramatically.

A university, like a parent, probably has greater influence through what it does than what it says. Consequently, it can do much to sensitize its component members by example and precept, by becoming a strong social and political force for racial equity. Although such an exertion of its powers undoubtedly can be extended in several directions, three especially come to mind: student teacher services, job placement services, and housing.

Every university involved in teacher preparation places its student teachers in schools throughout its state. These universities should insist that their student teachers be placed only in school systems and in individual schools that do not practice racial discrimination. In the area of job placement, commerce, industry, school systems, government, and other elements of the economy rely heavily on university placement services for staffing. If every university would systematically refuse cooperation to any school or business that practices racial discrimination or refuses to sign a pledge repudiating it, the result could be profund. Most universities also are involved directly or indirectly in student and faculty housing. A university can provide new students and faculty with lists of nondiscriminatory landlords and real estate agents and refuse to cooperate with those who practice discrimination.

The problem of the black challenge to higher education in the seventies is essentially that the universities have seen themselves and their responsibilities one way and the black students are seeing them now in quite another—and the black students are right! The universities have been part of a white Establishment run by whites for whites, with a white curriculum, a white social environment, and white cultural standards. Blacks have been accepted only if they were willing to adapt to this situation and become white black men. Such assimilation is no longer acceptable to blacks. They want to be themselves, and they are challenging the universities, along with the entire American system, to allow them what they deserve.

They want full and equal access to educational institutions, but they want the institutions to provide an education relevant to them and their needs. The universities can meet this confrontation only by changing their basic structure. They have been fundamentally white, they have excluded blacks for the most part, and they must now admit it. If they are to become relevant, they must recruit a proportionate number of black faculty members and students, find ways to compensate black students for the inadequacies and the irrelevancies of their earlier educational experiences, enact far-reaching and comprehensive curricular reforms, and find new and dramatic ways to increase the racial awareness of university communities.

The solutions are difficult but not impossible—the alternatives are chaos and destruction. Although it may be tempting to discount black demands and protests as unjustified and irresponsible, honesty requires us to recognize that what they want should long ago have been provided. After all, they are asking only that this country at long last become what it has always said it was—a land of freedom, opportunity, and justice for all.

PART THREE

SOME RESPONSES
TO PRESSURES

Racial Considerations in Admissions

ALEXANDER W. ASTIN

CONTROVERSY OVER RACE in higher education frequently centers on the admissions process. These conflicts, though focusing on black students or other student minority groups, raise certain more fundamental questions about the entire rationale of admissions as practiced in American colleges and universities. The purpose of this paper is to elucidate these basic questions in the context of racial considerations in college admissions.

Many people are concerned about the relatively low proportions of black students who are admitted to college and about the widespread de facto segregation that exists in our institutions. The basic facts about the racial composition of student bodies are now known. Among the 1.5 million new freshmen who entered college in 1968, between 6 and 7 percent were black.[1] Even though many colleges have gone to considerable effort recently to recruit more black students, our evidence indicates that the proportion of blacks among entering freshmen has changed only slightly since 1966.[2] In short, the representation of blacks among new college students is far below their representation in the college-age population (about 12 percent) and shows little evidence of increasing. Furthermore, those blacks who do attend college are not distributed evenly among the various types of institutions. Nearly half of the black freshmen, for example, attend predominantly Negro colleges, where the number of white students averages less than 3 percent.[3] Moreover, black students attending predominantly white colleges are

---

[1] John A. Creager et al., *National Norms for Entering College Freshmen—Fall 1968* (Washington: Office of Research, American Council on Education, 1968).
    In response to a question about racial background, 5.8 percent checked "Negro." Since we have evidence that some Negro students preferred to check "Other" in response to this question, the 5.8 percent is something of an underestimate. It is very unlikely, however, that Negro students who did not check "Negro" account for more than 1 percent of all students.

[2] Alexander W. Astin, Robert J. Panos, and John A. Creager, *National Norms for Entering College Freshmen—Fall 1966* (Washington: Office of Research, American Council on Education, 1967). Robert J. Panos, Alexander W. Astin, and John A. Creager, *National Norms for Entering College Freshmen—Fall 1967* (Washington: Office of Research, American Council on Education, 1967).

[3] Even this statistic is misleading: most predominantly Negro colleges enroll virtually no white students; at a few colleges—located mostly in the border states— whites constitute nearly half of the student body and thus raise the overall average.

concentrated in a relatively small number of institutions; more than *half* of all the institutions in the country enroll freshman classes in which blacks make up less than 2 percent.[4]

How Valid Are Traditional Admissions Criteria?

Traditionally, colleges have selected their applicants primarily on the basis of their secondary school grades and their scores on tests of academic aptitude. While other criteria—sex, geographic region, athletic ability, and so forth—are frequently taken into account, most institutions probably judge most applicants on the basis of evidence of academic merit. In the face of the expanding demand for higher education among secondary school youth, colleges have become highly sophisticated in applying these merit criteria, even to the point of eliminating large numbers of student applicants solely by means of computer analyses of test scores and grades.

There is little question that the average black high school student compares unfavorably with the average white on these merit criteria, particularly on tests of academic ability. Consequently, the blind application of such criteria in college admissions will result in (*a*) proportionately fewer blacks than whites being admitted and (*b*) partial segregation of the races, with few blacks being admitted to the most selective institutions.

The use of high school grades and aptitude test scores in college admissions is most often defended on the grounds that these measures predict subsequent achievement in college. And indeed they do, as recent reviews of the literature show.[5] A point that is frequently overlooked, however, is that these predictions are subject to a considerable amount of *error*: not all of the most promising students succeed in college, nor do all the least promising students fail.

Predicting academic achievement

Data from a recent nationwide study of academic achievement and survival in college[6] provide an opportunity to examine—in practical terms—the degree of error associated with predicting college achievement from

[4] Alan E. Bayer and Robert F. Boruch, *The Black Student in American Colleges* (Washington: Office of Research, American Council on Education, 1969).

[5] John R. Hills, "Use of Measurement in Selection and Placement," *Educational Measurement,* ed. R. L. Thorndike (Rev. ed. in preparation. Washington: American Council on Education). David E. Lavin, *The Prediction of Academic Performance: A Theoretical Analysis and Review of Research* (New York: Russell Sage Foundation, 1965).

[6] Alexander W. Astin, *Predicting Success in College* (New York: Free Press, in press).

high school grades and test scores. These data were obtained from 36,581 students (19,524 men and 17,057 women) who enrolled at 180 different colleges and universities in the fall of 1966. Table 1 shows the relationship between the students' grades in high school and their freshman college

TABLE 1: *Predicting Freshman College Grades from High School Grades*
(N = 19,524 men and 17,057 women)

Average Grade in High School	Number of Students		Freshman Year College Grades			
			Mean GPA		Percentage with GPA of 2.50 (*B* Grade) or Higher	
	Men	Women	Men	Women	Men	Women
A or A+............	1,262	1,686	2.94	3.08	76	84
A−................	2,035	2,732	2.67	2.83	61	73
B+................	3,324	3,893	2.41	2.59	44	56
B.................	4,247	4,174	2.18	2.34	29	37
B−................	3,121	1,982	2.07	2.15	22	24
C+................	3,094	1,644	1.92	2.02	15	15
C.................	2,312	927	1.77	1.83	10	10
D.................	129	19	1.61	1.73	9	16

grades. Clearly, a student's college grades are usually consistent with his high school grades. For example, boys who had *A* averages in high school obtained freshman year grade-point averages (GPAs) that were more than one full letter grade above the freshman averages obtained by boys with high school *C* averages. A similar tendency is apparent among girls.

Another way of looking at the relationship between high school and college grades is to examine the student's chances of obtaining a particular college grade-point average. The college letter grade of *B* or better (GPA of 2.50 or higher) would seem to represent a moderate level of academic "success." The results are shown in the last two columns of Table 1. About three-fourths of the men who had *A* or *A*+ averages in high school achieved at least a *B* average as college freshmen, whereas only 10 percent of the men who had *C* averages in high school did so. In other words, boys with an *A* average in high school were *seven times* more likely than were boys with a *C* average in high school to obtain a *B* average in college, and *A* average boys were more than *twice* as likely to obtain a *B* average in college as were boys with a *B* average in high school.

Though the relationship between high school grades and college grades is consistent, it is far from perfect. For example, one-fourth of the boys who had *A* averages in high school failed to make even a *B* average in college. Similarly, 10 percent of both the boys and the girls who obtained only *C* averages in high school managed to obtain a *B* average or better in their freshman college year. This substantial amount of error in prediction is reflected in the correlations of only .50 and .51 between high school and college grades for men and women, respectively.

How accurately do scores on tests of academic ability predict the student's college grades? To facilitate discussion, we divided our sample of students into eleven levels on the basis of their scores on tests taken in high school. These ability levels are shown in Table 2, together with the number

TABLE 2: *Predicting Freshman College Grades from Aptitude Test Scores*

Level of Scores on Academic Aptitude Tests	NMSQT Selection [a]	SAT V + M [b]	ACT Composite [c]	Number of Students	Percentage Obtaining an Average of *B* or Better
11	151 or higher	1470 or higher	32 or higher	323	74
10	143–150	1381–1469	30–31	1,200	67
9	135–142	1297–1380	29–30	2,437	63
8	127–134	1216–1296	28–29	3,328	56
7	119–126	1134–1215	26–27	4,730	50
6	111–118	1055–1133	24–25	5,079	40
5	103–110	980–1054	23–24	5,266	38
4	95–102	907– 979	21–22	4,522	31
3	87– 94	838– 906	19–20	3,515	25
2	79– 86	770– 837	17–18	2,413	21
1	78 or lower	769 or lower	16 or lower	3,768	16

[a] National Merit Scholarship Qualifying Test selection scores.
[b] Scholastic Aptitude Test, Verbal and Mathematics scores.
[c] American College Test composite scores.

of students at each level and the percentage who obtained freshman GPAs of *B* or better. There is, obviously, a positive relationship between how well a student performs on a test of academic ability administered during high school and his grades as a college freshman. A student at the highest level of academic aptitude (11), for example, had more than four times as much chance of obtaining a *B* average or better in college as did a student at the lowest level of academic ability (1): 74 chances in 100 versus only 16 chances in 100. However, test scores are less closely related to college grades than high school grades are. For example, 74 percent of the students at the highest test score level obtained *B* averages or better, as compared to 76 percent of the men and 84 percent of the women at the highest grade level (see Table 1). Moreover, students at the top level with respect to test scores represented a highly select group (only 323), compared with those in the highest average grade category from Table 1 (1,262 men and 1,686 women). An examination of the lowest-level categories in Tables 1 and 2 reveals a similar discrepancy favoring high school grades over academic aptitude scores as predictors of college grades. Of the 3,768 students at the lowest level of academic ability as measured by test scores, for example, 16 percent obtained B averages or better in college. However, if all the students who obtained high school averages of $C+$ or lower (more than twice as many as are at the lowest aptitude level) are grouped together, the overall percentage obtaining B averages or better in college is only 13.

The closer relationship between high school grades and college grades is reflected in the correlation coefficients: the correlations of freshman GPA with aptitude test scores are .35 and .43, respectively, for men and women, as compared to the correlations of .50 and .51 between freshman GPA and high school grades.

High school grades, then, are clearly the better predictors of freshman GPA. But another question arises here: Is a knowledge of the student's scores on aptitude tests superfluous, or will our predictions of college GPA be more accurate if we use high school grades and aptitude test scores *in combination*? To explore this possibility, we sorted all 36,581 students into 88 cells (8 grade levels $\times$ 11 test scores levels). The percentage obtaining

TABLE 3: *Chances in 100 of Obtaining an Average Grade of* B *(or Better) during the First Year of College as a Function of High School Grades and Aptitude Test Scores* (N = 36,581)

Level of Scores on Academic Aptitude Tests	Average Grade in High School							
	D	C	C+	B−	B	B+	A−	A or A+
11.............						58	71	88
10.............				29	37	56	70	84
9.............			31	34	40	58	69	85
8.............		15	17	33	38	53	71	84
7.............		11	18	30	35	53	73	79
6.............		15	19	22	33	50	70	73
5.............		13	18	24	37	51	64	77
4.............		11	15	23	33	50	57	63
3.............		10	15	20	26	46	53	
2.............		10	13	18	25	42	53	
1.............	4	8	11	15	24	36	40	

Note: Each cell shows the percentage of students who obtained a freshman year average grade of B or better, at a given level of aptitude (1–11) and with a given average grade in high school; percentages are not shown for cells which contain less than 50 students.

freshman GPAs of *B* or better, computed separately for the students in each cell, is shown in Table 3. Selecting any level of aptitude and reading across the row, one finds that the percentages get consistently higher as one goes from the lower to the higher grade averages. In other words, there is a consistent positive relationship between college freshman grades and grades obtained in high school, even when the student's level of academic aptitude is held constant. Correspondingly, if one selects any column of figures and reads up from the bottom, he will find that generally the percentages again increase. Thus, information about the student's scores on tests of academic aptitude is *not* completely redundant with information about his average grade in high school; it can be used to make more accurate the prediction of his academic performance in college.

The data in Table 3 once again underscore the substantial amount of error involved in predicting freshman grades, even when high school grades and aptitude test scores are used in combination. More than 10 percent of the most able students—those with *A* grades *and* aptitude test scores at the 99th percentile—failed to obtain even a *B* average during their freshman year in college. Similarly, among students who made only a *C* average in high school and whose test scores were below the 10th percentile, about 10 percent nevertheless managed to obtain at least a *B* average.

Predicting who will drop out

In a very practical sense, the student's ability to stay in college is a more appropriate measure of his "success" than is his freshman GPA. Though good grades will help him to gain admission to graduate school, to be awarded graduate fellowships, and even to secure certain types of jobs, they are irrelevant to any of these outcomes if the student drops out of college before completing his degree requirements. To the admissions officer, then, an understanding of the factors that predict staying in college versus dropping out is at least as important as an understanding of the factors that affect the student's grades.

To investigate the value of high school grades and test scores in predicting the student's chances of dropping out, we utilized the same sample of 36,581 freshmen. A "dropout" was defined as any student who failed to return for his second year of college. Before we performed this analysis, however, it was necessary to examine the relationship between freshman college GPA and dropping out. Figure 1 shows the percentages of men and women within each freshman GPA interval who did not return after the freshman years. As one would expect, the student's chances of dropping out

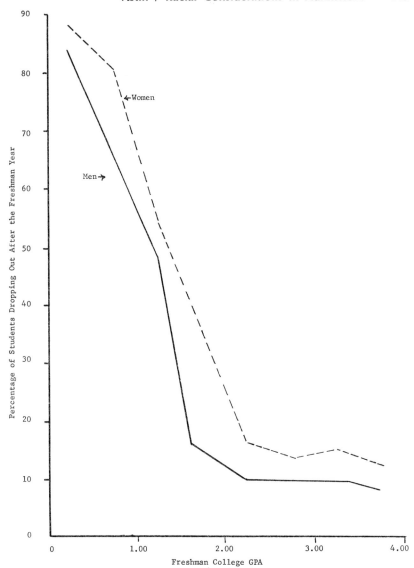

FIG. 1. Relationship between freshman GPA and dropping out of college
(N = 36,581 students)

increased as his freshman GPA decreased. Thus, among those freshmen
who had *A* averages, only about one in ten failed to return to college for his
sophomore year; by contrast, more than eight in ten of the students with
freshman GPAs close to *F* left college after their first year.

One finding that should be underscored is that the increase in dropouts from one GPA level to the next was not consistent. For example, students with GPAs of $C-$ (1.50) to A (4.00) were relatively unlikely to drop out; but the percentage of dropouts increased precipitously from the $C-$ level on down. (This tendency is indicated in Figure 1 by the lines descending at a very sharp angle and then leveling off almost horizontally. If the relationship between freshman GPA and dropping out were consistent across all grade intervals, the lines would be straight.)

That freshman GPA is related to the student's chances of dropping out is hardly surprising. If the student's freshman grades are poor enough, the college will simply not permit him to stay, even if he wants to. But the relationship between dropping out and freshman GPA did not occur only in the area of failing grades (GPAs from 0.00 to 1.00). On the contrary, the number of dropouts was relatively large for students at the $D+$ (1.00–1.49) to $C-$ (1.50–2.00) levels. This fact demonstrates that the relationship between dropping out and freshman GPA is not just a result of college regulations governing academic dismissal. Apparently, students whose freshman GPAs are below average (though not failing) are considerably more likely than are students with higher GPAs to decide not to return to college after the freshman year. Some of them may, of course, transfer to other colleges or even return to the same college after a period of time, but the fact remains that they are much less likely to return immediately than are their classmates whose grades are even slightly higher.

One obvious explanation of the marked differences in dropout rates that accompany relatively small differences in freshman GPAs is that students who receive borderline grades become discouraged and so decide not to continue on at the same college. In other words, the student's motivation may be substantially affected by the grades he receives. Another plausible, although not so obvious, interpretation reverses the causal relationship between freshman GPA and dropping out: it is possible that, once the freshman makes up his mind not to return to college for a second year, his motivation to perform well during the remainder of the term suffers. It seems likely that both relationships occur.

Since college GPA is clearly related to dropping out, the same characteristics that predict college GPA should also predict dropping out. The relationship between dropping out and high school grades—the best predictor of freshman GPA—are shown in Table 4. The percentage of dropouts consistently increased as the average grade in high school decreased, though this increase was not nearly as pronounced as in the case of college GPA:

TABLE 4: *Relationship between High School Grades
and Dropping Out of College*
(N = 19,524 men and 17,057 women)

Average Grade in High School	Number of Students		Percentage of Students Not Returning for Sophomore Year	
	Men	Women	Men	Women
A or A+	1,262	1,686	7	12
A−	2,035	2,732	8	14
B+	3,324	3,893	11	18
B	4,247	4,174	17	20
B−	3,121	1,982	20	25
C+	3,094	1,644	26	28
C	2,312	927	33	36
D	129	19	47	47

fewer than half of the students who had *D* averages in high school dropped out of college, as compared with more than 80 percent of the students in the lowest interval of freshman GPA. This lower degree of relationship is reflected in the correlation coefficients: college grades correlate −.32 and −.24 with dropping out for men and women, respectively, as compared with correlations of only −.18 and −.16 between high school grades and dropping out.

Does a knowledge of the student's scores on tests of academic ability add anything to our ability to predict his chances of dropping out? In Table 5, we have divided the students into eleven levels of aptitude test scores, separately for each level of high school grades. That a knowledge of the student's test scores, in conjunction with his high school grades, contributes to our ability to predict his dropping out is clear from an inspection of the data. As we proceed down the columns from the highest to the lowest test scores, we find that the student's chances of dropping out increase. (These increases occur in every column, except for students who had average high school grades of *C* and *C*+, in which case the percentages do not show the consistent increases found in the other columns.) As a matter of fact, the percentage increases from the highest to the lowest aptitude test levels are just about as large as they are going across the rows from the highest to the lowest grade levels. These trends are reflected in the almost identical correlations of dropping out with the two measures of aptitude: dropping out correlates −.18 and −.17 with aptitude test scores for men and women, respectively, as compared with correlations of −.18 and −.16 with high

TABLE 5: *Percentage of Dropouts as a Function of*
High School Grades and Aptitude Test Scores

(N = 36,581)

Level of Scores on Academic Aptitude Tests	Average Grade in High School							
	D	C	C+	B−	B	B+	A−	A or A+
11...............						12	1	6
10...............					6	6	7	5
9................			18	12	13	11	6	7
8................		31	19	15	10	13	10	9
7................		30	22	17	14	13	12	12
6................		26	24	19	15	14	12	12
5................		28	23	21	17	15	16	15
4................		32	26	20	22	27	28	24
3................		35	26	26	23	23	25	
2................		33	29	26	26	22	20	
1................	48	39	32	30	25	22	28	

Note: Percentages are not shown for cells containing fewer than 50 students.

school grades. Thus, these two measures are about equally useful in predicting whether a student will drop out, in contrast to their effectiveness in predicting freshman GPA, where high school grades carry much more weight than aptitude test scores. The correlations of both of these measures with college grades, however, is considerably higher than their correlations with dropping out. This discrepancy can be seen by comparing Table 5 with Table 3: variations in percentages of students who will get a B average or better range all the way from less than 10 percent to better than 80 percent in Table 3, whereas in Table 5 the percentages go up to only 48. Thus, *even the least able students are more likely to return to college than they are to drop out.*

In summary, these data show that the error involved in using high school grades and test scores to predict who will drop out is even greater than the error involved in predicting the student's freshman GPA.

Effects of the college

So far, we have considered the relationship only of high school grades and test scores to college achievement, independent of the type of college the student attends. In order to see how our predictions are related to the type of college attended, we examined the effects of a large number of institutional characteristics. As it turned out, only one of them—an estimate of the average academic ability of the entering freshman class which we have labeled "selectivity"—had any substantial effects on our predictions.[7] The levels of selectivity are shown in Table 6.

TABLE 6: *The Seven Levels of Institutional Selectivity*

College Selectivity Level	Number of Institutions	Corresponding Range of Student Mean Scores		
		NMSQT Selection	SAT V + M	ACT Composite
7............	9	129 or higher	1236 or higher	28 or higher
6............	15	121 – 128	1154 – 1235	26 – 27
5............	24	113 – 120	1075 – 1153	25 – 26
4............	44	105 – 112	998 – 1074	23 – 24
3............	45	97 – 104	926 – 997	21 – 22
2............	12	89 – 96	855 – 925	19 – 21
1............	11	88 or lower	854 or lower	18 or lower
No estimate available........	20	88	854	19

To show the true effects of selectivity on college grades, it was necessary to find students attending colleges of differing selectivity who could be "matched" on those attributes that are likely to affect their academic achievement and their persistence in college. To accomplish this end, we searched through our sample of 36,581 to find students who were equated with respect to their high school grades and aptitude test scores but who attended colleges differing in selectivity. Since we could not obtain enough such matches across all seven levels of selectivity to get a reliable picture, we combined the eight selectivity groups (seven levels plus "no estimate available") into three larger categories, as follows:

Broad Selectivity Grouping	*Original Selectivity Level*
Low	1, 2, and "no estimate"
Medium	3, 4, and 5
High	6 and 7

In this way, we identified eleven matched groups of students who exist in sufficient number at each of the three levels to permit us to make reliable comparisons. These eleven groups are listed in Table 7. Our criterion for including any group in this analysis was that it must contain at least 50 members attending colleges at each level of selectivity. The first group, for example (average high school grade of $A-$ and aptitude test scores at level

[7] Separate regression analyses were also carried using only institutions *within* each level of selectivity. In general, the predictive accuracy of test scores and high school grades was very similar at each level (see Astin, *Predicting Success in College,* for details).

7), was included in our comparisons because at least 50 such students attended colleges at each of the three levels of selectivity. Students with average high school grades of *B—* and aptitude test scores at level 7, however, were not included because there were only 43 such students attending colleges in the low selectivity category.

TABLE 7: *Effects of College Selectivity on the Student's Freshman Grade-Point Average*

(N = 11,368)

Student Group			Percentage Achieving *B* Average or Higher in Colleges of		
Average Grade in High School	Level of Aptitude	N	Low Selectivity	Medium Selectivity	High Selectivity
1. A—	7	962	89	82	62
2. A—	6	692	87	79	55
3. A—	5	538	89	67	46
4. B+	7	1,354	67	62	41
5. B+	6	1,208	76	58	35
6. B+	5	1,105	69	54	32
7. B	7	1,119	60	41	25
8. B	6	1,323	46	35	28
9. B	5	1,471	47	38	27
10. B—	6	681	28	24	15
11. B—	5	915	37	21	24

The data in Table 7 show that as we move from the less to the more selective colleges, there is a steady *decline* in the percentage of students receiving *B* averages or better during the freshman year. This decline occurs consistently in every group except the last one, where the percentage is slightly greater in the high selectivity group than in the medium group. In short, these data show clearly that the college's *selectivity has a negative effect on the student's freshman GPA*. That is, the more selective the college, the lower a given student's freshman grades tend to be. That these negative effects are not inconsequential is suggested by the fact that the student's chances of obtaining at least a *B* average during his freshman year are only about half as great at a highly selective college as at a relatively unselective college.

What do our data on the eleven matched groups suggest with respect to the effects of a college's selectivity on dropping out? Table 8 shows the percentage of dropouts in each of our eleven matched groups, separately for each of the three levels of college selectivity. *Without exception,* the dropout rate of each group declines at each increasing level of selectivity. A stu-

TABLE 8: *Effects of College Selectivity on the Student's Chances of Dropping Out*

(N = 11,368)

Student Group		Percentage Not Returning after the Freshman Year in Colleges of		
Average Grade in High School	Level of Aptitude	Low Selectivity	Medium Selectivity	High Selectivity
1. A −	7	31	12	10
2. A −	6	18	13	10
3. A −	5	27	15	14
4. B + ...	7	24	16	7
5. B + ...	6	28	16	9
6. B + ...	5	25	14	12
7. B	7	33	14	11
8. B	6	24	16	11
9. B	5	27	16	14
10. B −	6	23	21	12
11. B −	5	27	20	9

dent attending a college in the low selectivity group, for example, is about two or three times more likely to drop out after his freshman year than is a student of comparable ability attending a highly selective college.

The apparently negative effect of selectivity on dropping out is rather puzzling, particularly when one realizes that the student is likely to get lower grades if he attends the highly selective college. Since students who have below-average freshman GPAs are more likely to drop out than are students with above-average GPAs (Figure 1), it seems to follow that students in the most selective institutions would have higher dropout rates than students of comparable ability enrolled at the least selective institutions. But just the opposite result occurs: a given student is *less* likely to drop out if he attends a highly selective college than if he attends a relatively unselective one, *even though his freshman GPA is likely to be lower at the highly selective college.*

These findings controvert some of the most cherished folklore about the highly selective institution. Some people have suggested, for example, that one of the major liabilities of the more selective institution is that many highly able students who go there find themselves for the first time competing with other students whose intellectual and academic abilities are commensurate with their own; consequently, they become discouraged and drop out. The implication is that certain very bright students would have a better chance of survival at a relatively unselective institution, primarily because the less competitive atmosphere there would permit them to maintain the academic superiority that they had been accustomed to in high school and therefore to avoid the frustration and depression that they may feel in the highly selective institution. Not only do our data fail to support this line of reasoning, but also they suggest that the effect is just the reverse. Furthermore, it holds true for all eleven of our groups; obviously it is not confined to the most able students.

The reason that students are more inclined to leave the less selective colleges after their freshman year is not immediately apparent. Since they obtain higher freshman GPAs than do comparable students in highly selective colleges, they are certainly not asked to leave for academic reasons or because their achievement has not lived up to their own expectations. It is possible that many of them simply transfer to another institution rather than leave college altogether. Freshmen of moderate to high academic ability (which is roughly the span represented by our eleven matched groups) may be disappointed by the low level of competitiveness and of achievement at less selective colleges and may leave, either to seek a more intellectually stimulating environment or (if disillusionment is great enough) to withdraw from higher education altogether, at least for a period of time. Unfortunately, our data provide no direct confirmation of these speculations, which would seem therefore to constitute important topics for future research on college dropouts.

The "Atypical" Student in the Selective College

Many educators criticize the practice of lowering admissions standards for black students on the grounds that these students will be faced with unreasonable academic and social pressures that will greatly increase their chances of dropping out. These personal and academic difficulties are assumed to be especially severe in the most selective institutions.

What do our data show about how the academically "atypical" student performs in the highly selective institution? To arrive at some preliminary answers, we selected several groups of atypical students attending institutions in the top two levels of selectivity (levels 6 and 7). Specifically, six groups (three of men and three of women) were identified on the basis of their having (a) low test scores, (b) low high school grades, or (c) low test scores and low high school grades. The comparison of the six groups is shown in Table 9. The first group, for example, includes all men enrolled at these highly selective institutions whose high school grades were only C+ or below. Note that, with respect to performance in high school, this group represents the lowest 5 percent of our sample of men attending highly

TABLE 9: *Comparison of the Performance of Atypical Students and Typical Students in Highly Selective Colleges* [a]

Student Group	N	Percentage Obtaining B Average or Higher in College	Percentage Dropping Out after the Freshman Year
Atypical			
1. Men with average high school grades of C+ or less.......	161	14	14
2. Men with aptitude test scores (NMSQT) of 102 or less.....	140	27	9
3. Women with average high school grades of B− or less..	73	22	14
4. Women with aptitude test scores (NMSQT) of 110 or less......................	172	38	9
5. Men with average high school grades of C+ or less *and* aptitude test scores (NMSQT) below 110.................	50	12	12
6. Women with average high school grades of B− or less *and* aptitude test scores (NMSQT) below 110........	24	8	8
Typical			
7. All men in highly selective colleges..................	3,349 [b]	41	7
8. All women in highly selective colleges..................	1,857 [c]	60	9

[a] All colleges at selectivity levels 6 and 7.
[b] Mean NMSQT score = 130; mean high school grade average = B+.
[c] Mean NMSQT score = 129; mean high school grade average = A −.

selective institutions (161 out of 3,349). Only 14 percent of the group, as compared with 41 percent of *all* men enrolled in these colleges, obtained *B* averages or higher in college. If one scans the column of percentages of students who obtained *B* averages or higher, it becomes clear that each of these atypical groups had freshman GPAs considerably below the average for all students at the highly selective institutions.

However, an examination of the last column in Table 9 reveals that the dropout rates of the atypical students were only slightly higher than the overall dropout rates. In other words, the atypical student at the highly selective college, despite his substantially lower academic performance, is only slightly more inclined than is the typical student to drop out after the freshman year.

These findings have special implications for college admissions policies. First, if a greater number of disadvantaged students are to be admitted under less stringent merit criteria, it is unreasonable to expect that their academic performance will be as high as that of the typical student in the highly selective institution. Using the standard measures of high school grades and test scores, admissions officers and counselors should be able to anticipate fairly accurately just how far below the typical student these specially admitted students will perform. More important, since these atypical students are only slightly more inclined to drop out after the freshman year, *highly selective colleges could admit much larger numbers of students from disadvantaged and atypical backgrounds without substantially increasing their dropout rates.* Once again, these data illustrate the limits of our standard predictors of academic success.

Effects of Race on Performance

The standard admissions criteria are often criticized as being too "culture bound" and therefore not giving a true picture of the academic ability of the typical black student. Recent studies of students attending institutions in the state of Georgia,[8] however, suggest that such may not be the case. This research showed that grades and test scores predicted just as accurately for students attending predominantly black colleges as they did for students attending predominantly white colleges.

Our own data bear more directly on this question. These data were obtained from some 22,000 of the original sample of 36,581 students [9] described earlier. Information concerning students' socioeconomic status, race, and other characteristics was available from a questionnaire administered when the students first entered college in 1966.[10] Our sample included 776 black students, two-thirds of whom were enrolled in predominantly Negro colleges.

In order to test the appropriateness of the standard merit criteria separately for students of different races, we established three different groups: black students attending black colleges, black students attending white colleges, and white [11] students attending white colleges. (The number of white students attending black colleges was too small to permit valid compari-

---

[8] J. C. Stanley and A. C. Porter, "Correlation of Scholastic Aptitude Test Score with College Grades for Negroes Versus Whites," *Journal of Educational Measurement* 4, no. 4 (1967).

[9] These 22,000 students included all of those from the original sample of 36,581 students who returned a follow-up questionnaire mailed out in the summer of 1967.

[10] Astin et al., *National Norms—Fall 1966.*

[11] These "white" students might be more accurately termed "nonblack," since they include all who checked an alternative other than "Negro" on the racial background item (Caucasian, Oriental, American Indian, Other). However, since more than 90 percent of this group checked "Caucasian," we have used the term "white" rather than the awkward "nonblack."

TABLE 10: *Mean High School Grades, Aptitude Test Scores, and College Selectivity for Six Groups of Students*

	Men			Women		
	Whites in White Colleges	Blacks in White Colleges	Blacks in Black Colleges	Whites in White Colleges	Blacks in White Colleges	Blacks in Black Colleges
Number of students	*1,036*	*108*	*220*	*1,106*	*158*	*290*
Number of different institutions attended by the students	*151*	*57*	*7*	*163*	*67*	*6*
High school grades [a]						
Mean	5.0	4.7	4.3	5.6	5.3	4.3
S.D.	1.7	1.6	1.7	1.6	1.3	1.5
Test scores (NMSQT)						
Mean	114	98	76	109	95	66
S.D.	20	20	18	20	20	17
College selectivity (NMSQT)						
Mean	108	110	79	107	110	77
S.D.	14	15	5	13	15	5

[a] Based on an 8-point scale ($A = 8$, $A- = 7$, $B+ = 6$, $B = 5$, $B- = 4$, $C+ = 3$, $C = 2$, $D = 1$).

129

TABLE 11: *Actual and Estimated ᵃ Freshman GPAs and Dropout Rates for Six Groups of Students*

(N = 1,047 men and 1,021 women)

	Men			Women		
	Whites in White Colleges	Blacks in White Colleges	Blacks in Black Colleges	Whites in White Colleges	Blacks in White Colleges	Blacks in Black Colleges
Mean freshman GPA						
Actual...............	2.35	2.08	2.23	2.56	2.13	2.20
Estimated............	2.35	2.14	2.26	2.56	2.33	2.32
Percentage dropping out after the freshman year						
Actual...............	12.4	7.4	12.7	13.9	20.3	13.3
Estimated............	12.3	14.3	13.2	13.7	23.9	13.3

ᵃ Based on the students' high school grades, aptitude test scores, and college selectivity.

sons.) Each of these three groups was further categorized by sex, making a total of six groups. To reduce computing costs, we used 10 percent random samples of the two groups of white students (men and women) rather than the total groups (which numbered about 10,000 students each). Test scores, high school grades, and college selectivity for each of the six groups are shown in Table 10.

We first selected a random sample (1,047 men and 1,021 women) of *all* students without regard to their race or institution. Regression equations for predicting freshman GPA were developed for each sex, using the students' high school grades, aptitude test scores, and college selectivity since, as we have seen, selectivity is an important factor in affecting freshman grades. The regression weights obtained from the two analyses based on all students were then applied separately to the students in each of the six samples (three groups of men and three of women), in order to arrive at an "estimated" or "predicted" freshman GPA and probability of dropping out. Table 11 compares (*a*) the mean estimated freshman GPAs with the mean actual freshman GPAs and (*b*) the estimated percentage of dropouts with the actual percentage of dropouts for each of the six groups. The average estimated GPA for the two samples of white students are almost identical with their actual GPAs—a finding which is to be expected since white students comprised the bulk of the sample from which the initial weights were derived. However, for all four samples of black students, the estimated grades are slightly *higher* than the actual grades obtained by these students in their freshman year. The differences are small among the men, and somewhat larger among women, particularly black women attending white colleges.

These findings show that black students, particularly women, perform slightly below what would be expected on the basis of their high school grades and aptitude test scores. This overprediction obtains, regardless of whether the black student attends a predominantly black or a predominantly white college. In short, the traditional admissions criteria, far from discriminating against black students, favor them somewhat, in that they overpredict slightly how well the students will do academically during the freshman year.

The data on predicting dropouts (Table 11) give a similar picture: in general, the predicted and actual percentages are very close. It is of interest, however, that the dropout rates among black students attending white colleges are slightly *below* the rate that would be expected from their test scores, high school grades, and college selectivity. Although only the discrepancy for men is statistically significant ($p < .05$), these differences suggest some provocative speculations. Perhaps the typical black student attending a white college receives special tutoring and counseling that reduces his chance of dropping out, or perhaps he is simply more determined to succeed, because of the exceptional situation in which he finds himself, than is the typical white student in these colleges. Whatever the true explanation, it is again clear that the dropout rate of the predominantly white college will probably not be greatly affected if its enrollment of black students is substantially increased.

Are Admission Practices "Racist"?

Critics of current admissions practices correctly assume that the low proportion of Negroes among the students entering many of the more selective institutions is caused in part by the use of test scores and grades in admissions. Whether this de facto segregation of the races is evidence of "racist" attitudes on the part of these institutions, however, is another matter. Racism has to do with intention: if admissions officers apply merit criteria in a conscious and deliberate attempt to exclude black students, then the charge of racism seems valid. On the other hand, if segregation turns out to be an unintended by-product of the application of merit criteria, then the charge seems groundless.

Although a discussion of possible racist motives on the part of higher educational institutions may seem tangential to the topic of this paper, it is important to recognize that such arguments are frequently raised in discussions of admissions procedures. That de facto segregation among entering freshman classes is not a sufficient basis for concluding that racist motives are operating can be seen by examining other fields where merit is the primary criterion for admission. Two such areas are professional sports and jazz. It is well known that the proportions of Negroes in these two fields are much higher than their proportion in the population. But is it valid to conclude that this overrepresentation is a consequence of "racist" attitudes on the part of the persons who control access to these fields? Are whites discriminated against in screening candidates for these professions? Is favoritism shown toward blacks? Such conclusions would seem to be highly untenable, particularly in the case of professional sports where, until recently, blacks were excluded altogether. The overrepresentation of blacks in professional basketball and football is all the more remarkable when one realizes that most of the professionals in these two sports come from the ranks of college graduates. Negroes comprise less than 4 percent of all college graduates,[12] and yet they account for more than one-fourth of all professional football and basketball players. In short, then, one cannot infer that disproportionate representation of the races in a particular field of endeavor is evidence of racist attitudes on the part of the persons responsible for deciding who shall be admitted. Depending upon the field, a certain degree of disproportionality may result from the blind application of merit criteria without reference to race or color.

In some respects, it is ironic that the merit system of admissions has been attacked by persons concerned with equal rights and equal educational opportunity. As Jencks and Riesman [13] have pointed out, one remarkable feature of the American system of higher education during the past fifty years is its transition from a basically aristocratic system—one in which social class and family influence were the primary determinants of college attendance—to a fundamentally meritocratic system, in which people are admitted on the basis of what they can do rather than who they are.

Many colleges have tried to correct de facto segregation by abandoning or modifying the merit criterion so as to include a higher proportion of black students among their entering classes. One of the difficulties with such programs is that they are often administered covertly as "special programs for the disadvantaged," suggesting that their proponents still implicitly accept the merit criterion as the prime consideration in admissions.

Another problem is that the rationale for special admissions programs has never been clearly enunciated and defended by its advocates. Essentially, the introduction of such programs implies that a new value has taken precedence over the traditional one of merit. The proponents of double standards in admissions are in essence arguing that achieving a better racial balance in the student body is a more important objective than blindly applying a criterion based purely on merit. It seems to me that given the increased racial tensions and the pressures for black separatism that have developed lately, a strong case could be made for this point of view.

In addition to expanding educational opportunities, increasing the extent of racial integration in colleges can be defended on the pragmatic grounds that, in the long run, it would tend to promote racial understanding and thereby to reduce the likelihood of racial violence. An anonymous person of a different color is much easier to hate or vilify than is a friend, associate, or

[12] Alexander W. Astin and Robert J. Panos, *The Educational and Vocational Development of College Students* (Washington: American Council on Education, 1969).
[13] Christopher Jencks and David Riesman, *The Academic Revolution* (Garden City, N.Y.: Doubleday & Co., 1968).

neighbor, regardless of what his color might be. In this regard, the move within some colleges to establish separate curricula, dormitories, and social organizations for blacks seems to defeat the goal of promoting communication and understanding between the races by admitting more black students.

Maintaining "Academic Standards"

Opponents commonly raise the objection that even partial abandonment of the merit criterion in admissions would result in a lowering of the "academic standards" of the institution. While such a consequence is indeed possible, it is by no means inevitable. Part of the folklore of higher education is that academic standards are determined primarily by the abilities of the students who are admitted. This bit of folklore may apply to certain institutions that grade strictly "on the curve," but there is no reason why colleges cannot set any standards they wish, independent of their admissions practices. Standards have to do with the performance levels that the institution demands before it will certify that the student has passed certain courses or completed certain requirements for the degree. It is true that fewer students are likely to succeed ("be certified") if very high performance standards are maintained at the same time that admissions criteria are relaxed. Nevertheless, standards of performance can still be defined and maintained, whatever changes are made in the admissions process.

The problem of certification relates closely to the issue of *absolute* versus *relative* standards of performance in higher education. One difficulty with the grading systems used in American colleges is their relativity: an *A* grade at one institution may not be comparable to an *A* at another institution. Some of the more selective colleges apparently adjust certification standards to reflect their students' high absolute level of performance: the average freshman GPA in the most selective colleges is about 0.50 higher than the average GPA in the least selective.[14] Not all institutions and professors make such adjustments, however, so that a student *of a given level of ability* has a better chance of obtaining an *A* grade at an unselective college than at a highly selective one (Table 7). In view of such erratic grading practices, it is easy to see why graduate schools, employers, and others rely on admissions standards in judging the *academic* standards of the institution: admission criteria—in particular, average scores of entering students on standardized tests—represent objective measures which permit valid comparisons among institutions. The higher the admissions standards, the

14 Astin, *Predicting Success in College.*

higher (presumably) the academic standards. Clearly, admissions standards would not have to be used in this manner if institutions had absolute (that is, comparable), rather than relative, standards of performance.

Educating Students or Picking Winners?

In my judgment, *the model of selective admissions based on test scores and grades is inappropriate for institutions of higher education.* Presumably, educational institutions exist in order to educate students. Their mission, then, is to produce certain desirable *changes* in the student or, more simply, to make a difference in the student's life. Given these goals, they should strive in their admissions practices to select those applicants who are most likely to be favorably influenced by the particular educational program offered at the institution. Instead, the typical admissions officer today functions more like a handicapper: he tries merely to pick winners. He looks over the various candidates, evaluates their respective talents, and attempts to select those who are most likely to perform well. Handicappers, it should be stressed, are interested only in *predicting* the horse's performance—not in improving his performance, in trying to make him run better and faster. The problem here is that an educational institution is supposed to function less like a handicapper and more like a jockey or a trainer: it has a responsibility to *improve the performance* of the individual, not just to identify those with the greatest potential.

In another sense, college admissions officers have tended to operate like personnel managers in a commercial enterprise rather than like educators. Picking winners is an appropriate activity for businesses and industries, since their goal is to hire the very best talent so as to maximize productivity and profit. Similarly, competition among rival companies for the limited pool of available talent is consistent with the very nature of business. This business model, however—though it seems to have been adopted by many institutions—is not appropriate for education. The mission of the college is *not* simply to maximize its output of distinguished alumni by maximizing its input of talented students. Such a static view puts the college in the role of a kind of funnel, where what comes out is purely a matter of what goes in. Colleges and other educational institutions exist in order to *change* the student, to contribute to his personal development, to *make a difference.* Whereas the personnel manager is looking for applicants who can help the company, the admissions officer *should* be looking for applicants who can be helped by the institution.

That colleges are basically more interested in picking winners than in improving the student's performance is revealed by the rationale usually given for using high school grades and test scores in admissions. Institutions typically justify the application of these merit criteria on the grounds that they predict subsequent academic performance in college. Thus, applicants with poor grades and low test scores are not admitted because they are less likely to perform well than are students with high grades and high test scores. In short, the highly able student is admitted not because he has demonstrated greater potential for growth or change than the less able student, but simply because his achievement is likely to be higher.

Unfortunately, little is known about how to identify those students who are most likely to benefit from particular types of educational programs. But it is entirely possible that the character of student bodies would change radically if *potential for change* replaced academic aptitude as the principal criterion of merit in college admissions. It is not inconceivable, for example, that the very brightest students will achieve at a high level, no matter where they attend college. Thus, they may have very low potential for being benefited educationally by institutions; they would perform just as well in relatively unstructured situations where the only facilities were, say, a good library. Some of the less able applicants, on the other hand, may be highly susceptible to the influence of the college environment. The point here is that, with respect to making a difference in the performance of their students, many institutions may be squandering their resources by admitting only the brightest among their applicants.

Another argument frequently given to support the use of the standard merit criteria is that only the brightest students are capable of "profiting" from higher education. Presumably, this argument implicitly accepts the rationale for higher education just discussed: potential for *change* should be the principal basis for admissions. Recent evidence, however, fails to support this assumption, since students at all levels of ability showed similar gains in achievement during their undergraduate years, regardless of the type of institution they attended.[15]

Still another justification for using the standard merit criteria in admissions relates to the use of college admissions as a form of *reward*. Many parents, teachers, and students view being admitted to college as a kind of recognition for past achievement. This concept confuses the certification

[15] Alexander W. Astin, *The College Environment* (Washington: American Council on Education, 1968).

and the admissions functions. Clearly, it is appropriate for institutions to reward high achievement at the time of certification; but to treat the admissions decision as a kind of prize for good performance in high school is to distort the admissions function and, hence, the mission of the institution. In short, the use of the college admissions process to "pick winners" is not consistent with the *educational* mission of the institution. What seems to be needed is a serious re-examination of the entire rationale for admissions and increased research to assist each college in identifying those students who are most likely to benefit from its particular educational program. In this way, institutions can better fulfill their responsibilities to both the individual and the society.

Race as a Criterion in Admissions

Defenders of the merit system in admissions may argue that applying different admissions standards to different races is basically unfair and discriminatory. While there is truth in this argument, it should be pointed out that colleges have for years been willing on occasion to subordinate merit to other criteria in admissions, with very little outcry from the proponents of the merit system. The practice that immediately comes to mind in this connection is the use of sex quotas—the most extreme form being the single-sex college. Other forms of discrimination include setting higher merit standards for out-of-state applicants to public institutions, lowering merit standards for athletes and for the children of alumni, and varying merit standards for different regions (a device used by some selective institutions to achieve a "geographic mix"). With the possible exception of lowering standards for athletes, these discriminatory admissions practices have seldom been criticized as compromising the merit criterion. The point is simply that an acceptable rationale—either moral or educational—can be and has been made for waiving the merit criterion in favor of other criteria in the admissions process. If racial quotas are to be given precedence to merit criteria, it is imperative that the advocates of such quotas make their case immediately and convincingly.

Even if most colleges were to adopt racial quotas in their admissions policies, however, it is unlikely that a satisfactory degree of racial integration in student bodies could be achieved. The fundamental problem here is that there are simply too few black students in the total pool of college-bound students. A concerted effort by all predominantly white colleges to recruit more black students may serve simply to redistribute the inadequate pool that now exists.[16] Since most white institutions would probably apply the standard merit criteria within their black applicant group, their increased recruitment efforts might conceivably have a "trickling down" effect in that many predominantly black colleges would be forced to find new students to replace those recruited by the predominantly white colleges. It is doubtful whether these institutions have either the resources or the drawing power to identify and recruit substantial numbers of new students from among the non-college-bound population.

The point here is that competing for candidates within the pool of college-bound students has little effect on the size of the total pool. Clearly, what is needed is a much more concentrated effort on the part of colleges and universities to recruit many more black students from among those who might otherwise not attend college.

With respect to the broader social problem of racial tension, the importance of increasing the pool of black students attending colleges can hardly be overestimated. Consider, for example, that we live in a society where education, particularly higher education, is increasingly a prerequisite for entry into most of the higher status and higher paid professions. Consider also that one of the prime sources of racial tension is the reality that most blacks live in less affluent circumstances than most whites. If higher education is one of the principal avenues of escape from poverty and from ghetto life, then the current representation of blacks among college freshmen (6–7 percent) must be considered woefully inadequate. In short, we have a situation where the typical black is already far behind the typical white economically and where he is sure to fall still further behind because his chances of obtaining a higher education are substantially less than the white's chances.

Given the current economic chasm between blacks and whites, one could argue that the proportion of blacks going on to higher education should, for a period of time, be even *greater* than the proportion of whites. Instead, we have a situation where the economic gap is likely to widen with time. The undesirable social consequences that are likely to result from this increasing discrepancy can be avoided only if higher educational institutions are prepared to undertake major crash programs that will greatly increase the proportion of black students who go on to college. Simply stealing some other

---

[16] It should be stressed that the underrepresentation of blacks among entering college freshmen (6–7 percent versus 12 percent in the college-age population) is in part the result of high dropout rates among blacks in high school: only about 10 percent of the high school graduates are black. *Current Population Reports,* Population Characteristics, Series P-20, No. 182, April 28, 1969; "Educational Attainment: March, 1968."

college's black students will not do the job. Individual institutions must make an intensive effort to intervene at the secondary school level with programs designed to encourage black students to go to college. While such programs present many educational, economic, and logistical problems, these are minor compared with the increased racial tension that is likely to accompany a widening in the socioeconomic gap that already exists between the races.

Institutional Responsibility for Specially Admitted Students

A question which is still far from settled is how much responsibility for the student's progress the institution assumes when it admits him—frequently after active recruiting efforts—under merit criteria substantially below those used in admitting most other students. Should he simply be left to sink or swim as other students are? Should he be offered special programs of tutoring, remedial work, and counseling? If so, how should these programs be designed? How are they to be financed? How is the student ultimately to be assimilated into the regular academic program?

More important is the question of academic standards. Should the specially admitted black student be required to perform at the same level as other students if he is to receive academic credit for given courses and to earn a degree? It is likely that some concerned professors and administrators will be tempted to apply lower standards in evaluating the performance of black students so as to enhance their apparent level of achievement and thereby reduce their chances of academic failure and disappointment. While such double standards may have some desirable temporary effects—such as higher student morale and less institutional guilt—in the long run they would probably encourage the development of racist policies. Employers, graduate schools, and professional schools, for example, would want to know whether the students had earned a "black degree" or a "white degree." Such problems, which are inherent in any system that employs double standards of performance, highlight the need for differentiating clearly between *admissions* standards and *performance* standards.

Conclusions

In this paper, we have examined certain alternative arguments concerning college admissions policies and racial problems. We have attempted to explore some of the basic assumptions involved in the use of aptitude test scores and high school grades in college admissions and to present recent empirical evidence concerning the relative usefulness of these measures for students of different races. Our analysis and discussion seem to warrant the following conclusions:

1. The low representation of blacks among entering college freshmen and the de facto racial segregation that exists in many colleges is attributable in part to the use, in the admissions process, of high school grades and, in particular, of scores on tests of academic ability. As predictors of the individual student's chances of success in college, test scores and school grades are subject to considerable error. Thus, other criteria could probably be employed in the admissions process with only minor unfavorable effects on the level of academic performance and on the dropout rate.

2. Black students—whether they attend white or black colleges—on the average perform academically at the level that would be predicted from their high school grades and test scores. (The average performance of black women is slightly below expectation.) Dropout rates of black students attending white colleges, however, are slightly *lower* than is predicted from grades and test scores.

3. The goal of furthering racial integration in colleges basically conflicts with the use of purely meritocratic standards in admissions. If merit considerations in admissions are to be successfully subordinated to racial considerations, then the case for integration and increased educational opportunities for blacks needs to be made convincingly.

4. Predominantly white colleges that lower their admissions standards (with respect to required grades and test scores) so as to admit more black students are not likely to experience significant changes in their dropout rates, although the college grades of these specially admitted students will tend to be lower than the grades of other students.

5. A basic problem in attempting to achieve a higher degree of racial integration in American colleges is that the total supply of black college-bound youth is inadequate. Competing for students within this pool is not likely to increase the size of the pool. If significantly more integration is to be achieved, individual colleges must make a greater attempt to encourage non-college-bound black students to attend college.

6. The lowering of *admissions* standards does not necessarily result in the lowering of academic standards. In theory, at least, institutions are free to set standards of performance independently of their admissions standards. A major obstacle here is that performance standards (grades) are relative rather than absolute. The use of absolute standards of performance —which would be comparable across institutions—would obviate the need

to rely on admissions standards (average test scores) in assessing the "academic excellence" of the institution.

7. American colleges have pursued the use of meritocratic criteria in admissions so vigorously that the *educational* mission of the institution has become blurred. "Picking winners" may be appropriate for businesses and other enterprises that are primarily interested in exploiting talent, but it is an inappropriate model for institutions that exist to influence or *change* those people who are selected. Thus, the principal purpose of the admissions process should be to select the students who are most likely to benefit from the institution's educational program. Since recent research indicates that the mostly highly able students are not necessarily those who can be the most changed by the college experience, much more research on the problem of how to identify students with high potential for change is needed.

Commentaries on

Racial Considerations in Admissions

CHERYL D. ADAMS, NICHOLAS HOBBS
LOIS D. RICE, PETER M. MILLER

Considerations in Redefining Admissions Criteria

CHERYL D. ADAMS

THE ASTIN PAPER is a clear and helpful study of the admissions criteria used by most colleges in the nation. The data presented are, however, quite insufficient for the task of redefining admissions criteria.

First, the size and nature of the sample of black students is questionable—776 black students, 500 of whom were attending predominantly black colleges. Surely this sample does not adequately represent all black students attending college in 1966. That two-thirds were enrolled in predominantly black colleges becomes a fact of especial importance inasmuch as the data collected on students in black colleges may be completely inapplicable to special programs for blacks at white colleges. A black student on a black campus may have a higher level of aspiration and, therefore, may work harder than his black brother in a white college. Further, his overall performance may be better because of the lack of psychological interference. It would be misleading for a white institution to use data collected from a black college as a basis for its expectations of black students.

Second, the correlations are weak, as Astin himself admits and offers as evidence of the need for a redefinition of admissions standards. The point is worth repeating here, however, inasmuch as the correlations may be even weaker when applied to black students, where the sample itself is questionable.

A third limitation on the applicability of Dr. Astin's findings to a redefinition of admissions standards arises from the considerable change that has taken place since 1966 in the racial situation in the United States, the year on which the data on entering college freshmen are based. After that year, what may be called a "Black Pride" movement swept across the country. Its effects are most evident on college campuses, but as yet are minimal: an ill-defined and inadequate program in black studies, a mad rush for black students, a paternalistic tutoring program for inner city youth, and so on.

In particular, the rush for increased black enrollment at most colleges has a significant effect on the applicability of Mr. Astin's data on black students. In my opinion, for one obvious reason, the sample of black students is not representative of the black college student population today. In 1966, most college students were from socioeconomic backgrounds that facilitated going to college. Until 1967 few colleges offered special programs designed to provide financial and academic assistance to blacks. Therefore, at both white institutions and predominantly black institutions, a black student desiring a college education (1) had to come from an educational background that prepared him for college-level work and enabled him to meet the admissions standards, and (2) his economic status had to be such that he could finance his education. Perhaps at the predominantly black institutions admissions standards were less stringent and costs slightly lower, but essentially the two conditions had to be met.

Either condition would tend to exclude those black students being sought for special programs in most colleges today— students from low socioeconomic levels. Such students are likely to come from economically depressed areas where the secondary schools that purport to educate their students are notorious for their inadequacies—inadequacies that range from inferior facilities to antiquated teaching methods. A product of this kind of educational background has rarely tended to go to college, indeed has rarely bothered to finish high school. The paper notes that only about 10 percent of all high school graduates are black.

The second condition, adequate financial ability, is difficult enough for the average potential black college student: most black family incomes are insufficient to send a child to college. The financial situation is further complicated if there is more than one child to educate. A study made in 1962 makes the point: "The high correlation between family income and educational opportunity as measured by school attainment is further affected by the fact that the families with the largest number of children frequently come from the lowest income groups." [1] This study further

[1] Virgil A. Clift, Archibald W. Anderson, G. Gordon Hullfish (eds.), *Negro Education in America: Its Adequacy, Problems, and Needs* (New York: Harper & Row, 1962).

states that only one out of twenty children from low-income families attend college. Assuming that this figure did not substantially increase by 1966, then the black college students used in the Astin study were not from this low-income group, at least not in sufficient numbers to represent the majority of potential black college students.

Overall, then, the sample used in Dr. Astin's study represents those black students whose backgrounds closely paralleled those of white middle- (or even upper-) class Americans enrolled in colleges and used in the Astin study. Thus the student profiles offered are not typical of the black students being sought by many colleges today.

Another point needing attention is the conclusion that racial background has little, if any, effect on an individual's ability to score well on a standardized test. As I stated above, the black students used in this study probably came close to meeting the traditional admissions criteria. Therefore, their test scores are not representative of most would-be black college students. Mr. Astin has advised against the use of standardized tests as predictors of college success, but, as we have already found out, the data upon which he bases this warning is suspect.

I would like to offer an alternative reason for the need for a redefinition of admissions standards with regard to standardized tests. A very revealing survey taken by the Office of Education in 1942 explains the need for such a re-evaluation. In doing so, it points out the limitation in the cultural background of black students:

> Part of this limitation is due to the poverty, part to the cultural lag growing out of previous low status, part to the segregation pattern which excludes Negroes from libraries, museums, art galleries, lectures, concerts, and other cultural services, and which shuts them off from association with persons whose opportunities have been greater than their own. While many white students suffer from regional lack in this respect, Negroes suffer all the lacks of the white population plus the special deprivations imposed because of race.[2]

The twenty-seven years since this survey was published have not been enough to reduce this lag substantially. Of course, today there is the question whether or not the acquisition of this culture is relevant to the black man—a question that needs substantial research. But regardless of relevancy, black people are expected to have had the exposure to the white culture necessary to score well on a standardized test. It must be understood that this degree of attainment is almost impossible because the average black

[2] Ina Corinne Brown, "Socio-Economic Approach to Educational Problems."

student has no frame of reference to which he can relate the questions. They are completely outside his realm of experience.

One last point: The paper states that what may be needed is a duality in admissions standards—one set for blacks and one for whites. He goes on to question the efficiency of such a duality. I would like to stress that the cultural system in the United States has been based on a duality in the form of racist practices. Although I do not condone such duality, I feel that at this time it is not unreasonable to desire such practices in general university policy. In the future, when the inequities in educational preparation between blacks and whites have been minimized, then this duality can be erased. Until then it is essential that blacks be given the greatest possible opportunities to attend college.

In summary, while shedding light on the situation in 1962, the data offered do little to clear up problems in redefining admissions criteria. More intense research is desperately needed in this area.

Institutional Goals and Selection Procedures

NICHOLAS HOBBS

THE NATION has no greater internal problem than the full incorporation of the black man into the benefits, opportunities, and responsibilities of our society. Institutions of higher education, central as they are to society's functioning, could reasonably be expected to make a major contribution to the solution of the problem. Their most important contribution would be the education of Negroes in undergraduate, graduate, and professional schools in numbers at least proportionate to their representation in the population. We fall far short of this goal.

The major impediment to admission of blacks to colleges is their inadequate preparation for the experience, from early childhood on. But another impediment of substantial consequence is the procedure we use to assess the adequacy of their preparation and to predict their success in college. Although the first impediment will require years to remedy, the second impediment can be diminished by greater sophistication in the use of grades, test scores, and other predictors. Astin's paper—reasonably argued and abundantly supported by analyses made possible by the American

Council's research program—shows the necessity of making admissions procedures harmonious with educational policies.

Since World War I psychologists have argued convincingly, and with data to prove it, that certain kinds of human performances can be predicted with remarkable efficiency on the basis of past achievement or brief standardized samples of performance. Academic achievement proved to be one kind of performance that could be predicted with a high degree of accuracy, although other accomplishments, such as learning to fly an airplane or operate a lathe, could also be predicted with impressive precision. Appropriately enough, psychologists emphasized what they *could* do, not what they remained unable to do; their charts displayed how much better than chance their predictions were, not how far short they fell from high precision. Although the conscientious psychologist would point out that the most efficient batteries of tests could account for only one-fourth to one-third of the variance in the predicted performance, it is easy to overlook the fact that the preponderance of the variance—from three-fourths to two-thirds—remained unaccounted for. It is this large residual that Astin focuses on. What is "error" for the psychologist is "opportunity" for the educator. The challenge to the educator is to defeat the predictions of the psychologist.

But the very existence of a technology tends to determine the objectives of programs to which it is applicable. One hears an administrator note with pride that his college has been able to bring its average ACT scores at admission to 1200, or some such figure. Because a function can be measured, it becomes a goal in itself, not a means of achieving some clear educational objective. We can measure fairly well the ability to manipulate verbal symbols; thus this function gets emphasized in college programs both as predictor *and* criterion variables. Blacks, growing up in a symbol-impoverished world, get eliminated from the experience that should help overcome their deficiency. Were we able to measure and predict with equal efficiency the ability to manipulate social situations ("social intelligence"), one would expect a greater emphasis on social competence in education programs and a different composition of college populations. One is reminded of the observation that attributes of gentleness and compassion may be more important than intelligence in man's survival. Unfortunately we don't have a reliable test of these virtues; thus they get little attention.

Astin insists, rightly, that the purposes of a college or university should govern admissions policies and procedures more than they do. Even so, it is startling to read his blunt statement: "In my judgment, the model of selective admissions based on test scores and grades is inappropriate for higher educational institutions." I interpret this to mean not that efforts at prediction should be abandoned but that we need a better set of predictors to identify applicants "most likely to be favorably influenced by the particular educational program offered at the institution."

How is such a prediction to be made? One route would be to validate various plausible predictors against the criterion of responsiveness of the student to the program of the college. One would try to predict, not absolute achievement, but change in the student as a result of his college experience, along dimensions judged to be important by the college. This would require a much clearer and more widely shared definition of objectives than is evident in programs (as distinct from the catalogs) of most institutions for higher education. And what would the best predictors be? If our neat tests are not so good, there will be a strong tendency to turn to the interview as a screening device, as a predictor of a student's probable responsiveness, and this would be unfortunate. In most situations the interview provides a poor basis for predicting subsequent performance. Its great popularity as a selection device is exceeded only by its excessive inutility. Probably life history data, objectively recorded and then validated for specific college programs, would prove a relatively effective procedure in accomplishing the kind of prediction Astin thinks important. Finally, self-selection—the fact that certain kinds of colleges tend to attract certain kinds of students—could be planfully exploited to improve recruitment and selection. This undertaking would require that a college be aware of its purposes and of its character, and that these be made known, as best they can, to populations from which students are drawn. The best predictor, however, would be an opportunity for the student to experience the college program, to permit self-selection to work on the basis of firsthand knowledge. Dropping out of college should be an honorable alternative, not necessarily a sign of failure. Each college would then have an optimum dropout rate that would be greater than some earlier sought minimal rate. And black students would have a fairer chance to defeat our not-too-good predictors.

At this point a grave flaw in Astin's argument should be identified. His data are derived not from a randomly selected sample of high school graduates who might, under lenient circumstance, want to go to college, but from a population that both expected to be and was in fact screened on the basis of grades and test scores. Furthermore, the individuals involved not only wanted to go to college (presumably) but also believed (presumably) that they had a chance of being accepted by one or more of the colleges to which they applied. A rigorous, multiple selection process defines and limits Astin's sample. Astin's proposed lottery system (especially if accompanied by an adequate scholarship program) probably would result in a clogging of superior colleges with miserable students who both felt miserable and were in fact deficient in ability or preparation. Faced with such a dolorous situation, the high-level colleges would then probably set up tough introductory courses to reduce the number of miserable (phenomenologically and objectively) students. But courses for purposes of screening are expensive, and their predictive validity is uncertain. In the interest of efficiency and economy, as well as of the well-being of prospective students, the high-level colleges would probably then rediscover a remarkable fact: test scores and high school grades are pretty efficient predictors of college performance. Meanwhile, the less-demanding colleges, disturbed by an unusual quota of highly demanding students, and both alarmed and inconvenienced by their high dropout rate, would become the most vocal and insistent advocates of selecting students on the basis of test scores and high school grades. Windmills, though available for tilting, also grind grain.

Finally, there is the large issue of purpose: What end is to be served by admissions policies and procedures? This is a problem not of technique but of value. In the Air Force selection program in time of war it seemed fitting to define the selection task as reducing as near to one hundred as possible the number of cadets required to produce a hundred pilots. Individuals did not matter much. In the Peace Corps, in contrast, the selection task had to concern itself centrally with the individual who had volunteered to serve his country in time of peace; selection procedures had to give him maximum chance to do so. The college or university may have yet another goal: How can it function in unique ways to improve the quality of life in our society? Such a goal would mean the admission of students with a range of qualities not captured by high school grades and test scores. There is, as Astin makes clear, sensible social purpose to be served by the adoption of much more flexible admissions policies toward black students than prevails today in most colleges and universities. And we have some clues to constructive ways to open up admissions.

Furthermore, arguments for a more open policy for admission of black students must include one important consideration—what the black student can contribute to a college or university. The capacity to contribute is as important as the ability to profit in the complex equations of mutual choice at the time of admission.

A Larger Talent Pool

LOIS D. RICE

IN HIS PAPER Mr. Astin uses empirical evidence and moral suasion to urge the expansion of black enrollments in higher educational institutions. There is no quarrel with his goals. In fact, the temptation is to justify the paper by the writer's positive motives—to indulge the so-called "intentional fallacy," that oft-debated tendency among literary critics to judge a work by the author's attitudes rather than his art. This temptation will be avoided: indeed it must, for meaningful social changes have too long been thwarted, even reduced to pious utterances, because the art used to achieve them is insufficient to the task.

To improve the admissions process and increase black enrollments in higher education, the paper proposes that colleges and universities abandon the use of test scores and high school grades in their selection of students. Using data from his recent study of college freshmen, he argues that these criteria are subject to considerable error in predicting college success and dropout and that "the blind application" of such criteria in the admissions process is a major barrier to the enrollment of black students.

To those of us long-troubled by the effects of testing and selectivity on black students, Mr. Astin's position appears at first glance to be most tenable and actually supportive of these concerns. The study documents that black and other atypical students with less-than-desired credentials can succeed in higher education, even at selective colleges; that dropout among these students is less than the traditional measures of academic ability predict; and, without changing standards of performance, colleges could indeed change standards of admission to include far more black students.

His support, however, is more apparent than real. He does not consider the most obvious and logical alternative to selective admissions—open admissions. It is a curious omission, for much of this data and many of his conclusions sustain the open enrollment position. Instead, he advocates new admissions criteria. He would substitute for the intellective measures now used in selection some undefined and still undeveloped nonintellective measures to assess "student potential for change" within the academic environment.

This could be an appealing proposal:

if such measures could actually be developed (and to date researchers have found no justifiable mechanisms to determine potentiality for growth or change among students, black or white);

if such instruments would not contain old biases;

if higher education could revise its traditional offerings to foster climates for genuine change and develop new responses to possibilities for human growth;

and most important,

if such criteria would not create a new type of selectivity differing little from current practices, and no applicants were rejected for admission on the basis of such criteria.

I am not that optimistic.

I am not hopeful either that a significant segment of higher education will abandon traditional measures of selection, however strong the evidence developed against them or however loud the voices for open admissions. Mine, therefore, is a position of expediency. Short of open admissions, we should consider whether or not proper use of the merit criteria can foster greater access to higher education. Mr. Astin's findings provide some clues.

The very error of tests and high school grades in predicting academic success—Mr. Astin's great concern—can enhance the chances of admission for many black students. A high predictive accuracy would make the admissions process still more mechanical, preclude the essential personal judgments of admissions officers and talent searchers, and work against black students with low or modest credentials. Moreover, a higher predictive accuracy would undoubtedly imply a rather complete inability of institutions to "challenge good students or to help poor ones." (And while Mr. Astin would seem to desire greater predictive validity, I know—particularly in view of his own proposal—he considers that colleges and universities are capable of providing just such a challenge.)

Perhaps, most important, Mr. Astin (like Lynn[1] and Cleary[2] before

[1] T. Anne Cleary, *Test Bias: Validity of the Scholastic Aptitude Test for Negro and White Students in Integrated Colleges,* College Entrance Examination Board Research and Development Reports, No. 18 (Princeton, N.J.: Educational Testing Service, 1966).

[2] Robert L. Linn, "Reanalysis of the Data of Miss Cleary's Predictive Bias Study" (Mimeographed memorandum; Princeton, N.J.: Educational Testing Service, 1967).

him) finds that academic criteria overpredict the freshman year performance of black students. He states "the traditional merit criteria, far from discriminating against black students, favor them somewhat"—a conclusion hardly consistent with his recommendation to abandon academic criteria. Considerably more research is needed on the predictive validity of academic measures for black students—and particularly studies which will move beyond that magical benchmark of researchers—the freshman year. As Clark and Plotkin [3] and others have demonstrated, there appears to be a peculiar and quite exceptional growth of black students during the later years of college.

A once proper use of the merit criteria to foster access to higher education was talent searching. Throughout the years, we have been told of the limits of the pool of so-called talented black youngsters. For some years, Coleman, Kendrick, and others[4] have found that but 10–15 percent of black students would obtain a score of 370 or above on the verbal section of SAT—a result supposedly indicative of some ability to handle postsecondary training. Mr. Astin too speaks of the limits of the pool. Yet, all of these researchers have focused primarily upon the academic ability of black college-going or enrolled students who have found their way somehow *paid* into the pool. One experimental program—Project ACCESS—tested with the PSAT *free of charge* all students in the District of Columbia schools— a nearly all-black population. Results showed that some 33 percent of the senior boys and 34 percent of the senior girls exceeded the score of 360. (In late May 1969, each of the District secondary schools had at least 100 senior students who had scores at this level or higher but had no postsecondary educational plans.) Still a small pool but larger, nevertheless, than is usually assumed. Project ACCESS tested 70,000 black and brown students in six cities, and of this total it is estimated that 63,000 students were brought into the PSAT program for the first time—a program in which more than a million predominantly middle-class students participate annually as their first step toward college admission.

Despite my great concern about the adequacy of traditional tests for most black children, I am loathe, however heretical it may seem, to abandon measures so graphic of what still needs to be accomplished. The pool of so-called talented black students, however small, has not been exhausted.

[3] Kenneth B. Clark and Lawrence Plotkin, *The Negro Student at Integrated Colleges* (New York: National Scholarship Service and Fund for Negro Students, 1963).

[4] S. A. Kendrick, "The Coming Segregation of Our Selective Colleges," *College Board Review*, Winter 1967–68, p. 8.

And admission-type tests used outside the admissions process can obviously help to identify able youth and demonstrate too how the majority of blacks have been failed through educational and social injustices.

But are the merit criteria the only barriers to black attendance in higher education? Mr. Astin mentions few others. Neither does he account for the dearth of black students at nonselective institutions and open-door institutions. Civil Rights Compliance Reports collected by the U.S. Office of Education for the academic year 1968 indicate that of 61 junior colleges in selected urban areas, 39 had black enrollments of 10 percent or more and of these 16 had black enrollments exceeding 25 percent—a record considerably better than most colleges. But urban centers are predominantly black, and these data show that urban institutions have yet to extend themselves to their own communities.

The obstacles are more fundamental. They include:

· White America's view of the potentiality of little black children who aren't expected to learn, and don't—who aren't supposed to succeed, and fail;
· Teachers who do not teach; and
· Schools that do not adapt to the peculiar needs of children of poverty;
· Universities that don't train teachers to teach ghetto youngsters and consciously "protect" their teacher trainees from ghetto schools;
· Legislators who whittle away the funds so vital to the attendance of blacks in higher education and, over time, transform poverty-directed student aid to middle-class aid;
· Universities which price themselves out of the reach of the poor and still prefer to bet their own scholarship monies on winners;
· Years of institutional and national failure to provide black graduates of higher education a fair rate of economic return. (According to 1968 census figures, the median income of white high school graduates still exceeds the median income of black college graduates, and white college graduates still earn an average $4,000 more a year than blacks.)

The catalog could continue: the barriers are progressive and cumulative, and solutions at the point of college admissions, however necessary, are by themselves meaningless.

This is not to say that work and thought such as Mr. Astin's should go unattended or that the cry for open admissions should abate. It must be a loud cry for, somehow, those of us who seek this goal and the expansion of all opportunities are, perhaps without fully realizing it, placing a faith in higher education to respond to social ills.

Proper Functions of a College

PETER M. MILLER

THE ASTIN PAPER is unusual in that it presents figures to arrive at conclusions, and then proceeds—unsuccessfully, I think—to show that what they have proved is wrong or at least unimportant. The early tables show evidence of the ability of high school grades and standardized tests to predict college achievement. Then Astin argues that college achievement is not important, that many more low achievers can be admitted without harming the institution's quality, and that really it is not the high achiever that the college needs anyway.

My purpose here is to defend what Dr. Astin has shown first, and then indicate what may happen if we do what he wants us to, at least to the extent he advocates. This will lead me to disagree with his description of the function of college and to argue for continued reliance on evidence of merit. And finally I shall try to point out where I think the greatest effort at change and improvement must be made.

Little defense is needed of the early part of the paper, which gives clear evidence that high school grades are still the best predictor of college achievement, that standardized tests also are efficient, and that a combination of the two is superior. When anything can predict with 80 percent accuracy or better how a human being is going to perform (and react) in a college situation, it is doing a remarkable job. But Dr. Astin calls attention to the 10 percent of *A* students who do not get *B*'s and the 10 percent of *C* students who do and emphasizes what he calls this "substantial amount of error." I submit on the contrary that students subject to homesickness, girl trouble, possible disillusionment with a highly recommended college, uncongenial roommates, and the unpredictable effect of a sudden access to freedom are performing with remarkable predictability to get as many *B*'s as they do. Further I would be surprised if at least 10 percent of the *C* students did not respond to the stimulus of wider horizons and the freedom from high school shackles and achieve the *B*'s the tables show.

Having tried to undermine confidence in the measures of prediction, Astin then argues that not dropping out of a college is more important than achieving positively. He shows that grades and scores do not do nearly as well in predicting dropouts, and therefore wonders how many more poor students could be admitted to college and stay in. How long has it been since Dr. Astin has looked closely at the student who is just scraping by with a 1.9 GPA (when 1.9 is the lowest passing average)? If he had seen the apathy, the lack of achievement in the able student with the 1.9, and the misery of the poorer student who can barely make his 1.9, I think his conclusions would be different. A college must have a line of demarcation; but students just at the line, for whatever reason, are usually neither improving nor enjoying themselves.

Further, I cannot agree with Mr. Astin when he states that admissions standards are not necessarily related to the academic standards of a college. Any teacher worth his salt knows that he must gear his teaching to the level of student he has. Adulterate the quality of the students to any large extent, and the academic standards are bound to go down. A certain number of minority students with predicted low GPAs (the tables are not encouraging on their performing better in college) should certainly be admitted—for the good of society and for the specific good of the remainder of the students— and every effort should be made to help them perform better than the predictive measures forecast. And the number should be such that the college's ultimate product will not be debased.

I argue thus far from what I consider to be the function of higher education: to teach the teachable; to show new insights to the able; to promote mental growth; and ultimately, to prepare people to find new knowledge for the benefit of mankind. Astin says that college should *change* people, and I agree. Growth is change, and the people who have given indication in high school that they are growing mentally are the most likely prospects for significant, advantageous changes. Astin implies that the likely prospects can take care of themselves wherever they go, and that colleges should concentrate on students who have not yet shown promise because they offer possibilities for greater change. Changing them would be beneficial to all, but for the college to concentrate on these students, who either cannot or elect not to perform academically, will be to destroy itself.

The problem as I see it is that too many of the black and brown minorities coming through the schools are simply not prepared. The minorities themselves would agree to this and deplore it, though they might disagree violently on exactly what type of preparation they should have. Colleges at the present time cannot take many more of them without seriously lowering the level of performance of the students they enroll. It is all very well to seek recruits outside the minority college-going pool; but when you find that those you take cannot do your work, you must defeat yourself in either of two ways: change your work, or throw out the students you have recruited.

The problem may go back to the very beginning of schooling; at any rate it goes back fairly far. Some students at my own college who have engaged in tutoring projects in disadvantaged schools have found that, as early as the seventh grade, minority students are beginning to get out of the mainstream that leads to college. Whether they are forced out by poor preparation in earlier years or by failure on someone's part to motivate them properly, I am not competent to say.

The essential point is that students of all races must be taught from the very beginning that they can (and, in many cases, should) go to college, that at any rate they are college material. They must not be made to feel inferior because of their color or the language they speak at home. If they cannot speak English well enough to participate meaningfully in class, that problem must be tackled and solved at once. The result will be that in a few years, minorities, as well as Anglos, will be coming through the high schools with their potentials for college ready to be measured. The colleges that choose the most academically meritorious will be getting their share of minorities along with the rest.

Colleges can help in this educational revolution, but it will take more than the colleges to turn the trick. It will take parents of young children of whatever color, and indeed the entire United States citizenry, to bring about this educational revolution. It will not come overnight. Until it comes, the colleges will have to scrounge, to pick, to choose as best they can— much as they are now doing—to get the minority students whom they can help and who will help them.

Of course, colleges can do more than they are doing now (though not as much as Dr. Astin argues) in the way of minority admissions. But they can ignore the indices of merit only to their own great risk. They should not do so. It will not help society to have the colleges ruin themselves in a misguided effort to help minorities. The solution lies further away and is more difficult to get at: it lies in the workings of our entire public school system.

Allocating Limited Resources

DAVID G. BROWN

UNIVERSITY ADMINISTRATORS face hard decisions of *where* to invest dollars, time, and effort. How are universities to choose between supporting more black scholarships or a black studies curriculum, a stronger library in Negro history or a survey of ghetto housing needs, a militant black counselor or a predominantly black student union?

As these questions suggest, most universities are strongly committed to helping to solve the racial crisis; only the strategy of attack is in doubt. Because a typical list of black demands is like a never-ending scroll on which the granted demand goes out of sight only to allow a new demand to appear at the bottom, and because the university administrator cannot accommodate all needs, regardless of merit, for always his expenditure abilities are constrained by institutional income, he must somehow choose the projects that are most worthy of funding. This choice is my topic: Which alternative investments of university resources will be most productive in solving the racial crisis?

Premises

To facilitate the analysis, this paper proceeds from three premises. First, the topic—the campus and the racial crisis—must be faced. It is both immediate and perennial. The racial crisis constitutes a major social problem of the highest priority, solution of which requires discussion and action. Equally important is the continuing dilemma: Does society in the long run benefit most from a university community that alternates its effort among the problems of the day, or is a greater benefit contributed by a university community that remains aloof and works continually and with all its resources on eternal problems?

The second premise is submitted as a beginning answer. The campus must not be an ivory tower. The university has a stake and responsibility in overcoming the racial crisis. Time and talent must be directed toward solv-

156

ing the crises each age identifies.[1] Both society and campus are stronger when the campus is willing to help solve society's problems.

The third premise relates to the individual university: The only justification for adopting programs that assist and accommodate the black world is to strive to advance the dignity of the individual and of society. The administrator who institutes a black studies department or black scholarships or recruitment programs for black students as a "peace offering" will be sadly disappointed. Appeasement is self-defeating. The universities that have done the most to accommodate black demands are the universities that have had the most problems. In the minds of black protestors, accommodation to the first set of demands substantially increases the likelihood of success from a second confrontation over a second set of demands. And the adoption of programs favored by militant blacks attracts more militant blacks to campus. This accretion apparently typifies the situation at San Francisco State and Newark and Cornell, where the black student body has become more and more active. It is equally and more dramatically illustrated by universities such as Northwestern, where blacks who were enrolled in special programs for the disadvantaged led the movement.

Accommodation, thus, is often an invitation to confrontation. Every additional dollar spent on black studies, black scholarships, and black counselors advances the day that an individual university will have a major black-white confrontation and heightens the severity of the confrontation when it does occur. Blacks will not, and should not, leave the sympathetic university alone. They refuse to accept partial reparations.

The price of campus strife is not too high when social justice and human dignity are being purchased. Universities and colleges must devote substantial resources to numerous programs which have as their objective overcoming the racial crisis, and they must also prepare for confrontations.

Alternatives

For the past decade, because other institutions offered little hope in solving the major societal problems, resources were thrust upon universities. Project grants were given on the flimsiest proposals. Inappropriate tasks were accepted. A reason can be found to house almost any activity within a university. Too often, however, we in universities have been asking the wrong question. When we were asking, "Does this have anything to do with

---

[1] Of course a major portion of university time and talent must be directed toward problems that are not vogue, for often it is such attention that identifies new areas of inquiry and produces major breakthroughs.

what we're doing?" we should have been asking, "Is this the thing we do best?"

Radical departures are now evident. The days of easy dollars for higher education are gone. Other institutions such as industries and governments are showing that they too have an ability to attack the problems of the age. They too have a claim to the resources available. They too can serve best in certain realms. Upon universities, therefore, falls a new responsibility to choose carefully and to justify its requests. The case, made to private donors and state legislatures in the past, that the university can try to be everything to everyone is acknowledged as valid but irrelevant; it is newly realized that some activities are pursued inefficiently in universities and that universities themselves cannot provide panaceas.

Resource allocation to help solve the racial crisis is a pyramid of decision making. Society chooses to allocate so many dollars to the racial crisis and therefore not to color television sets or to the Vietnam war. Then society subcontracts part of the opportunity to various institutions, for example, the U.S. Air Force, the University of Michigan, General Motors, the American Council on Education, the State of New York, and the Black Panthers. Then the institution designs a particular strategy of attack on the problem.

Design necessarily follows commitment. Once the campus is committed to helping solve the racial crisis, alternative strategies must be outlined and ranked. The university decides where limited dollars will do the most good, where assigned faculty time will be most productive, how limited physical space may be best used. More students desire an education than the institution can accommodate: the university decides which group can best be served here and which groups elsewhere. In short, the university seeks to maximize the fulfillment of university objectives. In seeking the maximum, it is constrained by money, available personnel, academic spaces available, physical spaces assignable, and imperfect knowledge and judgment.

Universities committed to solving the racial crisis must choose among five basic strategies:

1. Educate more black students.
2. Expose white students to black problems and black culture.
3. Train students in service professions (for example, teachers of disadvantaged).
4. Manage and administer action programs.
5. Design, research, and evaluate action programs.

Consider each alternative.

1. Educate More Black Students

A college education for more blacks is the goal. It is a worthy one. From the college experience, black students may gain both the prestige of the degree itself and, more important, self-confidence, ability for abstraction, and relevant skills. But the barriers to attendance are many—financial, motivational, technical, and cultural.

Financial barriers

If educational access is to be provided for more blacks, universities must give education away, free of charge. The family income behind a majority of the black students who do reach college (an affluent group when compared with non-college-attendees) is less than $6,000. In contrast, only 14 percent of all white students come from families with incomes under $6,000.[2] Negro families are generally "in no position to make any contributions whatever to their children's college expenses."[3] Financial need is often total—tuition plus living expenses plus, in many instances, support for parents and siblings who expect family members of working age to contribute income. The need at a private university is $3,500–$4,000 per year for tuition, fees, and living expenses plus an additional $2,000 to cover the income not earned because the student is not working.[4]

Possible sources of scholarship funds are income from tuition, private donations, loans, and government grants. Grants are the greatest hope. Financing scholarships from tuition and regular donor income will not work. An example will illustrate: envision two gas stations at the same intersection, selling the same seat belts. One station sells near cost, at $5.00. The other charges $7.50 so that it may give some away to customers who can't afford to pay. The high motives of the second station will not sell overpriced belts. The $7.50 station will have no market and be forced out of the seat belt business. Because the quality of university educations cannot be as

[2] Alan Bayer and Robert Boruch, *The Black Student in American Colleges* (Washington: Office of Research, American Council on Education, 1969), p. 18.
[3] Christopher Jencks and David Riesman, *The Academic Revolution* (Garden City, N.Y.: Doubleday & Co., 1968), p. 442.
[4] This $3,500–$4,000 is the additional amount of "unreimbursed expenditure" that a private university undertakes when it accepts a "total need" student instead of a student who can pay his own way. Since the tuition component covers only 70 percent of the institution's costs, the total cost to the university is $4,200–$4,900. The lower range of figures is appropriate when considering the *substitution* of a needy student for a paying student; the latter range is the increased cost of accepting the needy student while continuing to serve the paying students.
Costs of education in public universities are similar, with a substantial portion of the lower tuition and income being offset by state appropriations.

easily compared as identical seat belts, universities do have some ability to price their services above actual costs. The flexibility, however, is limited and, to a large extent, already being exercised.

Nor are loans an attractive alternative. To date it has been extremely difficult to convince men who have never known steady jobs that repaying a loan is a real possibility. Financial aid officers report that the lowest-income students, both black and white, reject loan opportunities. To many who need it the most, borrowing money seems irresponsible.

The Ford Foundation's $7 million grant for National Achievement Scholarships (for talented and needy black students) represents a big step forward and a partial counter to the cutback in new Economic Opportunity Grant funds.[5] But these substantial grants are not enough.

State and Federal appropriations are the only feasible source of large-scale support. All states must join the majority that now appropriate funds for tuition equalization scholarships to students attending private universities. State appropriations to public institutions must reflect the need to provide needy black students with funds to cover tuition plus opportunity costs. Economic opportunity grants and work-study funds must be increased.

Without these increases, public institutions will be forced to generate scholarship funds by reducing expenditures per student and thereby lowering the quality of education. Since paying students will take their dollars to institutions where a dollar spent buys a dollar's worth of education, private institutions will have no alternative to the rejection of needy students. In the absence of special funds, increases in black scholarships cannot be considered by private universities except insofar as a transfer of current scholarship funds from white to black students is feasible.

Motivational barriers

To educate more blacks, money is necessary but not sufficient. Black students will have to be persuaded that college attendance is (1) possible and (2) worthwhile. This process means active recruitment. An example will illustrate. Drake University provided twenty-six four-year, all-expenses scholarships, each worth $10,000, for extremely needy students not planning to attend college. Eventually all twenty-six scholarships were awarded, but only after an intense search for takers. Normal channels were ineffective. The students sought had avoided high school counselors. They had

---

[5] For a description of the Ford program and 35 other scholarship opportunities for blacks, refer to "A Break for Black Scholars," *Ebony*, March 1969, pp. 45–56.

never considered attending college, never talked with anyone about the possibility, never heard of College Board tests, and they were actively hostile to the thought of college. Unusual obstacles impeded contact, such as the refusal of one parent to allow a counselor in his home to talk with his son. Only through churches, leaders among the disadvantaged, and Drake's own students and alumni were these prospects identified.

Black recruitment is expensive. To sell an education in white suburbia is cheaper and easier than to give one away in the ghetto. One factor is economy of scale: an admissions recruiter can spend one day at a large suburban high school and make himself accessible to a thousand college-bound students. The same time spent in a low-income neighborhood school of the same size may result in an exposure to only twenty-five college-bound students. A second factor is the grapevine: in high schools where there is the tradition of attending a certain college, former students are a university's most effective, though unpaid, recruiters. Breaking into a school is an expensive process. A final expense-increasing factor is that the typical black recruit must be convinced not only to attend "a particular" college but also to attend "any" college. The force of family and friends that pushes many whites to college is much weaker or is missing within the black community, where the percentage of fathers who have completed high school is only half as high and the percentage in semiskilled and unskilled occupations is triple the rates among whites.[6]

The wisdom of increasing institutional investment in recruitment depends largely upon the availability of financial support and the character of the program offered.

Technical barriers

To educate more blacks, money and motivation are necessary but not sufficient. Higher education will not serve black needs unless admissions criteria are bent. The modest requirement of a verbal score of 500 on the SAT eliminates over 99 percent of all blacks. The lower score of 400 eliminates over 90 percent.[7] If many blacks are to be enrolled, colleges will be dipping below 400.

Colleges will find they need to apply other measures of potential—measures more appropriate for persons reared in disadvantaged subcultures. The discounting of "board scores" afforded to foreign students is

[6] Bayer and Boruch, *The Black Student in American Colleges,* p. 18.
[7] John C. Hoy, "The Price of Diversity," *Saturday Review,* Feb. 15, 1969, pp. 96–97.

equally owed to blacks. And new measures that accommodate substantially varied cultural backgrounds need to be developed. The American Council on Education could provide a valuable clearinghouse of information on experiments with new evaluative criteria.

While developing new measures, the socially responsible university has only one option: to gamble on black admissions. Of course the nature and extent of the gamble will depend upon institutional characteristics. For Harvard the response is the "Gamble Fund" and a pre-enrollment catch-up program during the summer prior to the freshman year. For Rutgers at Camden, New Brunswick, and Newark, the gamble is an open admissions policy.[8] For Michigan State, the gamble is a special program of recruitment and counseling for more than 100 Detroit ghetto Negroes who are not normally admissible to the university.[9] At Illinois, Northwestern, Wesleyan, and Los Angeles similar experiments with more flexible admissions criteria are being pursued.

The time is now for every university to gamble by applying a different set of admissions criteria to a given percentage of each entering class. At the very least, higher education must grant access to all black students who can succeed in *conventional* curricula, even those whose test scores underrate their potential. For the campus, experimentation with new admissions criteria is cheap. An admissions committee may decide at any time to admit experimental groups of students according to new and different standards. If the students succeed, the new standards prove their worth.

There is another and vital consideration in the admissions gamble—the effect on students who do not succeed. If the students fail, new students may be admitted by different criteria. Small research expense, modest administrative inconvenience, and the low probability that the special program will mar the institutional image are very minor dangers to the university when measured against the potential crippling of the unsuccessful guinea pig. A failed student, by current practice, experiences great difficulty in gaining admission to a second, even less rigorous, college. Unknowingly he is the victim of the experiment.

So that experimentation can occur without crippling the students inadvertently caught in an unsuccessful trial, I advocate the nationwide elimination of *D* and *F* grades, at least at the freshman level. A student can be

---

[8] "Rutgers to Admit All Who Graduate in Three New Jersey Cities," *Chronicle of Higher Education*, March 24, 1969, p. 4.

[9] "Michigan State's Search for More Negro Students," *College Board Review*, Fall 1968, pp. 11–14.

told that his performance is unsatisfactory by simply not allowing credit for performance below *C*. "No credit" is sufficient penalty. The pains of adjustment during the freshman year do not need to linger until graduation. The sophomore year can be a fresh start.

More pertinent to the current discussion, the student who might have been inappropriately admitted to a program would lose only time, not his chance for a college education. The personal cost of the experimentation would be reduced, and the opportunity to develop new admissions criteria —ones more favorable to black students—would be introduced.

Cultural barriers

Not all problems are ones of measurement. Many blacks are appropriately excluded from college because they could not succeed in the programs currently being offered.

Few products are less differentiated than post-high-school education. Every type of student is forced into the same basic curriculum. Higher education is being mass-produced by one of the most expensive and least direct methods. Our foolish failure to tailor post-high-school education to student needs and potentials—especially now that students going on to college include some who have less inherent ability—is leading toward a very costly system of higher education that will be chronically and increasingly underfinanced. The situation is analogous to prescribing routinely the most powerful and most expensive drug to cure an undiagnosed disease, simply because the prescription works on one species of patient.

To educate more blacks will sometimes require accommodation to special backgrounds, values, and motivations. To accommodate new courses and new programs, new methods of instruction are needed.

For liberal white campuses, token programs for small numbers of black militants are an easy and visible, but often immoral, way to show concern.[10] A campaign for black enrollment should be based on the existence of programs that meet black needs. The cost of admitting talented black students capable of success in *standard* programs is minimal. Many campuses will wisely limit their effort to talented blacks.

Others, which have resources available, will, with equal wisdom, undertake special programs. Adequate service to students who have deficiencies in skills, motivation, and background requires more counseling, smaller

---

[10] For a more complete discussion of the moral issue, see **Paul B. Foreman,** "Race Confronts Universities: A Preface for Policy," *Journal of General Education,* July 1968, pp. 87–89.

classes, special sections, increased testing, additional supportive services, and much more expense. At Michigan State, for instance, the most conservative estimate is that the Detroit Project enrollees require educational expenditures $1,000 greater than the average freshman. Programs involving fewer students undoubtedly cost more per student.

In terms of cost, the appropriate "trade-off" for admission of a black freshman is closer to that of a white graduate student than a white freshman. Like graduate students, black freshmen require small classes, full scholarships, and individual programing. The campus that fails to back its special recruitment and admission program with special scholarship and academic assistance (including qualified, committed, and flexible staff) may be luring a student away from a college that could better serve his needs. Admission carries with it an obligation for relevant programing.

One programing alternative is segregated programs for "black students only," programs that highlight the role of black men in the scientific and literary advancement of man, programs that seek to nurture black self-respect by emphasizing the uniqueness of black culture. Berkeley deserves commendation for the creative and pioneering spirit that gave birth to its program. Most universities are, however, well advised to be cautious. There are good reasons to have serious doubts about the propriety of "Black is Beautiful" programs in an academic setting.

Universities cannot tolerate the manipulation of historical analysis to verify a predetermined bias, regardless of the worth of the position to be verified. Black dignity (as well as German supremacy) can be gained from history, but to study the French Revolution for the predetermined purpose of proving dignity is directly contrary to the impartial and dispassionate approach to knowledge that is the essence of intellectual inquiry. All subject matter must be approached with an open mind.

Nor can universities avoid relating the history they teach to the tasks they undertake. Separatism, the emphasis of differences among groups, has repeatedly led to bloodshed and hatred, while integration has stimulated human dignity and at least delayed bloodshed. With this background, how many experiments in separatism can be justified?

The fact is that black students will live in a culture where white values predominate. Becoming African is fine for those who will live in Africa, but American black students will live here. Bayard Rustin's penetrating question, "What in hell are such courses worth in the real world?" is painfully appropriate. To learn Afro-American cultures and values has real worth, but this learning must not supplant knowledge about the dominant culture.[11]

Equal to questionable desirability is questionable feasibility. Segregated black curricula require "separate but equal" facilities and programs. We can envision almost total duplication. For all the reasons that colleges enrolling fewer than 500 students are unable to participate in economies of scale, so also black-only programs, unless quite large, are headed toward serious financing difficulties.

To carry the feasibility issue further: for a college to generate the "critical mass" that allows the formation of a largely autonomous and separate black culture, approximately four hundred students will need to be enrolled.[12] Unless a university has or can attract four hundred, the black-only strategy will fail because of an absence of critical mass. It would be hypocritical for a university to design a curriculum that is dependent upon an extra-university culture when it could not provide that culture.

2. Expose White Students to Black Problems and Black Culture

Black America is a "foreign culture," even to black Americans. The son of a white lawyer from suburbia and the daughter of a black laundry worker from the ghetto can both grow from exposure to the black minority culture. To know and to understand the black man instills dignity within the black man himself and understanding within the white man. Drawing from the analogy with international education, strategies to accomplish understanding are at least three. First is the "rubbing shoulders" technique. Black students are brought to primarily white campuses to personify black America, just as Chinese students are brought to expose the student body to Chinese culture. For the white campus, the costs of this program are minimal and net benefits are high. Only the black students are potential losers. Those who wish to cross the color line have no problems, for the college environment provides ample opportunities to assimilate the host culture. Those who wish to remain in the black culture, however, may have acquired too many characteristics of the white culture to be accepted.

The second approach is academic exposure. Pursuing the analogy of Chinese area studies and courses on Chinese culture, universities may provide black studies departments, courses in black literature and in black art,

[11] Jencks and Riesman, *The Academic Revolution*, p. 430.
[12] Four hundred is not sacred. This estimate is the result of discussions with black students on several campuses whose judgment is that 200 believers in "Black is Beautiful" can maintain a community, and that 50 percent of all black students will be committed to the "Black is Beautiful" strategy.

lectures on the black labor market and black politicians, and speeches by leaders in the black community. Programs may be tailored to the individual needs and budget capacities of each campus, with full-blown graduate programs such as the ten-man departments developed at Yale and Berkeley costing over $200,000 per year.

Student demand is high: additional programing is clearly needed. The primary bottleneck restricting expansion of black lectureships, black literature courses, black area study emphases, and black studies departments is men even more than money. Twenty-five is a generous estimate of the number of scholars now qualified in the field.

For the immediate future, many campuses will need to rely on scholars in related fields and borrow speakers from a very few graduate centers. The critical need is to educate more scholars. This is a time for cooperation and restraint. Like all other disciplines, black studies scholars need supportive interaction among proximate peers. Geographic dispersion of these scholars, one to a state, would be almost certain to strangle the discipline. Today's experts should be concentrated in a limited number of high-caliber black studies departments so that they can graduate all of the black scholars that are needed by all of us. The demands for a black studies department in every college and university must be deferred, for acquiescence to these demands would be both an endorsement of mediocrity and a negation of the dream that the demands are meant to serve.

A third approach is direct exposure or involvement. Instead of going to China, white America is taken to the ghetto to observe what it is like to be poor and black. At Connecticut Wesleyan and Iowa Wesleyan, for example, each student is required to spend at least seven weeks engaged in voluntary service to a community. Old Westbury College grants up to forty-five hours of credit for service in the Peace Corps or VISTA. This approach has the advantage of authenticity and, if properly designed, low cost. When credit is given for "experience," it is usually awarded through a post-mortem in a faculty-led seminar. Once again, the Far Eastern tour and a semester in Hong Kong are relevant models.

Once again the major restraint is not money. In developing ghetto semesters and course credit for VISTA, the scarce commodity is administrative time. Defining the characteristics of an experience that is worthy of college credit, reducing anxieties among faculty with vested interests in current degree requirements and course offerings, cajoling internal budget switches from unproductive but traditional programs to these new programs —these are the needs.

Each approach has as its goal increased understanding and commitment. By nurturing within the white majority the lifelong desire and ability to attack the racial crisis, the campus can make its greatest contribution.

3. Train Students in Service Professions

In an eighteenth-century Western world, poverty and human need were objects of alteration by the church and the family, both institutions professing love but exercising little skill. In twentieth-century America, the role of the family is diminished and the church is represented by a professional theologian usually with seminary training. The seminarian is aided by a teacher specifically trained to work with the disadvantaged, by a lawyer specially trained in problems of the poor, and by a social worker specially educated in a graduate school carrying the name of his profession. By training these professionals who will help blacks, universities are making major contributions to the solution of the racial crisis.

The costs of professional education per student are, however, very high. At this point, expansion of existing programs would seem to be more in the national interest than the initiation of new programs. Over three-fourths of all seminaries, for example, enroll fewer than the five hundred students cited by a recent report of the American Association of Theological Seminaries as the minimum efficient scale.

Two hypotheses, both cost-reducing, need testing. First is the concept of a merged school of social service. In the field of administration, universities, including the University of California at Irvine, are training business, educational, public, and hospital administrators in a single curriculum with electives in specialized areas. By combining curricula, costs are cut and cross-vocational dialogue is encouraged.

Second is the coordination of need for paraprofessionals in service fields and undergraduate specializations in service. The number of colleges offering an undergraduate major in education far exceeds those offering specialization in social work or in public administration. Perhaps some of the shortage of social servants can be met by persons with only bachelor's degrees.

4–5. Design, Research, Manage, Administer, and Evaluate Programs

Special institutions such as United Community Services have been established expressly for the purpose of sponsoring and staffing action programs. These special organizations have necessary flexibilities that multipurpose institutions, such as universities, do not; for example, they are not constrained by academic freedom concerns, fixed departmental structures, tenure, broad and diffuse governance authority, and a commitment to rational and impartial inquiry. With all these special constraints, only rarely can and should a university manage and administer action programs.

More appropriate for universities are the roles of designer, consultant, and evaluator. From the library and the laboratory grow new ideas and new approaches, even the identification of new problems. From faculties are borrowed trained minds to serve on community boards and to advise on complex projects. From the scholars, society expects and deserves impartial analyses of the results of various action projects.

In this latter role, universities are without institutional equal. Conflict of interest is minimized, for universities rarely sponsor action programs. Undue outside influences cannot be effective in a climate of academic freedom. Wishful thinking and propaganda are not welcome in the community ruled by disciplined, dispassionate inquiry and rigorous analysis. Because other institutions cannot do it as well, universities must solicit opportunities to research and evaluate action programs. If these evaluations can be structured so that more blacks are educated, more whites are exposed to black culture, and more social servants are trained—all the better.

Which Programs to Support

Throughout this paper I have wanted to say "the data are insufficient," "no model fits." True, educators have not yet devised an input-output matrix of human development that neatly predicts relationships between efforts and results. True, even the first round of programs designed to attack the racial crisis are just finishing their first year of operation, and data are virtually nonexistent. True, neither the benefits nor the costs of various programs can be determined with any precision.

But the unavailability of data does not alter the necessity for deciding which programs to support. Rather than bemoaning the absence of data, an attempt has been made to relate those bits of hearsay and facts that are known. The alternative courses have been outlined, and the pragmatic and ideational bases for judgment have been broached.

The alternative emphases are clear: educate blacks, educate whites about blacks, train social servants, and evaluate action programs. Much is known about the costs and benefits of each.

A single institution cannot effectively emphasize all alternatives. Each college and university needs consciously to determine, in full consultation with its own black community, which emphasis fits its own experience and objectives, and then develop that emphasis. The institution's effort should reflect not only institutional objectives but also locale, personnel, and related and complementary programs. Each institution should do its own thing.

For the good of all concerned, some institutions will make their greatest contribution by limiting their own effort and participating in consortia. Resources are scarce, especially black scholars. For an institution to promise more than it can deliver will lead only to lost opportunities and frustration.

Commentaries on

Allocating Limited Resources

STUART A. TAYLOR, SANDY ENGLISH, NILS Y. WESSELL

That Most Profitable Educational Investment

STUART A. TAYLOR

THERE ARE obviously hundreds of thousands of black young people outside the colleges who should be involved in some meaningful experience of higher education. A new function of higher education ought to include the salvaging of these potentially productive and educable people. The day is long past when colleges and universities can justify being philosophically and intellectually exclusive, existing on an island away from real-life problems, issues, and people. If America had no racial problems, one could agree that the eighteenth-century academic pursuits would be infinitely deserving of our educational resources. But America does have a racial problem, and when educational administrators close their eyes to this, they miss the whole point. University administrators, like all senior executives, have the responsibility to allocate resources to those educational investments that promise the greatest return. The black American—still a victim of economic, social, and psychological violence—is the most profitable educational investment for America that university officials could have imagined. If institutions really want to make their resources pay off, they should invest in programs that will attract and educate black Americans.

Lack of Human Understanding and Intellectual Honesty

My task as a black academician is not to attack any one person or group of people. One might conclude that our educational system is largely responsible for the black rebellious youth who commit crimes against society *because* (1) university administrators often lack the most vital resource, human understanding and tolerance for the minority point of view; and (2) the lack of human understanding is filtered down through the universities, the small channels through which most of the powerful decision-makers in our society come. When we recognize the need to clean house in the president's office of our own individual institution, we will have taken the first step toward resolving the racial crisis in America.

A second resource I should like to discuss is that of intellectual honesty. One hundred and twenty years ago, Horace Mann referred to education as "the great equalizer of the conditions of men . . . the balance wheel of the social machinery." *Higher education has not been the equalizer for black Americans.* We need to deal with that. One reason higher education doesn't bridge the gap comes from the scarcity of professors and university administrators who have the personal integrity and honesty to teach the truth.

If a college education does nothing else, if it fails in all other respects, it should at least perform one very vital function: expose the students to the realities of the world in which they must live and function. We fail in that respect. Our educational system has produced professors and teachers who, down through the years, are guilty of cultural rape—more vicious than the physical version—in despoiling the black race of its cultural heritage. Seldom does a student, irrespective of his color, learn that the most venerable and most cherished of American institutions and traditions are racist in their operation and philosophy. Our legal institutions, which, we like to think, have the capacity to respond to the needs of the people, have often become rigid bastions of the status quo and work to the disadvantage of the ghetto dweller. The press and other communication media, which pride themselves on being spokesmen for the underprivileged and exposing injustice and inequality, perpetuate in a number of ways the myth that America is a white nation in which the black man is an intruder either unwilling or incapable of accepting positions of trust and responsibility.

Many of our institutions of higher learning have been exclusive white men's clubs to which black-skinned Americans are sometimes admitted, but rarely as full participants up the promotional ladder. How many university presidents dared to challenge their deans to get some color on the faculty rolls prior to the student revolutions? How many presidents, today, have the guts to tell the members of their boards of trustees—many of whom are ancient, feeble, from another time and another place, set in their ways—that such trustees are not capable of making relevant decisions, that their old way of life, their old standards, impede the progress of American education with its new function of salvaging black people who have no money for tuition, poor diets, a chip on their shoulders, bad manners, terrible high school grades, and all the rest. How many university administrators have the nerve to tell their professors that these people have just as much right to the professor's time and personal interest as the students from the traditional white, middle-class experience?

Scarcity of the Free Black Intellectuals

No doubt about it, the lack of human understanding and the absence of intellectual honesty on the university campuses have contributed to the scarcity of free black intellectuals. Every college and university wants at least one black Ph.D., but few people understand the functional role of a black professor. The black intellectual must deal intimately with the white power structure and cultural apparatus *and* the inner realities of the black world, at one and the same time. Under these conditions his mind is never free to do any one job well. In order to function with some minimum degree of success in these two opposite roles, he must be acutely aware of the nature of our educational and economic systems and how they monitor class stratifications. Very few men have the ability to be black and white at the same time and serve both groups with the same enthusiasm and loyalty. This is one reason why there are few black Ph.D.'s in teaching in the major universities. The so-called integrated intellectual environment on most major university campuses is not representative of black people's aspirations. The few who do aspire to become a professor at a major university soon realize that the psychological costs outweigh the economic benefits.

There is little understanding of what a black professor is likely to experience in the larger institutions. The tentative acceptance one finds in the predominantly white academic marketplace presents an illusion that integration is real—a functional reality for himself and his family, and possibly for all black Americans. Even if one does not wholly believe this, he is likely to give lip service to the aims of racial integration, if only to lessen his own cognitive dissonance and rationalize his own status in the nonblack academic community. When the voices from the black sector raise doubts about the meaning, the aims, and the real possibilities of integration, the black intellectual starts to question his own hard-won status. At the same time, those blacks outside the university begin to question the status of the intellectual: What is he doing in there? What is his function in relation to us? He must be a Tom.

Questions such as these arise only because the social and economic role of the black professor has never been defined by the black scholar. For the most part, the two or three black intellectuals who have been in the "super system" for decades have been rather free agents strangely isolated from the racial crisis. Their support and prestige comes from the white world. On the other hand, their cultural achievements, irrespective of how they "made it in the white man's world," are recognized primarily by the black people. Add to this a small group of black whiz kids who have no firm cultural base in the reality of either black or white world. The result: a rootless class of displaced persons who are refugees from the social poverty of the black culture with no legitimate claim to white culture either.

Black professors are rare resources today because anyone with dark skin who tries to place one foot in the black ghetto and the other in white academe is in serious emotional and psychological trouble. The academic marketplace, in which he lives and works, is based partly on a philosophy of integration that he knows does not work outside the walls of ivy, and those who openly support such idealistic philosophies are likely to encounter serious resistance and hidden barriers from both sides. There is violence and rumors of more violence to come on our campuses, all of which shake the black intellectual with his hard-won integrated status. This is especially dangerous when these academicians are asked by university administrators to become interpreters for the black world—most of which they know little about—to the white world, where they are intruders. Such a role places them on a vicious battlefield with no weapons, no loyal supporters, and no protection. Further continuation of this kind of exploitation will add to the racial crisis.

Scores of college and university administrators, who previously behaved as though their academic institutions were somehow apart from the communities in which they were located, are slowly becoming involved in efforts to resolve problems of social and economic injustice. Many of these same college administrators also are recognizing that their responsibility for education goes beyond merely accepting qualified students and professors without racial discrimination. Such commitments include the deliberate allocation of university resources to educational investments that have the greatest potential payoff: the most profitable educational investment at this time includes that large group of intelligent but discarded black Americans. The irony of it all is that some of the resources sadly lacking may not cost a dime—human understanding and intellectual honesty of major university administrators and professors.

Those administrators of the few major campuses that have one or two black scholars, are fortunate; they have a very scarce resource. However,

I urge them to free those black scholars from the terrible task of being a Tom or a spokesman for black sector to the white sector. Help the frightened black Ph.D. as he goes through the psychological and deintellectualizing exercise of freeing himself from white superior delusions. If he fails to go through these changes, he will not be able to relate to his black students or the black community, and his teaching will add to the hatred for blacks among his white students.

The major universities in America have direct access to the primary source of the racial crisis, that very large group of people with traditional white, middle-class values who want to maintain the status quo. If these institutions are serious about efforts to deal with the racial crisis, they will recognize the need to allocate more of their resources to that most profitable educational investment, the black American.

Pooling Resources for Opportunities

SANDY ENGLISH

I SHALL FIRST DIRECT my attention to Mr. Brown's remarks and then proceed with my own thinking regarding the question of "Allocating Limited Resources."

It has been argued that universities committed to solving the racial crises must choose among five basic strategies.

1. *Educate more black students.*

I agree with Mr. Brown for it is my firm belief that many blacks have not gone on to college simply because they lack financial resources. Much more money must be made available to accommodate the specialized needs of the black student. This, in my opinion, means that the Federal and state governments must earmark funds for black education. I single out the Federal and state governments simply because much of their aid has often been in the form of loans. Many blacks have advocated the philosophy of the "Black Manifesto" as a means of reparations. And, while I agree that the basis for this contention is sound, perhaps a more pragmatic approach would be to channel resources—whether Federal, state, or private —toward funding black education.

In short, if we are sincere about efforts to educate more black students, a pooling of resources is greatly needed.

Mr. Brown contends that "black students will have to be persuaded that college attendance is possible and worthwhile." I generally agree with this supposition. However, our colleges and universities have not fully tapped those blacks in high school who may wish to go on to college. No one questions that motivation barriers and the financial barriers are intertwined, but in light of the growing number of blacks finishing high school today, this factor is given greater emphasis than it deserves. One need only cite the case of a black male high school senior in Birmingham, Alabama, in 1959 seeking a college education: since no college was willing or perhaps able to offer him more than $300 for a school year—far less than what his needs dictated—he found himself in the military for three years immediately after high school. My experience leads me to believe that this example is typical of many blacks seeking higher education. And finally, I am certain that our colleges and universities have not enthusiastically sought those blacks who have had the proper motivation but lacked funds.

On admissions as technical barriers, briefly, the masses of blacks must be considered for admission to college on the basis of three criteria: (1) high school record, (2) motivation, and (3) recommendations. Any other factor, such as the SAT, will inevitably operate against a black's interest in going to college. Mr. Brown's suggestion that the D and F grades be eliminated and that credit be given in courses only for grades of C and better seems ideal. This practice would surely overcome some of the technical barriers. More important, it would avoid the need to create tutoring programs solely for blacks, for experience indicates that this kind of special program has its own countereffects.

Last, the matter of cultural barriers is raised. I tend to disagree with the notion of "segregated programs for 'black students only,' programs that highlight the role of black men. . . ." The role of the black man, whether in history or chemistry, should be incorporated into the entire university curriculum so that both black and white students will be thoroughly exposed to many of the facets of our society that have long been distorted or simply overlooked. This approach seems most realistic inasmuch as a black's purpose in going on to college is to fit himself better to function to the fullest of his capabilities in our society. Achievement of this purpose calls for continuous contact with his black and white brothers, unless we assume that sometime in the very near future blacks are to be granted a state of their own.

2. Expose white students to black problems and black culture.
I have already touched upon "white student exposure" and shall merely

restate here that whites can no longer close their eyes to the black world around them and vice versa. Much more can be done, however, to compensate whites (and blacks) for their involvement in black problems and culture, as suggested by Mr. Brown (college credit).

3. *Train students in service professions.*

This area seems most promising for cultivation, not so much as a solution to the racial crisis, but as a practical matter. All students would be better qualified to face the realities of our society if greater emphasis were given to the interrelationship between the various schools and professions. Recently, it was learned that many white social workers look down on their black clients and in some instances attempt to impose their white, middle-class values on the black client. In most instances, such practice stems directly from a lack of interdisciplinary training, both in college and graduate school.

4–5. *Design, research, manage, administer, and evaluate programs.*

My experiences with university research, management, and administration have led me to believe that the basic needs and problems of black students are often lost in argument, debate, and long, drawn-out research. Most administrators, professors, and professionals are sheltered by their own training and lack of exposure to the hard problems of the black masses. One administrator has alleged that he wants more blacks to come into his school, but before he will admit a black there must be some assurances that he can succeed. What more assurance can one have than that a student has an above-average high school record, motivation, and excellent recommendations? This administrator is still trying to resolve his impasse.

Which Programs to Support?

At this point, the question becomes: Which programs should be supported when resources are limited? First, let me say that although funds are limited today, many more funds could be made available if the Federal, state, local, and private sectors of our community would sincerely commit themselves to the proposition of more and better education for all blacks. To date, few have adhered to such a commitment. My recommendations are:

1. A national minority scholarship fund should be created, with assistance based on acceptance for admission to college and demonstration of financial need.

2. Loans should be reduced in part provided the loan recipient works in

certain parts of the Federal, state, or local government immediately after graduation for a given number of years (preferably two).

3. Funds should be granted by the government to centrally located schools to set up special programs related to the needs of blacks.

4. The government, universities, and others should give particular attention to the recommendations and suggestions of responsible black students.

5. The possibility and worthwhileness of college attendance should be emphasized from kindergarten to college.

6. The income level set as an indication of need for a student to participate in a college work-study program should be higher.

7. Funds should be granted less on the basis of academic record and more on financial need.

8. The practice of buying good students should be greatly reduced, if not terminated. In this way more funds could be made available for the needy, whether black or white.

These are but a few suggestions. However, this paper, along with the efforts of several others, will be a mere act in futility unless the commitment to educate blacks is undertaken nationally.

Some Difficult Choices

NILS Y. WESSELL

DR. BROWN'S PAPER presents comprehensively the options, barriers, and strategies which educational institutions must consider in planning programs and allocating resources in response to the extremely critical problems of our times. In my comments I shall single out only those aspects or implications that, to my mind, are of the greatest importance.

My first point underlies all educational efforts at all levels: we should speak of "determining priorities with respect to available resources" rather than of "allocating scarce resources." The former is more positive and even more realistic. If we begin by describing our resources as scarce, we begin on a note of pessimism or resignation, and may not be as innovative, imaginative, and venturesome as the problems of our times demand. I am not suggesting that we approach education with the attitudes of the flamboyant free spender; I am saying that we should not wear the mantle of a Scrooge. Somewhere between these two extremes is an approach or an attitude that is both realistic and farsighted, reasonable yet promising. Dr. Brown stresses the absence of data. I concur, but we should not conclude, as he does not, that we should, therefore, hold both planning and action in abeyance until data are available. Again let me state plainly: I believe it is critically important that the data be obtained by research and study, but not under a moratorium of testing new ideas and new approaches.

In the testing of new ideas and approaches, diversity must be our first concern. The diversity we proclaim for American education is more often rhetoric than fact. Educators are too ready to fall in line and follow a course whose popularity seems to have been demonstrated in other institutions. I am reminded of a study which proposed to catalog "tested" innovations in education. There is no such thing. Too often we are willing to adopt an "innovation" only if its sucess or popularity has been demonstrated—a clear contradiction in terms.

Many colleges and universities recognize only one or two of at least three roles they can and must play with respect to the nation's urgent social problems. The obvious role, the one most frequently recognized and quite possibly the most important one, is that represented by the phrase "education and training." Much of Dr. Brown's paper was directed to this role. Less frequently recognized is the role made possible by the use and application of the skills and talents residing in college and university faculties and student bodies. There are impressive exceptions, of course, but even when such skills and talents are enlisted in the cause, they are often provided only under a special grant or when additional compensation for additional services is offered. If men from the business community can contribute freely of their time in the public interest without compensation, why cannot college faculty members? The role rarely mentioned is that of the college or university as a corporate citizen. What is it doing in its own house to provide opportunities and to set standards for the community in which it is located? Again there are impressive exceptions to my implied indictment, but, overall, little seems to be under way. Is it because institutions are reluctant to publicize their activities, or is it because little progress is being made?

And finally, may I say that foundations too must determine priorities with respect to available resources. I found this hard to believe when I was numbered among those trying to separate foundations from their assets. It came home to me the first week I served as president of the Sloan Foundation; 90 percent or more of the proposals made to us must be turned down. There is no reasonable or sensible way to stretch our assets to enable us to respond affirmatively to more than one out of ten requests.

Like colleges and universities, foundations are faced with deserving requests aimed at meeting immediate crises as well as with meritorious proposals whose results cannot possibly be evident for years or decades. This is no theoretical dilemma. It is real. For example, how should a foundation choose between a research program in the biological basis of behavior, which might well have great promise for understanding the development of learning capacities in the young child but which might take years for any findings to be understood and applied, and another program which seeks to deal immediately with the educational or experiential deprivation which ghetto children bring with them to kindergarten?

Historically, foundations have tended to stress the *causes* of poverty, disease, and ignorance rather than the day-to-day treatment of these disorders themselves. Other figures of speech make the same point: foundations are concerned, not with palliatives or with rushing around to put out fires, but with the underlying conditions which produce ignorance or hunger or disease. Is it possible to maintain this posture in 1970? Twenty-five years from now, which approach will have done more to ensure equal educational opportunity—that which helps us understand the relation between endocrines, nutrition, and biochemistry and the learning process, or that which intervenes directly and sociologically by changing or enriching regular learning opportunities?

Another dilemma which is real and not hypothetical is represented by the choice between providing financial assistance to bright, well-prepared, and well-motivated ghetto college graduates anxious to enter professional school, and equally bright but educationally, culturally, and motivationally deprived youngsters? I am not sure what the right questions are. Do we speak of the more deserving or the more needy or the ultimate contributions to society to be expected, or other issues which have not even entered our consciousness?

Another very specific illustration of the necessity for choice is that between a request to support a black business enterprise in a ghetto and one asking that fellowships be made available to enable black students to enter graduate schools of business administration. Which is the more likely to change life in the ghetto? Which is the more likely to decrease the isolation of the ghetto?

It is clear also that many of the attempts to remove educational barriers seem instead, in the eyes of the disadvantaged, to erect additional barriers.

For example, requiring secondary school graduates to spend an extra fifth year in preparation for college may seem to be only a further thwarting of their educational aspirations, well intentioned though the idea may be. A similar misunderstanding and self-defeating effort may result from the provision of postsecondary educational and training programs which do not lead to the baccalaureate, such as the programs offered by technical institutes and junior colleges. Yet the fact remains that in any population, regardless of skin color, large numbers of individuals receiving such training are needed and develop marketable skills which are consistent with their talents. Such programs can also represent a significant advance in the goals and achievements of many of the urban disadvantaged and can create ambition and expectation for even higher levels of educational achievement and career advancement. The faculties in institutions offering such programs often are much better equipped to deal with the disadvantaged than teachers in colleges and universities which, for decades, have served only the intellectual and social elite.

I trust my apparent dogmatism in my earlier remarks is only that— apparent and not real. I know full well how much easier it is for a former university president like myself to sit on the sidelines and pontificate than it is to meet the daily and insistent pressures of the college or university administrator's job. As a private citizen and as a foundation executive I have a deep and sincere appreciation that there are numbers of administrators who are willing to assume the responsibilities and to face the frustrations. I will understand if they respond wryly by suggesting to me and other foundation officers that they would rather have our money than our gratitude.

Administrative Response to Campus Turmoil

THOMAS H. ELIOT

ONE OF THE DANGERS in a college president's trying to generalize about "student unrest" is his own limited experience. Either he has had peace on his campus, or he has had demonstrations whose shape and form were peculiar to his campus. Either way, he is in no position to second-guess any other president.

A second peril is timing. A president weathered a long demonstration, and his account of it was published in a major newspaper. Less than a month later, his students were engaged in another sit-in. Therefore, in trying to draw lessons from Washington University's demonstrations of December 1968, as I have been asked to do under the heading of "administrative response to campus turmoil," I pause frequently to knock on my wooden desk. We all know, by now, that a single person can cause fire and destruction, and that a few minutes can transform a peaceful campus into a battlefield.

The most I can do, then, is recount the events that occurred and try to find in them possibly useful hints—for my own future guidance and that of other chancellors and presidents—related to (1) university constitutions, structures, and policies, and (2) behavior patterns in moments of crisis. The second are profoundly affected by the first.

The national events of the spring of 1969 make the Washington University demonstrations seem tame—no destruction, no file-rifling, no guns. Fortunately many institutions have escaped the graver manifestations of campus strife—thus far, at least. Those which, like Washington, have a preponderantly white student body with a small and newly self-conscious black minority may find my account relevant. I cannot write knowledgeably about predominantly black colleges.

Washington University in the fall of 1968 had about 6,800 students, of whom 3,700 were undergraduates. Full-time black students numbered 138.

On December 5, 1968, two overlapping demonstrations began. The first was by about forty black students, most or all of them members of the

Association of Black Collegians (ABC). It lasted until December 14. The second was engaged in by a wide variety of other students, almost all white, in numbers that varied hour by hour and never exceeded 300. It was a disorganized affair that had dwindled into a lengthy "bull session" by December 7.

No property damage was done by the demonstrators. No one was held captive or physically harmed. No classes or other scheduled university activities were canceled or even impeded. For a short time considerable inconvenience was caused to administrators, as will be indicated below.

Student Participation, 1964–68

In dealing with these demonstrations, we were greatly helped by having paid close attention to the "student unrest" problem since the Berkeley outburst in the fall of 1964. In the intervening four years, we had:

1. Increased student representation on numerous university committees.

2. Established, through student initiative, a student judicial code and a student judicial board to handle minor offenses; and also established, by administrative action, a University Conduct Committee to hear appeals and to hear, de novo, cases involving possibility of serious penalties —suspension or expulsion. This Conduct Committee is composed of four professors appointed by me, and four students selected by the elected Student Assembly. The whole system was studied and approved by both the Student Assembly and the 20-member Senate Council, an elected body representing the faculties of all the schools in the university.

3. Established a University Community Council, consisting of two administrators named by me, four professors nominated by the deans and elected by the Senate Council, and six students chosen by the Student Assembly. This body, advisory to me, deals with policy questions affecting students. For example, it considered the disputed role of the placement service, proposed a policy, and recommended that its proposal and two competing ones be voted on in a campus-wide advisory referendum, which was done. At present it is wrestling with the ROTC problem. In May 1968, in the wake of the Columbia disaster, I asked the UCC to advise me on policy regarding demonstrations.

4. Placed two student government officers on the Trustees' Committee on Educational Policy and Student Affairs.

5. Adopted, with full trustee support, and adhered to a policy permitting students to invite and hear speakers of their own choice.

6. Taken the university out of the recognition business: politically oriented student groups are neither officially recognized nor prohibited.

7. Endured a couple of noisy but harmless protest rallies, and a small but effective "sing-in" aimed at a Dow Chemical recruiter. This last incident taught us some lessons with respect to the problem of identification and the need of procedural rules for the Conduct Committee to protect the rights of the institution as well as those of the students.

8. Maintained a high degree of informal communication between students and professors and administrators, including the chancellor.

9. By action of the Faculty of Arts and Sciences: (a) continued a joint College Planning Council (ten professors, ten students) until its major recommendations—for a compulsory system of faculty advising, a "pass-fail option" for a limited number of courses, and a new interdisciplinary general studies program—were adopted by the faculty, (b) established the general studies program under joint faculty-student direction; and (c) in 1968, began formal negotiations with a Student Assembly Committee leading to more effective student participation in faculty decisions, and admitted students to faculty meetings with a limited right to speak.

After the Columbia incident, the University Community Council (which included the SDS leader on campus) hammered out a policy statement concerning demonstrations. I endorsed it and, in so doing, wrote an introduction spelling out what the approved policy would mean in concrete terms. These statements were then included in the *Student Guide* which is distributed at the start of the school year. The Council reaffirmed a statement that unreasonable interference with the rights of others was "contrary to accepted standards," and that it was a "very serious offense" justifying a serious penalty. I described some of the modern kinds of "interference" and stated that a "serious penalty" is normally suspension or expulsion.

All of the foregoing steps were taken without any awareness that campus unrest, here and elsewhere, would soon take on racial overtones. We assumed that segregation was an evil (and worried about de facto segregation in some Greek letter societies). As late as the spring of 1968 the word "Negro" was freely used with no derogatory connotations. We were pleased with our M.B.A. program for Negroes and a Career Scholarship program for the disadvantaged. We sought to increase black enrollment and establish supportive services for blacks who needed them. Self-conscious black separatism was, therefore, a phenomenon we had not planned for. Nevertheless, the steps taken were not irrelevant; at the very least, they reduced the chances of major disruption allegedly in support of black demands. They are worthwhile in their own right and may eventually prove useful in relation to black students, especially if the latter's separatism is modified.

The Black Collegians' Demonstration

As noted above, in 1968–69 full-time black students at Washington University numbered only 138. Among these, some were in the special program for the M.B.A. for Negroes, which we began in 1967 in a consortium with Indiana University and the University of Wisconsin; 27 were freshmen, supported mainly by Educational Opportunity Grant (EOG) funds; and a few were upperclassmen on university scholarships.

The black demonstration was triggered by an incident on Thursday, December 5, involving an M.B.A. candidate who accused campus police officers of improperly arresting and manhandling him. On that afternoon, about 40 black students converged on the "dispatching room" (otherwise an outer office and waiting room) of the campus police.

I went to that office to talk with them, or rather to listen to them. Emotions were high. They demanded that two campus policemen be suspended and three discharged outright. They also recounted numerous incidents, stretching back over a year, which they said indicated a pattern of discriminatory harassment of blacks. I told them that I would not discharge a student or anybody else without a hearing. I said that they had shown cause for a hearing, and that it would be held as promptly as reasonably possible, on Monday, December 9. The black students refused to leave the campus police office. Dispatching became difficult (chiefly because of the emotional tension and the danger of a more serious incident) so we moved the dispatcher to another office.

I returned to my office and conferred there for several hours with colleagues well-acquainted with the black students (including the heads of our M.B.A. and Career Scholarship programs), and a junior administrator and a graduate student, both black, who were friends of many of the demonstrators. Personal visits were made, but brought no progress: there were "many other issues," but nothing could be discussed until the officers were fired.

After spending an uncomfortable night in the campus police office, early on December 6 the ABC students cleaned up the office and walked over to a large accounting and files-and-equipment suite in the basement of Brookings Hall, two floors directly below my own office. They were admitted by an employee and remained "in possession" for eight days and nights. However, on that Friday and the following Monday, employees worked there for a part of each day. On Tuesday, December 10, the necessary papers, files, and desk equipment were moved to a nearby office, luckily available, and regular university business proceeded unhampered.

On December 6, the ABC sent upstairs to me a brief "Black Position Paper," raising "issues and areas" that are now familiar in the lexicon of "demands": a black studies program, more black students, amnesty, and so on. But this document said that these issues could not be discussed until a "prerequisite" had been met, namely, the firing of three officers.

After preparing a reply on the specific "issues and areas," I took it to them, but they refused to talk about these issues. I explained why I would not satisfy their prerequisite, and we had an interesting, courteous, and seemingly unproductive conversation about the nature of justice. That was my last face-to-face conversation with them until the night of December 13–14. We frequently reminded them of our readiness to negotiate personally, but they preferred to exchange carefully drafted documents.

I was able to get an alumnus and trustee of the university and a nationally known legal scholar, Professor Paul A. Freund of Harvard, to serve as chairman of the panel which was to hold the hearing on the complaints against the police. I also appointed two faculty members (one of them black) and offered to name two nominees of the ABC. After a protracted exchange of notes, I agreed to three. Through this same note-exchanging process, I informed the ABC that the accused officers had been given no assignments pending the hearing, so that they could prepare their defense, and that if the panel recommended their discharge, their pay would be stopped as of December 5. The ABC considered this a sufficient satisfaction of their prerequisite, so that the way was open to discuss deeper issues.

It took a considerable time, however, for the ABC to formulate its arguments on these issues, especially as most of the demonstrators attended the first Freund panel hearing on Monday, December 9. Therefore, we took the initiative. We spent December 10 working on a document of our own, and delivered it at the basement office that evening. It was published in full by the *St. Louis Post-Dispatch* the following day and by the *St. Louis Globe Democrat* on December 12. It read, in part, as follows:

> The demonstration by black students persists despite some exchange of views. . . .
> Let us put this into the larger, nationwide context. America has a race problem. We have had one for many years. Events in Watts, in

Washington, in Detroit, and in Newark testify more forcefully than can the statements of any professor. But the important thing is the feeling of black awareness, and the opportunity which this gives our universities to enlarge their horizons of human understanding. Many black students coming to a predominantly white university like Washington University are thrust suddenly into an almost totally white community. Despite all the good will in the world it is difficult to find on most university campuses a faculty or administration that grasps what it means to be black in America or that has a deep and sensitive awareness of black history, black culture or black outlook. Social customs of white American students seem alien and cold, perhaps even degrading to black students.

Thus American universities that pride themselves with being all-encompassing have for a long time overlooked the vital black culture at our very doorstep. We are the poorer for this omission. Just as the university hopes to broaden the outlook of the black student and offer new opportunities to him, so we white people in the academic community have an opportunity to broaden our outlook and to increase our sensitivity. We have the chance to take another step forward against provincialism and narrow vision.

Black students here are demonstrating for what they believe to be right. In a real sense, so long as there is no disruption, they can be said to be demonstrating for us all, updating us to a new level of understanding and awareness. Their demonstration thus far has been peaceful, restrained, and courteous. Occupancy of a basement office has caused minor inconvenience, but has not disrupted the business operations of the university. . . .

Whatever else these demonstrations may have done, they have shown the need for better communication between black students and white administration. The university has much to teach its students and much to learn from them. It is the university's business to be universal. Since the university has much to gain from increased understanding of black students, and the larger black experience, I am asking the Board of Trustees to constitute a committee of Trustees, faculty, and students both black and white, with community advisers, to develop ways for Washington University to broaden its appreciation of and receptivity to minority groups and minority cultures in the United States. . . .

On December 11, the ABC presented me with a long and thoughtful "Black Manifesto," containing ten demands, to which we replied. On December 12, the ABC notified us of continuing dissatisfaction with our reply on four of the ten points raised in the Black Manifesto. At 11:30 on the night of December 13, they asked me to meet with them at midnight in the basement office. I did so, and explained why we had made the replies that they had found unsatisfactory. They left Brookings Hall early the following afternoon, again after carefully cleaning the premises.

The Issues in the Black Demonstration

Some of the issues were easy to handle. For example, a Black Studies program was demanded; the Faculty of Arts and Sciences had already voted to establish such a program. Provision for an assistant financial aids officer was already included in next year's budget; the strong case made against relying on the Parents' Confidential Statement as a basis for determining the scholarship "need" of many black applicants convinced me that the new appointee should be black. The demand that financial aid should not include "burdensome loans" ceased to be an issue when they suggested that loans should not exceed a specified percentage of all aid, a suggestion which conformed to our established policy. We readily agreed to a demand for "sensitivity seminars," as consistent with our own statement noted above.

One demand that has caused great difficulty elsewhere was not pressed insistently. This was for exclusive ABC control of the Black Studies program. It was pointed out that the ABC would be represented on the committee in charge of the program. Another familiar demand, for amnesty, I simply dismissed as irrelevant. Where no disciplinary action is necessary, there need be no thought of amnesty.

The sticky points, which we discussed at my final after-midnight conference, related to demands for a great increase in the number of black students (25 percent of all new enrollment in 1969), a new black admissions officer, and administrative control over social science research involving black individuals or groups as the subjects of such research. I told them that, despite the cutback in Federal EOG funds, we were budgeting funds for some 90 freshman scholarships (but that, on the basis of past experience, we might get only 50 black freshmen with these funds), that foundation grants were being sought to support a new program of transfers from the local Junior College, and that I was personally eager to see our graduate and professional schools more actively recruit black students. I had already scheduled a meeting of our deans for this purpose, and I now invited the ABC leader to come to that meeting (which he did).

I declined to appoint a new black admissions officer, pointing out that since the spring of 1968 we had been seeking a black director for our Educational Opportunity program who would have a close connection with the admissions office, and that two of the junior administrators mentioned above work part-time for that office. I listened with surprise and interest to the bitter complaints about "human subjects" research. In response however, I could only try to explain the difference between basic and applied research and the essential independence of the investigator. I said that

I would see to it that scholars engaged in relevant investigations were informed of how the black students (and presumably many other black people) felt, and would express my own views, but that I would not tell them what to do.

There remains to be mentioned only the original issue—the charges against the police. In the first hearing, on December 9, the six-member panel heard evidence as to the alleged pattern of harassment, and subsequently wrote a constructive report recommending steps (which we are taking) to improve our campus police system and especially to reduce the likelihood of interracial tension. The lawyers for the ABC and the police then agreed that, to hear the specific charges against individual officers, a new three-member panel was needed. This was because I, rather than the defendants (the accused police officers), had appointed half the original panel. The attorneys agreed on Professor Freund as chairman. The police officers named a professor who was a former mayor of St. Louis. The ABC named a part-time student and employee of the Central Educational Methods Research Laboratory. This panel heard the case on December 16 and concluded unanimously that the evidence did not justify disciplinary measures against any of the officers.[1]

The White Students' Demonstration

A few activists were quick to seize upon the black students' protest of December 5 as an excuse to organize a demonstration of their own. That evening, about 20 students entered my outer office (the door was open) while I was conferring with colleagues in my inner, or private, office. They used telephones and messengers to alert the campus, and by ten o'clock from 200 to 300 students (the number fluctuated) were sitting in the outer office or standing in the corridor outside it. They said that they wanted to support the blacks' demands. When I told them that the blacks were demanding that people be fired without a hearing, they spent some time thinking up demands of their own. Meanwhile numerous faculty members had come to my office, uninvited but most welcome, offering to help.

Eventually a deputation entered my private office and presented several demands to a roomful of administrators and professors. I granted none, but pointed out that one demand, that ROTC be abolished, should be addressed

---

[1] On Feb. 27, 1969, my quarterly letter to the faculty summarized the steps being taken to implement the decisions made in December. Such implementation is essential if recurrent demonstrations are to be avoided, but a detailed account is beyond the scope of this paper.

to the Faculty of Arts and Sciences, which gave academic credit for ROTC courses.

Students and some professors stayed all night in the building and most of the next day. My private office was undisturbed. The "demonstration" took the form of an around-the-clock "dialogue," which continued for two more nights in a large lounge across the quadrangle. On the evening of December 6, the Arts and Sciences Faculty voted to abolish credit for ROTC. This vote, which almost certainly would have come out the same way under more peaceful circumstances,[2] was much criticized for appearing to be a surrender to student pressure. It did take any remaining steam out of the demonstration.

The steam never got very bad. To be sure, when on December 6 the head of the ABC emerged from the basement and urged the white students to leave the building, they refused to do so. (So much for the sincerity of the original organizers' claim of "supporting the blacks.") But when one of the few vehement extremists urged "taking the building" and ejecting administrators or holding them prisoner, they refused to do that either. The great majority wanted not violence, but discussion; not raw power, but a feeling of more direct participation. Thanks to the patience of several dozen tireless professors, these goals were achieved.

Issues for Consideration

Peaceful occupancy

Some people say that disciplinary action should be taken against student "trespassers" who enter and stay in premises "where they don't belong." There is much public sympathy for this view. More than one university president has been praised for announcing that students who disobey an order to get out in a few minutes will be arrested or suspended or expelled.

This sounds so simple. But it leaves countless questions unanswered.

Who gives the order? Even if he is an administrator or professor expressly authorized to do so, what restrains him from exercising his authority arbitrarily? Ten students, by appointment, come to a dean's office to complain about a department head. The dean, tired and irritated, soon tells them that he has heard enough and asks them to leave. They reply that they haven't finished their story. He orders them to leave in five minutes. They refuse. The ten students are going to be fired?

---

[2] In May 1969, the University Community Council conducted a campuswide advisory referendum on ROTC. In this referendum, by secret ballot, a large majority of the Faculty of Arts and Sciences again voted for denying credit.

What premises, other than private offices, are going to be ruled as out of bounds for students, and at what times? Who decides this? Someone—theoretically the president, I suppose—determines that the library shall be closed at eleven o'clock. Racing against a deadline, an earnest student is finishing a term paper at the library, surrounded by reference books. He keeps on working there, ignoring an assistant librarian's order to leave. Are you going to expel him?

Perhaps improper or defiant occupancy should, by itself, be a ground for expulsion. The examples above suggest, however, that a simple rule to that effect may run counter to many deeply felt convictions about the nature of colleges and universities. Therefore, it could do more harm than good. To call mere occupancy "trespass" and make it a campus crime takes us back toward the days when students, like children, should be seen but not heard, and presidents and deans and professors could assume that they would be submissively obeyed. Those days are gone.

Disruption

A campus crime, in the area we are discussing here, should be only an action that does discernible harm. "Trespass" by students can be accepted by the academic community as a cause for discipline if—but only if—it significantly interferes with other people's rights or disrupts the operations of the institution.

The events at Washington University raised real questions about what "significant disruption" is. Students, both black and white, entered buildings and offices whose doors were open to them. Then they stayed. Their staying caused inconvenience. It was not easy for accountants to work efficiently with students sitting in. On one day I refrained from using my telephone much because of the chance that students in the outer office would listen on the extension. In both instances I might have claimed "disruption" and ordered everyone to leave. However, my colleagues and I preferred to avoid an unnecessary confrontation (for the order would have been disobeyed) by defining the result of the students' conduct as minor inconvenience rather than serious disruption. Wholly aside from tactical considerations, I think that our interpretation was the more accurate one.

On Tuesday, December 10, we seemed to be close to crossing the line from inconvenience to disruption. That morning the black students, declaring that they needed to be undisturbed as they prepared a lengthy document, closed the door of the accounting office in the basement and locked out the three employees. Fortunately another large office was available nearby. We sent a note to the ABC, asking them to open up so that we could transfer the necessary papers, files, and equipment to this larger office. They did so. If they had refused, there would have been a clear case of disruption.

Disruptive seizure

This leads us to the issues presented when needed facilities are effectively taken over by student demonstrators and made unusable. As a matter of principle, such sit-ins are disciplinary offenses. But the severity of the discipline may depend on the nature of the facilities. A faculty discipline committee may be harsh when classrooms or libraries are occupied, less so when a business office is. (The vagaries of discipline committees and systems are discussed below.) The practical question is how to deal with disruptive sit-ins. In February 1969 the University of Chicago successfully sat the demonstrators out, patiently enduring 16 days of isolated disruption. Brandeis had a rather similar experience. I have no doubt that the president, in each case, received much gratuitous advice to bring in the police and throw out the miscreants.

This is a matter where no rule of thumb is appropriate. There is a strong body of opinion that the intrusion of the police automatically makes a bad situation worse. On some campuses, indeed, it has strengthened the militants' support; elsewhere, when students have committed acts of violence and the police have acted with great restraint, it has received widespread campus approval.

Given a clear case of serious disruption, all kinds of factors must be weighed in deciding what the police role should be, among them: (*a*) the imminence of serious physical damage to persons or property if the demonstration continues, and, conversely, the possibility that the calling of the police will itself lead the demonstrators to destroy the contents of the building they occupy; (*b*) the belief, often strongly held by administrators as well as professors, that the autonomy of the institution is threatened by the entry of the police, and that the university should handle its own disciplinary problems; (*c*) public insistence on campus "law and order," implemented in some cases by the police's authority to move onto the campus without invitation; (*d*) the vulnerability of the facilities seized: whether, for instance, they include fragile artifacts of great value, library card catalogs, or confidential files; and (*e*) the geographical and ethnic situation: an urban campus, easy of access to outsiders, can be turned into a battleground very quickly, once force is used; if the demonstrators are black, and there is a large black population close at hand, this campus battle could develop into an urban riot.

Discipline procedure

Serious disruption should lead to serious penalties—suspension or expulsion. Yet, over and over, we have read of demands for amnesty being granted, suspensions being lifted before they begin, easily proven charges being dropped. This pattern defies rational explanation except in terms of a retreat from the concept of the rule of law. Not from legal safeguards for the accused: students and professors alike fervently insist on due process, and the courts often back them up. But due process assumes a fair hearing. A fair hearing, it seems to me, requires judges who will decide in accordance with the evidence and impose sentences consistent with the gravity of the offense.

This brings us to the question of the administration of campus justice.

Clearly, all students should be informed in advance, and in writing, that serious disruption (which can be illustrated by examples) may result in suspension and expulsion. If such a rule can be promulgated by a regular faculty-student committee (in our case, our University Community Council) so much the better: the rule has an acknowledged *legitimacy* that unsupported presidential pronouncements may lack.

Clearly, there should be a standing disciplinary committee or judicial board, preferably including students as well as professors. Such a body is not a court, but it needs legal guidance, for its proceedings must, again, have acknowledged legitimacy.

There are several major obstacles to firm enforcement of the rules through severe disciplinary action. The first is that some professors and students on discipline committees may be incapable of making an objective decision divorced from their own political opinions. Hatred of the war can lead such a "judge" to excuse an act of disruption such as the protracted imprisonment of a Dow recruiter. The second is the Selective Service Act. When a boy expelled from college is going to be drafted, perhaps to be sent to Vietnam, expulsion takes on an extra dimension. There is an added reluctance to impose this penalty. Similar in impact, though less important for the moment, are the statutes that would deny public funds (scholarships, student loans, research and training grants) to campus offenders. Like the draft, the possibility of this additional penalty tends to make discipline committees unwilling to enforce the rules. Such laws thus weaken campus "law and order" instead of strengthening it.

Even without the handicaps provided by the draft and Congress' heavy helping hand, the larger the numbers involved, the more difficult it is to achieve fair and firm enforcement. Positive identification is made next to impossible when numerous students pass their ID cards around. Individual hearings for hundreds of students wear the discipline committee out and are sometimes so prolonged that any disciplinary action comes to seem futile.

Finally there is a special problem. Do we believe in equal justice on the campus, or, in compensation for past wrongs, are we to treat some students more equally than others? At one college, black students totally disrupted a class. They were not disciplined. Surely, if they had been white, they would have been disciplined. I'm not second-guessing this forgiveness of the blacks, but I am wondering (1) how long white students will accept a double standard adverse to themselves, and (2) whether discipline committees will be willing to punish anyone if some are automatically exempt from punishment.

Possibilities for Guidelines

The harmful effects of student unrest may perhaps be mitigated if an institution adheres to the following guidelines, policies, and procedures:

1. The institution makes a constant, conscious effort to maintain administration-faculty-student communication. The more joint committees, the better; just talking is not enough to satisfy students' desires for effective participation.

2. A joint council, advisory to the president but so regularly supported by him that its decisions have acknowledged legitimacy, should formulate an explicit warning that serious disruption, described in the warning, will be met with serious discipline. (This, I think, is much more useful than minatory public statements by presidents or boards of trustees, though such statements may have a salutary effect on some timorous campuses.)

3. The policy with respect to police intervention should be flexible. Established bodies—a faculty council, a joint policy committee—can be asked to endorse a general statement leaving it up to the administration to decide whether and when to call the police (or to seek a court order that could lead to police intervention), with the understanding that police will be called in clearly perceived instances of immediate physical danger. Police intervention to end a disruptive but peaceful sit-in should at the very least be preceded by consultation with these established bodies.

4. A joint discipline committee should be selected to ensure, as far as possible, objective judgment and fair procedure. This committee, the joint

council, and a representative faculty body should consider the wisdom of formally authorizing the suspension of a student pending the hearing of his case. Hearings have sometimes been disrupted by the accused and his friends: therefore, suspension pending a hearing may be the best way to get the hearing held and thus preserve due process.

5. Administrators should go very slow in deciding that a demonstration is seriously disruptive. Patience and tolerance of incivility are preferable to angry confrontation. "Trespass" by itself is not necessarily disruptive.

6. It is obviously desirable to have campus justice administered equally regardless of race, creed, or color. A discipline committee can be asked to do no less. It is possible, however, that on some campuses the patience and tolerance mentioned above should be extended to black students more than to white, so that the disciplinary machinery would be less promptly invoked.

7. Both promises of "amnesty" to disruptive demonstrators and insignificantly light penalties gravely undermine the whole basis of rational campus conduct.

These suggestions are offered with a full realization that they may be of little or no immediate use to institutions whose campuses are now battlegrounds. Some may be inadequate for, or inapplicable to, very large state universities. They certainly do not guarantee peace or "law and order," and so do not meet the demands of those who would turn the clock back and subvert the university in the name of law and order. But they may suggest some of the ways by which the current unrest can be contained in constructive channels and the sharpness of the repressive reaction blunted.

Commentaries on

Administrative Response to Campus Turmoil

MORRIS B. ABRAM, ELIZABETH DENERSON SCOBELL
WESLEY L. HARRIS, SR., ROBERT WENDELL WHITMORE

The Jeopardy of Disruption

MORRIS B. ABRAM

THERE IS MUCH in Chancellor Eliot's paper with which I agree. I feel, however, that the purposes of this discussion would be better served if I comment briefly on points where there may be some disagreement.

Dr. Eliot has written insightfully (and the results, no doubt, prove he acted wisely) about the disruptions at Washington University in December 1968. I use the word *disruption* quite deliberately, although he applies the term *inconvenience* to the sit-in by the students in the administrative offices and the later locking of the door of the accounting suite so that three employees were barred from their own offices. (He obviously would have considered the latter action a disruption had the employees not received permission to remove their files to another place and continue their work.)

Quite apart from the question of the discipline which can and should be imposed for such actions, I think we ought to "tell it like it is." I would call what Chancellor Eliot describes here a disruption—for, in my judgment, when any member of the university community is deliberately prevented from performing his function in his assigned and accustomed place, there is a disruption and an offense has been committed.

What one man can do—outside the law and under an appeal to conscience—another can do. When one man's rights are not safe, another's will soon be in jeopardy. A student has no more right to evict an accountant than an accountant has to sleep on a student's bed as an uninvited guest—even though the student is offered a thermal sleeping bag and invited to rest peacefully on his own floor.

195

When black students held the communications center at Brandeis in January 1969, the university's teaching and research missions continued with very little inconvenience (despite a call for boycott, class attendance exceeded normal levels). Yet the forcible occupation of the building was promptly—and I think properly—condemned by the administration and faculty, and the Student Council passed a resolution proclaiming "its opposition to the seizure of Ford Hall as a tactic for political objectives."

I believe that a majority of the members of the university community desire and expect that a setting free from violence and coercion will be maintained for the functioning of the university—although this majority is now, perhaps, a diminished one. But even if only a minority desired this, it too has rights which ought to be recognized even if they cannot always be fully protected.

In this brief commentary I can only mention certain aspects of the immensely complex subject of civil disobedience. When students at Brandeis hear about some of my past activities as a lawyer in Atlanta, they sometimes ask me, "Since you acted for and supported Martin Luther King, Jr., while he was engaged in civil disobedience, why do you not show the same understanding of civil disobedience by the students?" My answer is that when I first knew Martin Luther King, he could not vote in the only meaningful election in Georgia, could not send his children to the nearest public school, and could not eat in the department store where he bought his clothes. A university is not perfect, but it is not to be compared to a society that denied so much to Martin Luther King—and no student at Washington University, Harvard, or Brandeis has any grievance against the university to be compared with Martin Luther King's very real claims against society.

Moreover, Martin Luther King never asked for amnesty. One of the last things he did before his death was to return to a Birmingham jail to serve a sentence (which he undoubtedly thought unjust) for a nonextraditable offense. He did this, I think, because he realized that the law is an envelope which protects us all, and he was unwilling to destroy its symmetry or render it impotent even when he felt its final judgments wrong as applied to him.

The failures of Washington University—even as candidly admitted by Dr. Eliot—do not seem to me to fit into the category of a cause for civil disobedience. Nor do I think the numerous channels of communication and avenues of appeal previously made available by the university were properly utilized—as they should have been—by the students. Nor do I believe the steps the students took were necessarily for the correction of any complaint. The pattern of occupation triggered by one incident, followed by escalating demands, represents a growing danger which must be faced frankly by the university community, for decisions within the university simply cannot be made on the basis of who can mobilize the most force at a given time and place.

I acknowledge that black students, at Washington University as at Brandeis, have special and unmet needs, and that faculty, administration, and white students may not comprehend many of their sensitivities and problems. Much of this unshared burden the black students bring with them as they matriculate; it comes from outside disadvantages and discrimination. The university cannot fully lift this burden, but most good universities do try. However unsuccessful in this area universities are—or may appear to be—of all the institutions in a predominantly white society, they are generally the least discriminatory, the least repressive, and the most willing to respond.

A Deeper Look at Causes of Turmoil

ELIZABETH DENERSON SCOBELL

MY IMMEDIATE REACTION to Dr. Eliot's presentation is that he and other administrators at Washington University should be commended for the intelligent manner in which they reacted to the crucial events of December 5–13, 1968. Fortitude and compassion were evidenced in the handling of a very tense situation; however, I am amazed that Dr. Eliot and other administrators were unprepared for the demonstrations staged by black students. He says that close attention had been paid to student unrest ever since the 1964 Berkeley outburst and some positive steps had been taken to involve students in policy making. He says further, "We calmly assumed that segregation was an evil (and worried about de facto segregation in some Greek letter societies)." (I like the choice of the word *assumed* in that statement.) He mentioned unrest at Columbia and referred to riots in some major cities, but I wonder why no attention was paid to Northwestern University, where black unrest in the spring of 1968 centered on Greek letter organizations and housing. This probably marked the beginning of the black separatist spirit which now permeates many campuses.

Reflecting on the Northwestern demonstrations, I well remember the communications media reported that black students there wanted separate dormitories and dining facilities—period. No reasons were given other than this was another outgrowth of the black power movement. Only in the Northwestern student publication did I see the whole or at least more truth revealed. Black students at Northwestern, as in most other predominantly white institutions, resented the administratively approved, segregated fraternities and sororities and, in gist, said to the administration: "Either you require these organizations to desegregate and live in integrated housing, or provide separate housing with dining facilities for black students." After all, is not segregation condoned and perpetuated through these same societies?

I have been conditioned to mistrust the white press, especially in its reporting of news pertaining to black people; therefore, I checked the *St. Louis Argus,* a weekly Negro newspaper, to see whether their version of what happened at Washington University coincided with articles referred to by Dr. Eliot in the *St. Louis Post-Dispatch* and the *St. Louis Globe Democrat.* The *Argus* enumerated several incidents where black students claimed they were treated differently from white students: they were constantly being asked to present their identification cards when the same demand was not made of white students. It seems reasonable that identification cards of 6,700 students would be at least spot-checked before those of 138 students who stand out vividly for physical reasons. According to the *Argus,* the incident that triggered the demonstrations differs somewhat from other reports.

> A Negro student, serving in the capacity of resident advisor, interceded to prevent a fracas on campus. After reporting the brawl, he was subjected to foul treatment by answering security guards, and a letter he later forwarded to all university officials relating the occurrence, raising certain questions on Washington University's general policy, was completely ignored by Administrative officials.

I have very pointed questions that I should like to raise with the panel that reviewed the charges brought by these students. It seemed odd that Dr. Eliot makes no mention of the correspondence from this young man. Why was this not investigated? It seems too sudden that their demonstration was halted and they withdrew from the accounting office which they had occupied for several days. What were the findings of the committee? It is unfortunate that neither they nor any black students involved in the demonstrations are represented in this report.

Apparently the Washington University events differed in several respects from those on other campuses that have had disruptions. At all times some type of dialogue or communication was maintained between students and the administration. Except for one broken window, there was no property damage; classes and business operations continued. No one received bodily harm, and neither local police officials nor National Guard troops were brought into the picture. And when the occupied offices were vacated by the students, they were left clean and orderly. For these things, we commend the administration and the students. Other administrators should look closely at Washington University and learn a lesson in being "cool" when faced with some of the same problems and the necessity to make decisions.

Students also should examine the events at Washington, since they are becoming more and more vocal in expressing their wishes for a part in policy making and in expressing their opinions about the relevance or lack of it in the curriculum and about the teachers. Somehow, responsible participation has to be developed, not through loud outbursts or by making hurried decisions. More times than not, the worthwhile moves are accomplished thoughtfully and deliberately, not hurriedly.

Almost half of the American population is under twenty-five, and population estimates indicate that by 1972 a majority will be under twenty-one. Imagine what life in these United States may be like if, within the next four years, college and university students join forces with other persons in this age group. More and more, this portion of the population is becoming vocal on many issues. High in priority on the students' grievance lists are the Vietnam war, ROTC, and government-sponsored research grants and contracts connected with the war. There are increasing outbursts concerning subjects taught and their relevance in the late 1960s. The relationship of the college and university to the needs of the larger community in all its facets is a moral issue that occupies an important position in the lives of many students and is evidenced in their joining the Peace Corps, Vista, and other service volunteer groups. Identification with the problems of black people and other minorities is growing. With the solidarity that campus living provides, it is altogether likely that we have seen only the beginning of student unrest, demonstrations, and outbursts.

I am reminded of a Negro college president who, I am told, when faced by a group of angry students after a fellow student had been shot in a racial confrontation in a neighboring town, reacted as too many officials do. One student who was very articulate was asked by the president how old he was. The student replied that he was twenty. The president, protruding his chest and shaking his finger for emphasis, replied, "I'm sixty-one, and I've taken a whole lot in my lifetime. Why are you so impatient?"

Do we actually believe that today's young people are going to "take" what we "dish" out to them without question and without rebellion?

Constructive Disruptions

WESLEY L. HARRIS, SR.

My COMMENTS are directed to what I believe to be an enlightened and effective response by college administrations to *constructive disruptions* of colleges and universities by African-Americans. Constructive disruption of an academic institution depends upon the institution and may take the form of sit-ins or a show of arms. The point is this: disruptions are absolutely necessary for changes in the social, cultural, and financial structures and curriculum of American academic institutions. Constructive disruptions are strongly encouraged if African-Americans are to be graduated from "white" academic institutions as useful citizens of the world.

The enlightened and effective response by college administrations *must* not in any way limit the human potential of African-Americans. The proper response to constructive disruptions of a campus by African-Americans would attempt to change the hollowness of American academic institutions vis-à-vis the nonwhite peoples of the world. Also, the response should be flexible without continued constructive disruptions. I shall amplify these suggestions.

To my knowledge the so-called campus turmoil initiated by members of the African-American academic community has resulted from unbearable, inhuman tension. Continued existence in this state will weaken the African-American student's ability to analyze the aims of present American institutions. The African-American student revolt is real and designed to make strong and useful African-Americans *within* potentially more viable American institutions. The college administrations must face these realities with a desire to restructure academic institutions along more humanistic lines. Hence, there is no need to form a committee charged with finding solutions to "immediate problems." Such committees usually interpret the immediate problem as that of saving the institution for future destruction.

Rarely have college administrations initiated changes without considering their actions as capitulation to militants. Can American college administrations initiate changes which the entire academic community views as non-piggish? No comment is needed on the purpose of university committees charged with planning the future of the university.

Because the unbearable, inhuman tension experienced by African-American students in white academic institutions is but one example of the inability of American institutions to appreciate human differences, the response to African-American "student unrest" should contain a means of formulating policy and exercising prerogatives that will elevate America up the ladder of perfection where humanity occupies the top rung. An enlightened and effective response to the unrest of African-American students does *not* consist of the formation of an Afro-American studies program while simultaneously maintaining investments in companies which are doing business in southern Africa. The enlightened and effective response is positive, definite, and total.

Finally, American academic institutions must evolve to the state where they can respond effectively and in good faith without resort to constructive disruptions resulting from human needs. For an academic institution, no timetable can be defined for the attainment of this state; however, this should be given highest priority in the university committee charged with planning the future of the university.

The suggestion by Dr. Eliot of forming joint committees—"the more joint committees, the better"—indicates that he has misinterpreted the spirit of African-American students. Participation without change is simply putting on a heavier white mask. His suggestions on discipline and the role of police during campus unrest are well taken except that of suspension of a student before a hearing. Also, may I add that amnesty should be granted to all African-American student participants in constructive disruptions of a campus.

A New Sense of Responsibility

ROBERT WENDELL WHITMORE

THE TOPIC "Administrative Response to Campus Turmoil," if limited to response in a crisis, is too narrowly conceived to be useful to the larger topic of the challenges of student unrest, for the latter go beyond tactics or stratagems.

Obviously, by now everyone knows that campus turmoil is a possibility anywhere, from the most sheltered and isolated college to the most imposing academic fortress. It is equally obvious that any campus community needs free-wheeling scope to deal with crisis situations as they arise. Formulas, regardless of how carefully conceived, cannot be very useful. Yet, I would hope that no university presidents are left so out of touch with the course of events or so unprepared as to be forced by surprise or fear into impulsive action (unnecessary calling of police, inflammatory or "out-of-hand rejection of consideration" statements, etc.).

Given these assumptions and the political expertise of the average university president, one would expect an institution to maintain a continuing equilibrium. To those presidents of institutions that have suffered extensive damage and long periods of seemingly irrational disruption, this optimistic and perhaps naïve observation must be hard to accept. My optimism is reinforced by the fact that at the American University, though portents have been ominous, the outcomes of our disruptions have been productive. But my optimism holds only if given concepts are fully understood by those in power—especially college presidents—and their consideration is not confined merely to crisis situations when strategy replaces reason. For the consideration of college and university leaders, I have prepared the following:

Code of Understanding

1. There is no fixed doctrine or theory that is necessarily good the next day. As life is a process, so is education an ongoing endeavor. Everything institutional leaders do must be questioned. They must be willing to subject their theory to scrutiny. Because what they do affects all segments of the community, the franchise to scrutinize must be universal.

2. Administrators—not just of universities—in order to protect themselves, tend to limit their intimate associations to their staffs. Unless admin-

istrators reveal themselves to others, their position in the community will lack credibility. University administrators must submit themselves to the threats inherent in openness.

3. Every person has something to teach educators. If what he teaches displays ignorance, then educators have found someone who needs to learn. If what he teaches has substance, then they have found that everyone is ignorant of some things.

4. Spontaneity and creativity demand that a person be himself. A university needs individuals, from the board of trustees member to the incoming freshman, who neither fit a mold nor follow a given pattern.

5. Primary goals in life do not have to include contentment, wealth, or power. It is to be hoped that more and more students are less and less concerned about finding a high-paying job, and are concerned instead about realizing their own humanity and developing compassion, sensitivity, and personal freedom. Colleges and universities should strive to see that education serves ends that are more meaningful, using means which allow struggle, scope, and humanness.

In regard to the concept "change," we must skip over the questions, "How can I most easily deal with a sit-in?" and tackle the problem of avoiding such situations through constructive redirection and channeling of energies for progressive change.

The word *community* (already used several times) has become a vogue way to describe the groups that take part in university life. Since the demise of in loco parentis, the student has been led to believe that he has certain responsibilities and certain rights within the microcosm of his university. In short, the concept of citizenship has replaced the concept of parental sanctuary. A new sense of freedom is eliciting a new sense of responsibility. Where there are weaknesses, students want to help create strengths. Where there are wrongs, students want to make rights. Where there is injustice, students will strive for reform. Where there is discrimination or racism, students will react. How the channels of communication and participation are developed will dictate how students communicate their needs or exercise their concerns.

Students must admit to their lack of wisdom and knowledge. But no one can dispute the creativity of the student mind and the critical way in which he can look at an environment that is new to him. His transience is his greatest liability and greatest asset. His call for immediacy can be unreasonable, or it can move the institution that otherwise would remain bogged down in timidity. If he calls for immediacy, it is because he hasn't been involved meaningfully in the decision-making process and doesn't realize how painful and complex change can be. In short, a university decision-making process designed to serve students, yet doesn't see the wisdom of consulting and involving students to make that process more efficient and more effective, is excluding its most obvious resource. As a secondary consideration for those who are interested in strategies, failure to use this resource can create problems on which strategists can try out their wares.

Dr. Eliot's paper indicates that he should be congratulated for an intelligent, fair, and courageous effort in handling the incidents of unrest on his campus. Although the section on "Student Participation, 1964–68" was not detailed, the steps taken were somewhat progressive and forward looking. However, certain questions arise:

Does student representation mean representation with vote? Do the students represent different interests and minorities on campus, or do they tend to be of the so-called silent majority? What effect does university nonrecognition of politically oriented student groups have on student participation? Is the black student group a political organization? What procedural rules are needed in such cases as the Dow Chemical sing-in, and what did the conduct committee come up with in this regard? In what ways was a high degree of informal communication maintained between students, professors, and administrators? In what ways has more effective student participation in faculty decision making been instituted? Does admission of students to faculty meetings with limited speaking privileges really constitute meaningful "student participation in faculty decisions"? Before the Thursday, December 5, incident, had the black students approached the administration? What attempts were made to communicate with black students?

Let us now move to comments on the section "Possibilities for Guidelines."

Except for the first, the guidelines deal with two matters: (1) disciplinary action for those who cause disruption, and (2) policy with regard to police intervention. The first guideline deals with maintenance of administration-faculty-student communication but is spoiled by an Agnewism—"The more joint committees, the better; . . ."

Dr. Eliot defines disruption as an action that "significantly interferes with other people's rights or disrupts the operations of the institution." This is perhaps a useful definition in times of crisis, but what the institution needs to protect against is long-term disruption. This can take the form of an institutionalized fear, the kind of fear which diverts our full energies from the proximate as well as long-range goals—goals which give our universities the potential to educate men adequately in our complex, dynamic, and troubled world. Right now our universities are pathetically inadequate in many areas. Our rallying call should be the challenge of educating the twentieth-century man. Whether or not we are successful in this endeavor will be crucial in determining which course history will take. Ad hoc committees to wave banners and take over buildings as well as joint committees to discuss various aspects of strategy and tactics are symptoms of a faltering social grouping.

We must find new ways of developing until we can work together to formulate bold new approaches to education. It is time that the leadership for change comes from the top. Let quiet reason—not turmoil—guide the course. Unless buildings are being taken over, administrators should forget about strategies and tactics and get to the business of building towers on the foundations that have been so ably protected. There will be controversy about which towers should stay and which shouldn't, but simply that towers can be built will display the soundness of the foundation. A struggle for survival can be replaced by a drive for achievement. Together, administrators, faculty, and students can seek answers to questions. Together they can use those answers to build realities to what have been our dreams.

Faculty Response to Racial Tensions

AMITAI ETZIONI

THE RESPONSE of most faculty members to the mounting drive for black studies programs is, not surprisingly, marked by confusion: the term "black studies" encompasses programs and aspirations whose variety hardly permit an undifferentiated response. Some of the conceptions, especially those that challenge academic freedom and societal values, will likely continue to arouse broad and bitter opposition. Others that seek to enrich scholarship through research and study in such subjects as the sociology of the ghetto and the history of the Negro-American community are winning wide support. Still other programs view black studies as requiring separate black social communities on white campuses, an approach which some consider resegregation but which may also be viewed as a sociological prerequisite for ultimately successful integration at other social levels and later stages. In short, thoughtful reaction requires a differentiated response.

The analysis here presents some of the issues faculty members must consider in four different areas: *admission* of students from disadvantaged backgrounds; *compensatory education* for those admitted without full qualifications; *specialization* in ethnic studies; and *separate facilities* for the social life of students of a minority group. Factors that will influence the directions of faculty responses in each of these areas are explored.

The analysis here is based on materials other than a study of the way faculties have reacted to these four key aspects of programs for students from disadvantaged backgrounds. In the situation of considerable flux, we doubt the usefulness of reporting a study that would show X percent of professors prefer one version of black studies while Y percent prefer another. Our analysis derives from sociological research and theory on related

The contributions of Carolyn O. Atkinson to this paper closely approximated those of a coauthor; her modesty stopped her from sharing the by-line. I also gratefully acknowledge the comments of Sarajane Heidt, Murray Milner, Martin Wenglinsky, all members of the Center for Policy Research, and of Harry A. Marmion. For elaboration of the theoretical points made, see Amitai Etzioni's *The Active Society: A Theory of Societal and Political Processes* (New York: Free Press, 1968).

issues in the fields of race relations, social mobility, societal change, and educational reorganization. All these areas have implications for our inquiry and a fund of theoretical material and empirical findings with which to inform it.

Before we attempt to outline criteria by which one may conceptualize, differentiate, and assess the consequences of the ideas, programs, and actions of this new movement, we must stress that almost all the conceptions advanced thus far emphasize *black studies* rather than *study by blacks*. The highest priority is given to the demands of black students (and faculty) for the inclusion of certain kinds of courses in the curricula offered by predominantly white colleges and universities. Secondary attention—often at the end of a long list of curriculum demands—is given to seeking the admission of more black students to these institutions.[1] As these lines are written, students at City College of City University of New York are demanding that half of the entering class in 1970 be black and Puerto Rican. This kind of demand, which may become more widespread, has only recently reached the top of the list of demands even at this institution.

In our judgment, only a minority of the black high school graduates who enter college will major or concentrate in black studies. Rather, the main issue concerning the majority of black students will be the substance and quality of the general education they receive, not the one or two courses they may elect from the black studies program. Hence, *the major need of the black community and the society is to expand considerably the numbers*

---

[1] A typical list, the demands of black students at the University of Wisconsin, follows: "(1) An autonomous black studies department controlled and organized by black students and faculty which would enable students to receive a B.A. in black studies. (2) A black chairman of the black studies department who would be approved by a committee of black students and faculty. (3) That at least 500 black students be admitted to the University next fall. (4) That 20 teachers be allocated for the initiation of the black studies department with the approval of black students. (5) That amnesty, defined as no reprisal or chastisement, be given all students who participate in boycotts or other such actions in reference to our demands. (6) That a black co-director of the Student Financial Aids Office (scholarships, loans, etc.) be appointed with the approval of black students. (7) That black counselors be hired by the Student Financial Aids Office with the approval of black students. (8) That scholarships be provided for all athletes up until the time that they receive their degree. Some athletes have to go for a fifth year. (9) That the existing black courses be transferred into the black studies department. (10) That it be established that black students with the black faculty have the power to hire and fire all administrators and teachers who are involved in anything related to black students. (11) That it be established that control of the black cultural center be in the hands of black students. (12) That all expelled Oshkosh [State University] students who wish to attend the University be admitted immediately. (13) That proof as defined by black students that the above demands have been met be given to black students by the administration" (*Washington Post,* Feb. 14, 1969).

of black students admitted to college and to assure the effectiveness of this expansion by providing the needed bridging education. Almost none of the documents and reports of oral presentations[2] of advocates of black studies include a demand to provide students of disadvantaged backgrounds with bridging education. Yet the need is not only that black students be admitted to colleges but also that they shall graduate *and* have gained an education that will be effective and meaningful in the changing society they will enter and whose transformation they will help accomplish. Bridging education is being promoted by others in the education field, and—we shall see—is a complex and difficult matter. But these factors neither explain nor justify the almost total disregard by the black studies movement of the need for such education.

Instrumental Education for Black Students

For the black studies movement, it is simpler to imply that a program designed to build black identity and pride will provide a viable education for black students than it is to confront the deeper, more complex issues. Many black students, it seems to us, both desire and need more than liberation from psychological shackles. What they may need is discussed below. What they desire is instrumental education in *addition* to black studies. Data from surveys on current and potential students of Federal City College[3] show that 66 percent of the respondents said that black studies were "extremely important" and 24 percent said that they were "important."[4] At the same time, the report that "most of the 90% black student body were interested in pursuing careers in business, teaching, and science-related fields,"[5] suggests that interest in the expressive aspects of education do not supplant more instrumental concerns.[6]

Consistent with these findings are those from a study of high school

---

[2] Many of these are reported in the daily press and the *Chronicle of Higher Education.*

[3] Federal City College, a land-grant college which opened in the fall of 1968 in Washington, D.C., is an urban college whose student body is 90 percent black and was chosen by lot.

[4] Peter G. Nordlie et al., *The Role of College-Community Relationships in Urban Higher Education* (Washington: Bureau of Research, Office of Education, 1969), 2:101.

[5] *Washington Post,* March 6, 1969.

[6] *Instrumental* education refers to education acquired as a means to other ends than the sheer acquisition of knowledge as such. *Expressive* education is a goal in itself. The distinction is analytic in that most courses have some elements of both but, for a given population of students, it is usually easy to tell which aspect is dominant. We here class the courses (or classes) according to the predominant element.

seniors in Washington and applicants to Federal City College who were asked what kinds of courses and curriculum they thought FCC should develop. The results [7] were as follows:

FCC should develop a curriculum that includes primarily traditional courses in the liberal arts and sciences, such as algebra, zoology, history, and so on.

Seniors, 22.3 percent; applicants, 31.5 percent

FCC should develop a curriculum that includes primarily courses on community needs and urban problems, such as race and cultural relations, urban legal problems, and so on.

Seniors, 14.7 percent; applicants, 15.4 percent

FCC should develop a curriculum that includes primarily courses in preparation for the world of work such as data processing, medical technology, and so on.

Seniors, 24.9 percent; applicants, 21.7 percent

FCC should develop a curriculum which includes courses on issues and problems of contemporary society as well as classically academic courses.

Seniors 35.5 percent; applicants, 27.3 percent

FCC should develop a curriculum that includes primarily courses that emphasize African history and culture.

Seniors, 2.5 percent; applicants, 3.5 percent

Although our informal contacts and observations offer no hard evidence, they and the logic of the situation suggest that these findings are not atypical. They imply that if a student is able to choose among programs, he is more likely to opt for one which is also strongly instrumentally oriented rather than chiefly expressive.

Do black studies provide the education that is desired and needed? To what degree do they accomplish this, and through which of the varying conceptions of black studies? The following sociological criteria may serve as guidelines for reviewing and comparing various conceptions of black studies.

Education, it is often said, ought to prepare students for life in the society into which they will graduate. But our society is changing both of its own accord and in response to the pressure exerted by its underprivileged members through growing political awareness and action. Thus, the question must be asked: for which society are students to be prepared—the society that the Kerner Commission saw as "racist" and as moving toward a bifur-

[7] Helen Astin and Ann Bisconti, *The Role of College-Community Relationships in Urban Higher Education,* 3:8, Appendix.

cation into separate and unequal parts; an Afro-American statehood; or society closely approximating the assimilation-integration model, in which the black minority eventually blends into and becomes indistinguishable from the white majority? None of these alternatives offers either a realistic or a normatively justifiable view of the society for which current students can and ought to prepare themselves.

This is not the place to discuss in detail the near future of American society; nor would it be wise to build an educational program on highly specific assumptions about the future. Yet some remarks on this highly intricate and speculative subject will clarify a framework within which the following discussion can be assessed:

1. The society will be an affluent one. A GNP of $4.5 billion and a per capita GNP of $12,000 per year are predicted for the year 2000.[8]

2. Racial and other forms of discrimination will certainly not disappear, but will probably decline, especially in the area of economic opportunity. The number of good-paying jobs available to persons from disadvantaged backgrounds will increase.

3. Most of these positions will require vocational, semiprofessional, or professional skills of the kind provided by *instrumental* college training. A projection for 1975 shows 88.6 million professional and technical employees in the United States (a growth of 64 percent compared to 1960), with only 13.7 million positions for clerical employees (a growth of 40 percent), 6.1 million for sales personnel (+ 39 percent), 15.5 million for operatives—semiskilled workers (+ 29 percent), and 3.8 million for laborers (+ 3 percent).

To some extent, the mere possession of a college degree will continue to be an advantage in the labor market. But to state that ours is a "credential society" and to imply that how well one is trained matters little so long as he has a degree is a dangerous half-truth. Degrees matter, but so do competence, recommendation letters, the institution that awarded the degree, and so on. And the larger the proportion of the population having college degrees and the more that degrees are granted "automatically" to students who remain in residence or participate in a special studies department *without* acquiring full instrumental training, the greater the likelihood that graduate schools, civil service, corporations, and other employers will develop secondary screening mechanisms and tie their rewards to other criteria and achievements. High school diplomas as a credential underwent a simi-

[8] Herman Kahn and Antony J. Wiener, *The Year 2000* (New York: Macmillan Co., 1967), p. 10.

lar transformation, and the beginnings of the process for college degrees are already visible. How quickly this can happen may be seen from the following:

> Those who finished these courses [designed by Hutchins at Chicago] received a B.A. But other colleges, particularly graduate schools, rarely recognized this as a true B.A. and often required the Chicago College graduate to take a year, and sometimes two, of additional courses before they admitted him to graduate work.[9]

To some extent, the development of additional screening mechanisms can be retarded by the political pressure on employers, and underprivileged groups and their allies can be expected to continue that pressure. But the prediction must remain that substantial differences in *instrumental qualifications* will significantly affect the allocation of resources in the future society, of which students from disadvantaged backgrounds both desire and deserve a greater share.

Instrumental Characteristics of General Education

The stress here on the instrumental function of undergraduate education may raise the question: Are not the colleges the seats of general education, with instrumental training occurring primarily in the graduate and professional schools? Undergraduate colleges do provide some straight instrumental preparation: (1) Their graduates are hired as teachers and social workers on the basis of the B.A. degrees awarded them. (2) They serve as preparatory schools for professional schools (courses in mathematics for future engineers). (3) They communicate values, information, and "discipline" that are prerequisites for success in the existing society. (4) For undergraduates who go on to graduate work, a major in philosophy, English, or French (and so forth) is preprofessional if study is continued in the same or a related area. (5) Many educationalists like to discuss the fine general education programs of Harvard, the University of Chicago, and Columbia and to imitate them; yet the instrumental aspects of the same teaching materials increase when they are used at Wayne State, Bowling Green, San Jose State, or wherever working-class students are enrolled in large numbers. The instrumental function becomes even more predominant in the case of students from disadvantaged backgrounds, especially if they have a subculture of their own.

Of course important expressive elements are included in liberal arts education, but for most students such education is much more instrumental

---

[9] Daniel Bell, *The Reforming of General Education* (Garden City, N.Y.: Doubleday, 1968), p. 30.

than is often implied. The future society *may* give less weight to technological and economic considerations and be more concerned with the quality of life—culture, community relations, and leisure. It will not in any event be a society in which most citizens live like Chinese mandarins—in which those with chiefly a generalist, humanist education will be rewarded to the same extent as those also able to program a computer, run the accounts, or practice law.

Some advocates of black studies programs stress that their aim is not only to train lawyers, doctors, and other service professionals, but also to foster an intense commitment to practice one's vocation so that it is meaningful and helpful to the members of one's community. Even if the desirability of such an orientation is accepted, the community commitment still must be additional to, and cannot replace, instrumental competence. (How such preparation can best be provided and kept relevant to the community's needs is discussed below.) And even if a society were sought in which instrumental training were unnecessary or irrelevant, sociologically it is unlikely to come to pass. Thus, to prepare a subpopulation of college students only or primarily in noninstrumental ways would be to undermine their positions in the society in which they will live. And to neglect the provisions of bridging education would effectively perpetuate the disadvantages that created the need for such education in the first place.

Instrumental qualifications by themselves will make a difference, but society will not suddenly begin to reward people only for merit. It may be expected that increased attention will be paid to merit and, therefore, training more people from disadvantaged backgrounds will strengthen the movement in this direction.

The Correcting of Perspective

Advocacy of instrumental preparation in no way argues against the creation of black studies programs; rather, it provides a basis for assessing various conceptions of such programs. We hold as our central tenet that students from disadvantaged backgrounds need *instrumental bridging education,* if only in such areas as syntax and grammar [10] and mathematics, to

---

[10] It has been argued that "ghetto English" is not "bad" English but rather an argot with a vitality and tradition of its own, and that to attack it simply as "bad" English is to sustain the image of the Negro as inferior. But if people who have grown up using a different version of the language are forced to speak only "the King's" English, they may become unable to express themselves spontaneously. It may well be important to permit the use of specialized argots in intimate social relations and teach the "other" English in effect as a second language, to be used in instrumental interactions.

do well instrumentally in the society. Many programs have attempted to provide bridging education—precollege summer classes, additional remedial classes during the semester, counseling, tutorials, and so on—and have encountered problems. As studies of Head Start (and the Coleman Report) indicate in a different context, it is not yet clear that effective techniques and formats for bridging education have been found; some programs are too regimented, and others help to instill stigma rather than overcome it. Nevertheless, redesigning, strengthening, and expanding these programs must be prime goals of any attempt to provide effective and meaningful education for students from disadvantaged backgrounds.

Although most members of the black studies movement disregard bridging education, they do focus on the expressive needs of black students. Advocates of black studies suggest, if we summarize their statements, that: (1) corrected perspective toward self and society is essential for instrumental achievement; (2) a corrected perspective toward self and society is meaningful as an end in itself; and (3) black studies are the way to make such a correction. The validity of these positions depends to a large extent on how they are advanced. To take the first statement first, the findings and analyses of social scientists overwhelmingly support the statement that building self-confidence—overcoming an image of self as inferior, backward, or incompetent—is prerequisite to the successful development of instrumental skills. Such a correction of perspective and the education it entails do not substitute for instrumental training; both kinds of education are necessary. Since most Negroes will seek a place in American society with varying degrees of satisfaction and success, they must become prepared to live in it. Designing an education based on the assumption that they will choose to retreat from the American society seems unsupported by existing evidence and indications.

Moreover, expressive and instrumental education tend to enhance each other. For instance, just as a person who defines himself as a failure will do less well on an examination than someone with self-confidence, so will a person who does well on several examinations become less likely to maintain a self-view of failure. And while one needs to be proud rather than ashamed of his heritage, it is also important for black students to be able to point to a large number of success models, like black scientists, pilots, heads of Federal agencies, and so on.

For those already committed to the view that social groups must advance on both "legs," it may be difficult to conceive of an approach that focuses on expressive (or "psychic," or symbolic) efforts. Actually, such an approach has many roots and followers. Thus, in Maoist China there is a strong element of anti-technology, propsychism.[11] The designing of the war against poverty in 1964–65 placed considerable emphasis on organizing and educating for community action rather than on providing jobs, houses, and income. In part, a budget squeeze necessitated an economical program (community action costs much less); in part, political theory suggested that community action would provide the power base required to advance other goals. In part, though, a social psychological theory, an "Americanization of Fanon," suggested that correcting Negroes' perspectives on self and society would provide the necessary leverage for changing self and society, and community action was to change the perspective.

Just as the development of China (or any other nation) needs commitment *and* technology, the American poor need autonomy *and* jobs, and, similarly, black students need expressive education *and* instrumental training, both because each is an end in itself and because each supports the other.

Some may hold that emphasis on instrumental training implies that black people must become black white men, working at meaningless jobs in bureaucratic posts or on the assembly line and subscribing to the consumer fetishism of suburban society. The reason lies elsewhere. The jobs available to the untrained or poorly trained are much tighter than those for the skilled and professional; one realistic way to be freer in our present and near-future society is to be instrumentally qualified. Nor is there any reason to suppose that a well-trained person would therefore be ashamed of his background, subculture, and community. Or that such a person would not limit his work and consumption so as to leave time and energy for cultural activities, public action, and reflection.

Thus the discussion comes to the question of the most effective sociological context for both the correction of perspective *and* instrumental training. So far as expressive education is concerned, the earlier the correct orientation is presented, the less damage will be produced in the first place. When correction is needed, however, the earlier it is introduced, the more effective and less painful it will be. Hence, some ethnic studies should be introduced

[11] Lifton puts it thus: "The methods of the Great Leap Forward, to be sure, had a compelling external logic: putting into use the human labor with which rural China abounds as a substitute for the large machinery she lacks, and thereby creating both national and local self-sufficiency, or as the official slogan has it, 'walking with two legs.' But it turned out that the 'legs' were largely psychic, and while psychic legs are of the greatest importance, they cannot substitute for either bodily or technological ones—especially in the making of steel" (Robert J. Lifton, *Revolutionary Immortality* [New York: Vintage Books, Random House, 1968], p. 103).

into the high schools and even primary schools and become a standard part of the curriculum. Schools whose students are largely from disadvantaged backgrounds might devote more time to ethnic studies, while largely middle-class white schools might include this topic in classes on American history or society. (Or perhaps the same curriculum could be used throughout the educational system, with adjustments for class and ethnic variation.) The optimal situation would find the colleges needing only to "finish" a process that started much earlier. A major contribution to that end would be for teachers colleges and liberal arts colleges that train teachers to give increased attention to the preparation of teachers of and teaching materials for precollege-level ethnic studies.

Until such steps are taken, undergraduate colleges [12] will have to provide this expressive education for their students. Such education can take various forms, ranging from inclusion in general liberal arts courses (such as Columbia College's Contemporary Civilization and the University of Chicago's program) to a major segment of courses on American society, to specialized courses for students interested in pursuing study in greater depth.

The need is for ethnic studies rather than solely black studies, because Spanish-Americans, Japanese-Americans, and other ethnic groups have needs similar to those of black students. Again, lower-class WASPs have some parallel needs as well, especially for bridging education, and other minorities—Jewish, Irish—may increasingly demand resources as ethnic studies come to take their place in the curriculum. It is neither practical nor desirable that all kinds of ethnic studies be provided in one set of courses, program, department, or college; the point is that the needs are broader than offerings only to black students. A general increase in such programs would, however, certainly be in accord with the American tradition of pluralism.

To protect the institutions, which are already under great financial and manpower pressures, three principles should be applied in the development of ethnic studies: priority should be given (1) to those areas of study that as yet have no ethnic program, and (2) to disadvantaged groups. (3) Resources should be allocated to any ethnic program roughly in accord with the "demand" for it on the part of students and faculty.

To return to the functions of ethnic studies, they will at best provide the cognitive bases for the needed correction of perspective. For example, a course in black history which studies precolonial Africa and the civil rights movement cannot alone be expected to have major psychodynamic conse-

---

[12] On graduate studies, see below.

quences. Rather, such consequences might be achieved by such means as a whole program of black studies for undergraduates, black teachers teaching instrumental subjects to black classes, and segregated social groupings—"colleges" within the white university.

To assess these suggestions, we seek to apply two sociological principles —the limits of pluralism, and the dynamics of group integration.

The Limits of Pluralism

The often-used dichotomy between an integrated society and one in which two groups live almost completely separate from each other (a dichotomy which prevails in the discussion of this area [13]) does not exhaust the possibilities. On the contrary, most modern societies are pluralistic on some levels and universalistic on others. Some differentiations among groups are highly intolerable; others are less so; and still others are not only acceptable but even valuable for the society as a whole and each of its members. Without embarking here on a general theory of society, a few highly schematic points do have direct bearing on the issues at hand.

1. Societal differentiations are the more intolerable as their magnitude becomes greater and if the cleavage is expanding. The differences among the races in the United States on these dimensions are smaller than in many Latin countries and seem to be shrinking, although rather slowly.

2. Differentiations are the more intolerable as the extent to which they are encompassing becomes greater; that is, a low position in one sector (economic, for example) supports similar positions in others (political power, education). Broad-scope, parallel differentiations render difficult both the correction of a disadvantage in one area by additional achievement in others and the blurring of group lines. Pluralism then tends to become unlimited, all-encompassing, and dangerous, and the society is divided into sharply drawn, self-conscious camps.

3. The specific sectors into which the differentiation among groups of members has penetrated are significant here. There are roughly four such areas, which will be discussed in the paragraphs that follow.

Cultural pluralism is enriching rather than damaging to the societal fabric. Progress in this area is achieved by recognizing many alternatives as

---

[13] See, for example, a lengthy report of Bayard Rustin's views by Thomas S. Brooks, "A Strategist without a Movement," *New York Times Magazine*, Feb. 16, 1969; Robert S. Browne, "The Case for Two Americas—One Black, One White," *New York Times Magazine*, Aug. 11, 1968; Nathan Hare, "The Case for Separatism: Black Perspective," *Newsweek*, Feb. 10, 1969; Roy Wilkins, "The Case against Separatism: Black Jim Crow," *Newsweek*, Feb. 10, 1969.

legitimate and of equal status rather than by seeking to homogenize or impose one set of cultural norms. Thus, for instance, both black and Nordic types of beauty can be recognized without inflicting psychic deprivations on either group. Robert S. Browne gives the following example, which is a good analogue for many others:

> Millions of black parents have been confronted with the poignant agony of raising black, kinky-haired children in a society where the standard of beauty is a milk-white skin and long, straight hair. To convince a black child that she is beautiful when every channel of value formation in the society is telling her the opposite is a heart-rending and well-nigh impossible task. [And he continues:] . . . In the American ethos a black man is not only "different," he is classed as ugly and inferior.[14]

This situation can be countered by claiming that the opposite holds, that black is beautiful while white is ugly. But such an approach is not the only alternative. It can be argued even more cogently that a rich society, rich in spirit, sees beauty in a large variety of different styles, colors, foods, and so on. Thus, it does not follow that complete segregation is needed to solve this and similar problems.

A measure of *social pluralism* is inevitable. There is no nation, no community, in which people do not interact selectively in their interpersonal and social circles. In this area of social process, public authorities can provide little positive guidance, although legal, economic, and other barriers to free social interaction can be removed. And as we see it, a measure of voluntary social differentiation is much less damaging *per se* than assimilation-integration theory suggests. So long as free interaction is provided in other sectors, voluntary differentiation among friends and mates is not a serious threat to a society in which subcommunities live together peacefully and with mutual respect. Actually, during the transition from our separate and unequal to a pluralistic-integrated society, some differentiation of social circles may be needed as a source of emotional security (this point is discussed below).

Economic differentiations are far more dangerous than informal social ones, especially when they have accumulated for many decades, are based on ascription rather than achievement, and the prerequisites for achievement are concentrated in the hands of select groups. Here it is necessary both to remove the barriers based on ascriptive attributes and, to the extent that the assets needed for achievement have been accumulated, to provide

[14] *New York Times Magazine,* Aug. 11, 1968.

the disadvantaged with extra resources to help them catch up to equality of opportunities, a process we call "universalization." [15]

Finally, there is a hard core of *ultimate values*, national symbols, universal rules, and monopolization of the legitimate use of force which constitutes the limits of pluralism, the universal societal bonds which tie the member groups into one supra-unit or society. When differentiation significantly penetrates into this area, the society will tend toward disbanding. Such a situation led to our and other nations' civil wars.

An individual or a group may be committed to particular values which it views as having priority over membership in the nation; it may even seek to secede and form a new state in Africa or the Deep South—or the ghettos of our cities. But it is an empirical observation that such a secessionist group can hardly expect the support of the society it seeks to divide or leave. On the contrary, sharp retaliatory measures are to be expected as secessionist activities challenge the most deeply held commitments of many other citizens. It also follows that those who seek cultural and social autonomy and economic universalization weaken their positions considerably when they use the language of nationhood. Their posture of seeking, not the legitimate societal goals of subculture, equality of opportunity, and improvement of the quality of life through a transformation of the society's structure, but rather the severing of the universal societal bonds to form their own nation simply alienates most members.

This view of society as much more able to accommodate pluralism on some levels than on others, as in effect welcoming separation in some areas and insisting on integration in others, has two major levels of implication for the assessment of black studies. It has consequences for the view of the society for which students are educated, and for the view of the campus which—like a micro-society—has its own pluralisms and universal bonds. Three of the implications are illustrated here.

First, the teaching of black studies as a negation of America, a rejection of its basic values, and a legitimation of symbols which run counter to those

---

[15] ". . . in an address to the board [College Entrance Examination Board], Harold Howe II, the U.S. Commissioner of Education, observed that a new doctrine had been established in elementary and secondary education with the premise that 'equal educational opportunity does not result from treating all pupils equally.'

" 'Now it is time,' he said, 'to ask what the colleges have done, and what they propose to do, in order to reflect this new philosophy in higher education.'

"The Commissioner urged colleges to 'read the disadvantaged background into college entrance examination scores before making decisions on admissions.' He also suggested that colleges might add 'a whole year of pre-college compensatory work' to their regular curriculums" (*Chronicle of Higher Education*, Nov. 8, 1967, p. 1).

of many members ("all white men are devils") is secessionist.[16] The "positive" teaching of black studies—as advancing black values, as adding a major component to American pluralism and thus making it less constrictive—is in accord with the pluralistic-integration model.

The demand that all students be exposed to the same curriculum is assimilationist; the demand that any group of students be given a totally separate program of studies is secessionist. The provision of black studies with the requirement that those who "major" in them also take some courses to ensure their familiarity with the general bases of American civilization is in line with pluralistic integration.

It is easy to offer psychological and sociological explanations for the extremist positions taken by some leaders of the black studies movement. But this discussion is concerned more with the consequences of various positions than in their motivational and experiential bases. Pluralistic programs are those which aim at the limitation of interracial conflicts, the recognition of shared values and rules on the campus and in the society at large. It is hoped that the total rejection of the white world and the demand for total autonomy are only transitory stages, a step on the road from being oppressed and suppressed to that of membership in the society as a semi-autonomous community, proud of its own positive values.

Second, a group's orientation to national symbols (such as the Constitution and the flag) and core values (for example, the value of the individual) is a key indicator of its position on this general issue. Secessionist are those programs, classes, and other activities that encourage black Americans to reject summarily such values. Assimilationists demand homogeneity of commitment. Pluralist integrationists acknowledge that these values and symbols are *now* more accessible to some Americans than others but, rather than rejecting their universal validity, draw on strengthening the commitment to those values to further legitimate the demand that all Americans be accorded equal access. Thus, the critical orientation is not dampened by stating that we believe in the Bill of Rights and the Constitution; our critical orientation is aimed, first of all, at the existing societal institutions.

Some of the core values themselves may be challenged, for instance, the excessive emphasis on individual opportunity and material affluence. Such

[16] We use the term "secessionist" rather than "separatist" because, although all forms of secessionism by definition challenge the unifying bonds and core values of the society, there are many forms of separatism that do not have these consequences, and could in our view be considered pluralist rather than assimilationist integration.

a challenge is in accord with membership in a society as long as it is sought for all members and not only for one subcommunity.

Browne presents a case for "two Americas—one black, one white." But typical to most, though not all, of these statements, he really seeks an equal and legitimate subcommunity status rather than a separatist state or society.

> The separatist would argue that the Negro's foremost grievance cannot be solved by giving him access to more gadgets—although this is certainly a part of the solution—but that his greatest need is of the spirit, that he must have an opportunity to reclaim his group individuality and have that individuality recognized as equal with other major cultural groups in the world.[17]

We see no sociological reason that "a *complete* divorce of the two races" is necessary.

Third, the campus, like the society, has some universal rules which are morally and judicially binding on all members. The assimilationist sees no particular reason to exempt black studies from the universal rules implied in the concept of academic freedom, for example, the protection of teachers from being fired because of their views. The secessionist seeks an autonomous black program, even college, in which commitments to black values are the criteria for hiring, firing, and so on. Here is not only a demand for blacks to control programs in which blacks are studying but also to select the "correct" kind of blacks.[18] This approach cannot be tolerated by a university if it is to survive as a free institution. The pluralist would say that if these rules have a discriminatory effect, they would be altered for all students, but such an effect cannot serve to justify special dispensations for any subgroup.

Dynamics of Group Integration

The preceding analysis also suggests that informal selection of blacks into segregated friendships, lunch groups, and courting is to be expected to be common, especially when class differences are added to racial ones, as when lower-class black students join a middle-class white campus.[19] The campus, like the society, is not a large small-group, in which the basis of cohesion and solidarity is a close personal relationship among each and every member. On the contrary, a limited amount of interpersonal and group separation, so long as it is voluntary, may be quite useful to integra-

---

[17] *New York Times Magazine,* Aug. 11, 1968.

[18] James E. Cheek, a Negro, referred to "reverse racism" in this context (*Chronicle of Higher Education,* May 6, 1968).

[19] For a report from Cornell on this point, see Ernest Dunbar, "The Black Studies Thing," *New York Times Magazine,* April 6, 1969.

tion on the *next level*—the classrooms—and fuller integration *later,* once the educational, psychological, and economic differences between the racial groups have been reduced.

Intimate social groups are usually formed among persons very similar in many attributes; even among whites, homogeneity tends to prevail. This iron law of sociology can hardly be expected not to apply to black-white relations. We do expect some interracial intimate groups, but they will be much less common than intraracial groups at this stage.

Separate intimate relations provide a sociological foundation for the emotional security that is generally needed for student life, a life that is quite tension-provoking in our achievement-oriented society and especially so for persons from disadvantaged backgrounds who have more ground to cover.[20] The black studies movement can be viewed as an attempt to meet the need for emotional security, and the more such security is provided in social circles, the less the likelihood that pressures for less demanding curricula or separate classrooms or "colleges" will be brought to bear. Similarly, the more that effective bridging education is provided, the less threatening the regular classroom will appear.

Last but not least, the separate black *social* group, under indigenous (rather than appointed) black leaders and in the framework of Afro-American or black centers, provides the most powerful vehicle for the correction of the perspectives of black students *and* for integration on the next level and in the next phase. Psychodynamics suggests that individuals who are isolated from their natural groups and removed from their leaders tend to rigidify their positions. Conversely, if the group's perspectives change, especially if the change is guided by the group's own leadership, the individual members find the necessary emotional support to "let go" of their old positions and make the transition to new ones. This transitional phase is always problematic in that once the old perspective is "unlocked," it may be changed not in a constructive direction but rather toward a new distortion. Without *group* changes, however, deep changes are unlikely to occur.

It also follows that these intimate social groups are best able to provide the noncognitive elements of the needed transformation. If the university provides the buildings for such efforts or salaries for the instructors (as it does for other extracurricular activities), whether it grants no credit or some credit for these extracurricular activities—these are secondary matters that can probably be best decided on the basis of local circumstances. The

[20] At Northwestern University, "Negroes, particularly those from the inner city, had long tended to stick together socially" (*Chronicle of Higher Education,* May 20, 1968, p. 4).

main point is keeping the classroom devoted mainly to cognitive work and as an integrated student society, while the more expressive work is carried out in the black social groups.

The U.S. Department of Health, Education, and Welfare recently challenged the setting-up of black dormitories and threatened the withdrawal of Federal funds from colleges which allowed their buildings to be used in such a way. Yet, first, there are many ways in which a separate black social life can flourish—black social centers, a free choice of roommates, even separate subfloors—other than making race a basis for admission to a building. Second, HEW will have to re-examine its guidelines to see if they are based on assimilationist or pluralistic integrationist assumptions. Pluralism is in accord with the core values of the American traditional society as well as sociologically viable. Assimilation, which occasionally is implied in the liberal civil rights tradition, seems to have some of the normative and sociological connotations black separatists excoriate.

It follows that the shortest route toward a genuinely pluralistic, integrated society may be one which entails a step which may seem backward to the assimilationist integrationist. Namely, in accordance with the universal rules of academia (which may themselves be transformed for all students), black social centers may be created in addition to other existing ethnic ones. And within the limits of universal shared core values, a plurality of subcultures may be more fully legitimated and supported.

Toward Black Studies

So far, we have deliberately focused our discussion on bridging education, undergraduate black studies, and social centers. Graduate programs and research specialization in black studies should be fully supported as well. There is already a significant body of scholarship in this area.[21] There is no need to be a purist here. Perhaps some subareas within the realm of black studies are not as rich in volumes as is, let us say, Shakespearean literature, but many other areas are not better endowed than black studies and quite a few are less so. Moreover, scholarship flourishes when scholars are available, which requires "chairs," funds, libraries, museums, and so on—resources which until recently were very scarce for black studies.

As noted earlier, not every college ought to provide the same set of courses and programs of undergraduate *and* graduate black studies; after all, many colleges have no graduate programs and some are much nearer

---

[21] See, for example, Arnold M. Rose, "Graduate Training for the Culturally Deprived," *Sociology of Education,* Spring 1966, pp. 201–8.

to the ghettos than others. We must leave to a future publication the question of the ways in which different kinds of colleges may introduce different types of black studies.

The creation of graduate and undergraduate black (and other ethnic) studies will create many jobs for persons of disadvantaged backgrounds; it must, hence, also be viewed as a step toward eliminating inequality of higher education, in which there is an increase in students from disadvantaged backgrounds but very little commensurate increase in faculty and research staff. Institutions might thus both expect and welcome a whole subsystem with its own internal differentiation of quality, variation in form (for example, instrumental versus expressive emphasis), and so forth.

Ultimately though, black *studies* (as distinct from social centers) will have a mainly cognitive and largely instrumental role; and the main task of introducing large numbers of students of disadvantaged backgrounds into the society and educating them to help transform it will be performed by bridging education and black social groups and not by exclusive curricula or challenging universal bases of the campus or the society. A larger increase in admissions of students from underprivileged backgrounds, effective bridging education, ethnic studies, and ethnic social centers will make universities more responsive to the underprivileged parts of the society and to the majority of the students strongly committed to social justice. These reforms may well not satisfy everybody and should not be introduced in the hope of eliminating all tensions and conflict. But the preceding sociological criteria do suggest that such reforms do not undermine any basis of the society or the academic community and, hence, may be regarded as not only responsive to legitimate needs but also in accord with a vital, self-reforming society.

Sociological factors and considerations that may influence the reactions and actions of faculty to the demand for black studies have been analyzed. They by no means exhaust the range of possible responses or the areas of involvement. For instance, there remain the questions of faculty service to the community off the campus; the role of community service in shaping university policy with regard to expansion of the campus into low-income neighborhoods; the ways universities may have to be reorganized in the faculty's view if they are to provide community services or bridging education. These and other subjects remain to be treated in a future discussion, as the dialogue continues and serves as a propelling factor in university reorganization commensurate in scope and depth with those of challenges and needs we face.

Commentaries on

Faculty Response to Racial Tensions

DOUGLAS F. DOWD, DEBORAH PARTRIDGE WOLFE
ROBERT D. CROSS

Education as Cooperative Inquiry

DOUGLAS F. DOWD

TO SET THE TONE, I shall start with what might logically come as a conclusion to my discussion of Professor Etzioni's paper.

In the society, indeed in the world, a struggle has begun between the old and the new, the powerful and the powerless, and in that struggle we are finding that what we possess in the way of democracy is more formal than real. The higher learning well reflects the hierarchical state of affairs in the larger society, for nobody pretends that on campus either decision making or the process of learning takes place among equals. The world is in trouble, and so is the university, and whatever else might be true of both, both are enduring a challenge to authoritative structures. In the outer society, as on campus, those without power or authority have rightly begun to wonder why present patterns should persist, when present patterns are those that have brought us to the dangerous state of affairs within which so many tremble.

On campus, for at least the social sciences and the humanities (areas within which black studies programs are designed) there is substantial reason to wonder whether most of what is being taught is worthwhile, indeed, substantial reason to assume that it may range between the useless and the dangerously wrong. The time seems to have come when the role of the professor should be that of working side by side with students, in an apprenticeship role with the aim of gaining understanding. We professors know one thing well: how to inquire. If we know the answers to deep and troubling social questions, we have hidden our knowledge very successfully.

If the process of cooperative inquiry, rather than of authoritative teaching, is the process we should develop, then education becomes a matter of growth more than of reaching stated levels. The best student in the class would be he who grows the most, not he who can write the best answer to set questions. Thus where each student begins—his prior education—is not as important as how much he grows. Placing the emphasis on intellectual growth takes it away from "bridging" and "compensation," and it also does something else: it enables us more rapidly to overcome the educational crimes of the past and to move to something like a democratic university—and perhaps even toward a democratic society.

I shall turn now more closely to Professor Etzioni's paper. He offers a serious sociological contribution toward understanding the influences on black students of studies programs, admissions criteria, and social arrangements. He does not comment explicitly on faculty response to racial tensions, nor shall I. Rather I shall examine some points with which I disagree.

The paper is unduly conventional in its emphasis on compensatory education, bridging, and career preparation. Indeed, in today's tense conditions, such an emphasis can add unnecessary new tensions—as has happened in many institutions where well-intentioned faculties have responded to new situations in established ways. I do not believe that every time a black or white student group raises demands, the faculty should jump accordingly; I do believe that so widespread a movement as black studies deserves the utmost in consideration and creative imagination as a faculty response. Furthermore, in any discussion of an educational development that is part of a political development, it is necessary to comprehend the felt needs of those carrying such developments to the edge of realization. After all, it has been the most determined and militant black students who have brought these issues alive, and it is their definition of their problems to which first—not sole—consideration should be given. Thus, the opinion surveys of high school seniors and applicants to Federal City College (cited in the paper) can be both accurate on the view of the students surveyed and inadequate to allow us to understand the dynamics of the process.

The most energetic and concerned black students are trying to foster at least an educational revolution for themselves and for future generations, and it would be unwise to judge them as either wrong-headed or romantic at this point, as it would have been foolish to write off Sam Adams or Tom Paine in our colonial history because they spoke for a minority. The majority will always opt for the conventional, and their needs are seldom derided within their status quo. If it is the desire of black students for higher education that is our focus, we may be sure that there are growing opportunities for the majority point of view to find satisfaction. (It should be noted that the turbulence caused by militant black students—a minority —is one reason that change of a more conventional variety is being expedited.) But that observation says little about the desirability of black studies programs or what Professor Etzioni sees as complementary (perhaps competing) programs for "bridging" and "compensation," to which I now turn.

To repeat, I believe the initial focus of this kind of discussion should be on the proposals of those who provide the thrust toward change, for they have forced the issue and will continue to do so. These students resist strongly the term "disadvantaged" when used to characterize them, for its use connects integrally with the perspective that speaks of bridging and compensation. The black students who demand change are angry, and see themselves as members of an exploited and oppressed group. In this connection, "disadvantaged" is more than a euphemism; it is a historical interpretation, amounting to apologetics, and leads to educational proposals that sharply disagree with both the politics and the educational proposals of the black students themselves. At least two matters require elaboration here: (1) why the problem of bridging and compensation is secondary, rather than primary; and (2) the relationship between successful black studies programs and the more conventional means by which black youngsters can receive quantitatively and qualitatively adequate education.

Professor Etzioni correctly speaks of the "almost total disregard by the black studies movement of the need for such [bridging] education." Activist black students are concerned, however, with the almost total disregard by predominantly white educational institutions—and even black ones— of the need for black students to appreciate their own historical roots and development so that they may be better able to transform their oppressed conditions. The black studies movement does not speak of remedial education; that is the function of those who control primary and secondary education—to make such education unnecessary. Reforms along these lines are likely to be speeded up by the emergence of more sweeping proposals, among which are black studies proposals. We need not fear the impact of so-called white backlash in these respects, for the primary and secondary education of black youngsters is so bad already that it can become only marginally worse; and where it isn't bad, there is no need for bridging and compensation.

But, Professor Etzioni might respond, what about black students now entering colleges from inadequate educational backgrounds? Here at least two things may be said, one factual and one conjectural. First, at Cornell University we have deliberately sought out black students from urban and rural backgrounds who have not had the curriculum, the grades, or the scores that would normally be considered appropriate for admission to Cornell. Such students have been a sizable minority of the black students at Cornell, and their performance has been equal to the average of their entering (white and black) class as regards grade averages, dropping out, and the like. These have been students whose math and verbal performance were such that in the past no sane admissions officer—sane by conventional standards—would have admitted them. The criterion we have used most strategically for such students has to do with their motivation. If they need help in one skill or another after they arrive, like any other students, they can get it. We have, and need, no special program for this purpose. I should add that about two-thirds of the black students at Cornell are in the Arts College, which has the highest standards of admission and performance in the university. And I would add something more: this experience has opened our eyes to the strong probability that our admissions standards for white students require serious questioning.

Turning now to the more speculative aspect of this question, black students' demands for curricular additions have sensitized both white students and faculty to the very tired quality of much of the existing curriculum and to the degree to which much that now exists has been a response to special-interest groups in the past—farmers, corporations, governments, and, in the case of Cornell, the hotel industry (to mention no others).

I doubt the correctness of describing black students' desires for black studies programs as being based so much on "expressive" needs. Their need is to overcome the systematic miseducation that they (and we) have had concerning their (and our) history, their (and our) place in this society, and their (and our) needs and possibilities. We have had crash programs in math and science, among other things, in the past, and black students need their own crash programs run by and for black people; and I think their claim on our educational resources is more worthy of attention than those that earlier responded to Sputnik. But let me end by examining the controversial and conjectural questions surrounding open admissions and associated curricular developments.

The demand for open admissions for black students—and others as well —has been given attention. The objections raised are often expressed in terms of a lowering of standards, and at least two things are wrong with that objection. First, many, probably even most, colleges and universities have made the possession of a high school diploma the sole criterion for admission. If this is a mistake, it has been a widely practiced mistake that should have been objected to long before the demand was raised by black students. Like so many other matters in our society, attention is given and standards are raised only when people outside the mainstream begin to ask for what those within it have long enjoyed. Second, and more important, the large-scale admission of seemingly ill-prepared students to colleges could be the development that would enable us to reconstruct the higher learning along lines more promising than those now in existence.

A Faculty Member Responds

DEBORAH PARTRIDGE WOLFE

AMERICA CLAIMS to be one of the world's great democracies. We believe that such a democracy is not merely majority rule, or blind conformity, or ruthless individualism, or paternalistic guarantee of individual happiness; rather, it is participatory group life, enjoyed by free individuals possessing maximum opportunities for participation. Its chief characteristic in regard to individuals is "respect for personality." In regard to the group, its chief characteristic is the flexible and evolutionary nature of group institutions.

We further believe that in order to develop and maintain such a democratic society, education must be available to all. Believing that education is a social process, Dewey in his *Democracy and Education* sets up this criterion for educational criticism:

> The two points selected by which to measure the worth of a form of social life are the extent to which the interests of the group are shared by all its members and the fullness and freedom with which it interacts with other groups. An undesirable society, in other words, is one which internally and externally sets up barriers to free intercourse and communication of experience. A society which makes provision for participation in its good of all its members on equal terms and which secures flexible readjustment of its institutions through interaction of the different forms of associated life

is in so far democratic. Such a society must have a type of education which gives individuals a personal interest in social relationships and control, and the habits of mind which secure social changes without introducing disorder.[1]

In brief, Dewey is pleading for a type of education that will be appropriate for the development of a democratic society. According to him, such a society would provide for *free and full participation of all its members* in the determination and pursuance of common interests; its essence would be a willingness to "share" in planning. According to this view, therefore, democracy is more than a theory and a practice of government. It is a way of life and applies to school affairs, church matters, home affairs, economic matters, and all other aspects of life as well as to government. This criterion for education implies "the ideal of a continuous reconstruction or reorganizing" of experience, of such a nature as to increase its recognized meaning or social content, and as to increase the capacity of individuals to act as guardians of this reorganization.[2]

It is not surprising that increasing demands for black studies have been made by that segment of America's population which has felt directly the inadequacies of America's dream through the "internal and external" barriers which have been set up both in and out of school. Likewise, it is not alarming that college and university faculties, rooted in medieval European curricula and patterns of organization, argue that students don't know enough about education to plan the curriculum and possess even less wisdom about selecting faculty and determining policies. And yet Harold Taylor has said:

> When Black students make demands for Black Studies programs, when they demand a share in the decisions about who will be their teachers, and when they back up their demands by taking over buildings, they are not imitating Nazis or Fascists. They are using the sit-in as an instrument for making changes in university attitudes and policies which should have been made long ago. . . . What is most important about the demands of the Black students for a new curriculum is that they are challenging the whole conception of how faculty members have been making up the curriculum in the past.[3]

I would go still further and say that we should thank the students for helping us face American education's greatest challenge. Abba Lerner

[1] John Dewey, *Democracy and Education* (New York: Macmillan Co., 1966), p. 115.
[2] Ibid., p. 376.
[3] Taylor, "The University in Society," *Channel 13 Program Guide,* August 1969, No. 10, p. 5.

titles his article analyzing this issue "Black Studies: The Universities in Moral Crisis." [4]

Points of Agreement

With this general philosophy in mind, I agree with Dr. Etzioni on the following points.

"The major need of the black community and the society is to expand considerably the numbers of black students admitted to college and to assure the effectiveness of this expansion by providing the needed bridging education."

In his article "Almost All-White," appearing in the *Southern Education Report,* John Egerton reports that "Less than two of every 100 students attending one of the 80 senior, majority-white state universities in this country are American Negroes. Less than one of every 100 students graduating from those institutions is a Negro, as is less than one of every 100 faculty members." [5] Such salient facts demonstrate that in a society where nearly 12 percent of the population is black and less than 2 percent in the public state colleges are black, there is a moral issue before us. Even though Etzioni stresses the need for bridging education, I wonder if the need for better guidance earlier in the student's life and articulation of programs and goals between high schools and colleges do not play important roles in lowering the numbers of eligible black students.[6] I am equally concerned that there is an implication that all black students are disadvantaged and therefore need bridging education. I am happy that the City University of New York has set September 1970 as the target date for open admissions to the university under carefully conceived guidelines.

There is a need to begin black studies before college; in fact, they should begin in the elementary school.

With this general principle, I heartily agree. Black studies should begin with the child's entrance into school whether he is black or white. They should be integrated into the total curriculum, in history, in music, in art, in literature, in fact in every subject area just as it belongs naturally and historically. It should be a part of the universal understandings of every American.

[4] Lerner in *Humanist,* May/June 1969, p. 9.
[5] Egerton, "Almost All-White," *Southern Education Report,* May 1969, p. 2.
[6] See Deborah Wolfe, "New Criteria for Selection of Marginally Qualified Disadvantaged Student," *Journal of Higher Education,* July 1969.

An increase in ethnic studies would be in accord with the American tradition of pluralism.

Cultural pluralism is the strength of America and must be viewed from a positive vantage. Priority should be given to black studies for the three reasons given by Dr. Etzioni: (*a*) too few black studies programs are available; (*b*) disadvantaged groups should be integrated as soon as possible; and (*c*) students and faculty (both black and white) are demanding such studies. In addition, because blacks constitute the largest racial minority and have been limited in their democratic participation, the start should be made with black studies if we are to develop the kind of society about which we talk. This start does not imply that full consideration should be denied other minorities; after all, all of us are a minority in one way or another, at one time or another.

Likewise, there is need for emphasizing the universality of man. "There is a hard core of ultimate values, national symbols, universal rules, and monopolization of the legitimate use of force which constitutes the limits of pluralism, the universal societal bonds which tie the member groups into one supra-unit or society."

With this basic principle I agree. I find no inconsistency with this need and the need for greater emphasis on black studies. As Etzioni indicates, most modern societies are pluralistic on some levels while universalistic in others.

"Black students need expressive education and instrumental training, both because each is an end in itself and because they support each other."

Most advocates of black studies share this feeling. The desire for developing black studies in no way indicates that black students and faculty wish *only* black studies, as can be noted in the statistics given from data collected at Federal City College. In fact, I know of *no* college or university where either students or faculty recommend the elimination of a broad spectrum of disciplines. Certainly this principle is in keeping with the purposes and structure of the university, for when one majors in a subject or an area, he is expected also to study outside that field. For example, Oberlin College in announcing the creation of the interdisciplinary program in Afro-American studies, which began in the fall of 1969 after a three-year period of student and faculty work, defined its purposes:

1. To foster an understanding of the unique "Black Experience" in America as it is reflected in

    a) Afro-American modes of cultural expression;
    b) Afro-American social and political institutions; and
    c) historical developments within the cultural, social, political, and economic contexts of American life as a whole.

2. To enrich the educational offerings of Oberlin College by providing all students with the opportunity for extensive work in this vital area, and thus raising the concerns and contributions of black Americans into their rightful prominence.

3. To increase the relevance of an Oberlin education to the black community and the larger society of which it is a part.

4. To heighten awareness and appreciation of African history and cultures.

In order to reach these goals, students participating in the program must fulfill the following requirements: (1) at least six hours in any combination of the Core Courses: Images of the Black Man in African, Western Civilizations, and Research Workshop in Afro-American Studies; and (2) four courses from at least three of the following areas: history (two courses offered); behavioral sciences (five courses); humanities (three courses); education (Education in the Black Community); and music. Other related courses offered include nine courses in a wide variety of areas. Certainly this is a liberal education (both expressive and instrumental).

"The separate black social group . . . provides the most powerful vehicle for the correction of the perspectives of black students and for integration on the next level and in the next phase."

Black students must know who they are and possess a positive self-image. They must have an appreciation of the tremendous contributions blacks have made throughout the history of civilization—as the birthplace of what is now referred to as Western civilization. As Professor Green of Michigan State University has said:

> The problem of college and the black student is critical. For years, college life in America has been largely dysfunctional for black students and functional for white students. . . . One highly significant change has occurred among black college students. They have completely changed their reference point. They no longer think white. Black students are beginning to think black. In essence, they no longer aspire to or cling to a white model but readily identify with their black heritage and culture. This represents an important change in perception and attitude, since, in the past, becoming educated meant that black college students had adopted

all of the attitudes, values, i.e., profit motive, etc., commensurate with white middle-class life.[7]

Points of Disagreement

"In our judgment, only a minority of black high school graduates will enter college to major or concentrate in black studies."

In my judgment this is incorrect. In the past, few students majored in African studies because few courses were offered by the colleges and universities, especially by those predominantly white, and little use could be made of such a major, even if you went into teaching. However, with the awakening of America and its institutions of higher learning (an awakening largely to be credited to black students), American educators at any level will not be able to omit this area from the curriculum. Witness the recent investigations made by the Congress on the treatment of minorities in the textbooks of our land, the provisions of the Civil Rights Act, and the work of the Civil Rights Commission. Yes, there will be a place for those majoring in black studies.

"Bridging education is being promoted by others in the education field and—we shall see—is a complex and difficult matter, but these factors neither explain nor justify the almost total disregard by the black studies movement of the need for such education."

Most black educators have noted the need for strengthening the general background of many black students who come from inferior high schools, taught by inferior teachers, in inferior surroundings, and with limited materials. The literature is replete with examples of this concern. To name only two: Edmund Gordon and Doxey Wilkerson's "Compensatory Education for the Disadvantaged" and the entire Summer 1967 issue of the *Journal of Negro Education.*

"To state that ours is a 'credential society' and to imply that how well one is trained matters little so long as he has a degree is a dangerous half-truth."

Of course, all of us agree with that, but I have listed this under points of disagreement because I hear an inference that black studies programs are inferior, not worthy of a degree. Every college professor knows that a course or a program is as good as the faculty that teaches it and the

[7] Robert L. Green, "College and the Black Student," *Working Papers for: Revolution in the Inner City,* mimeographed report of an Intercollegiate Conference Sponsored by the Oberlin College Alliance for Black Culture, p. 1.

library that furnishes the documented materials. I am willing to wager that some of the black studies programs will be the best programs on the campus, especially when it is realized that students will take the courses because they *want to,* not because they are *required to.*

"Since most Negroes [*we prefer the term 'black' for psychological and sociological reasons*] *will seek a place in American society . . . , they must become prepared to live in it. Designing an education based on the assumption that they will choose to retreat from the society seems unsupported by . . . evidence . . ."*

The pressure to institute black studies programs does not carry with it the assumption that blacks wish to remove themselves from American society. On the contrary, many black educators believe that what we need to develop is not necessarily an integrated society but a multiracial society, in which individuals can maintain their identity, maintain their blackness, maintain their whiteness or redness without social or economic sanctions. We should push for a multiracial society in which differences are appreciated and respected.

"Schools whose students are largely from disadvantaged backgrounds might devote more time to ethnic studies, while largely middle-class white schools might include this topic in classes on American history or society."

This statement is erroneous and dangerous. Black studies are *about* black people, but *not just for* black people. In fact I agree with a young black college student attending one of the "better" colleges in the United States when he said:

> When one looks at the entire situation he finds black-student demands being met by courses that, by right, should have been in the curriculum in the first place; in effect, those who truly benefit are white students as their education becomes more pertinent to the world scene.

It was gratifying to learn that at Michigan State some of the white students established a group to support the Black Student Alliance and to end white racism. The emergence of this group is highly significant and important. White students must act if they are to contribute to the amelioration of social injustice in American life.

Areas of Omission

I shall list three areas not treated by Dr. Etzioni that I deem highly important, although because of time and space limitations I shall not discuss them.

1. Present procedures for selecting faculty almost preclude finding truly "prepared" personnel for black studies inasmuch as most universities have not awarded doctorates for African and Afro-American studies. There must be more flexibility in this area.

2. The black colleges and universities have been in the vanguard in this area for many years. Black colleges still enroll the largest number of black students and can serve as real leaders in the field of black studies. In a study made by Hanes Walton, Jr., in 1967–68 of "African and Afro-American Courses in Negro Colleges," he found that 43 offered courses in Negro history, 22 offered courses on Africa, and 3 had full-fledged African studies programs, one leading to an M.A. in that field.

3. The greatest need for change is to be found in faculty attitudes. Prejudice still abounds among faculties, and there is great lack of knowledge about the black man. (After all, these teachers are the products of universities which had no black studies.) Too much cannot be said in favor of sensitivity training for every *faculty* member. Students learn not only what they are taught, but also what they feel. (Feelings are facts.)

Finally, if we are to achieve the kind of democracy in our education Dewey recommended as one "free and with full participation of all its members," and "one that is constantly reconstructing and reorganizing its experiences," then we should welcome the surge for black studies on our campuses.

Meeting the Needs of Black Students

ROBERT D. CROSS

I FIND MYSELF largely in agreement with the thrust of Professor Etzioni's paper, and wish, first, to underline two main areas in which I generally endorse his findings. Then I shall move to two aspects of the black studies movement which I think engender the most faculty (and administration) concern.

Etzioni rightly insists that the demands of society must affect, though not completely determine, the direction in which our colleges and universities move. His analysis of the interrelationship between what I would call liberal arts education and what he calls instrumental preparation is unfortunately abbreviated, but I don't question either his sense that society will be importunate in requiring a great increase in instrumental skills or his description of the kind of skills which will be demanded. I accept, too, his unstated premise that most black students will want their college education to help them acquire some of these skills in order to fit them for the real economic action of the future.

I am less sure than Etzioni that America in the next few decades, any more than America in the past, will be unambiguous about the norms of pluralist democracy. To me, the genius of American history has been that immigrant groups—with the conspicuous exception of non-Europeans— have been allowed to remain differentiated socially and culturally during the years that they moved politically and economically into the mainstream of our society. The professed ideal of America has been the melting pot—rapid, total assimilation. I hope that America will regard its black citizens—now that the second, and more profound emancipation is taking place—in accord with its experience, and not its popular logic. I believe deeply that cultural pluralism is more likely to produce civic peace, individual freedom, and a benign evolution toward a truly egalitarian society than are policies that amount to marching orders toward immediate, total assimilation. Cultural pluralism applied to campus life means, I think, integrated classrooms (*especially* in black studies) and a considerable amount of voluntary social separation. Most colleges have, for years, provided centers for foreign students, without compelling foreign students to frequent them or preventing the other students from participating. A similar logic has justified Newman Clubs, Hillel Clubs, and, at least in their modern version, fraternities and sororities. Logic also provides a compelling argument for providing a social-cultural center for those black students who wish to have one. Because a great deal of learning goes on in dormitories, I hope that there will be no need for racial separation there, whatever the legal position turns out to be.

Etzioni somewhat underestimates the depth of the desire of many black students for expressive education, education that may help strengthen their sense of personal identity and ethnic pride. As he and Arthur Lewis and many others have contended, this sense is more readily and deeply inculcated long before young people are ready for college by family or by schoolteachers, whose relation to students is less fragmented and piecemeal than that of college faculty. Still, many black students do arrive in college feeling these needs acutely, and probably this situation will continue for many years to come. Colleges understandably might prefer to disavow a responsibility better assumed by others; but in a society which makes attending college virtually a requirement, and in an academic world where no college wishes to exclude any source of potential talent, it is probably inevitable that every college will have to respond to this residual obligation. Every college will have to concern itself to an important degree with much besides the cognitive, which Etzioni believes is its proper domain.

I think Etzioni also underestimates the degree to which advocates of black studies have assumed leadership in the long-overdue protest against the traditional curriculum and pedagogy of American colleges. Some of this protest stems from the desire to influence more directly the affective, or expressive, domain, referred to previously. But much of it arises out of doubt that colleges have claimed even that limited autonomy from society's demands that is properly theirs and from the suspicion that where the college seeks to serve either society or the individual, it does not do so very efficiently or thoughtfully. Some advocates of black studies, of course, expropriated these criticisms of present practice rather indiscriminantly, and their own proposals are not always free from the blemishes they excoriate. But the black studies movement has found allies and emulators because they recognized that black studies amounted to a criticism of practice much in need of critical review.

A large proportion of faculty and administration malaise about black studies seems to stem from these last two considerations. Both the insistence that collegiate studies be responsive to the affective needs of students *and* the insinuation that black studies may be only the first stage in a radical reconsideration of curriculum and pedagogy are likely to seem profoundly threatening. Some faculty members are wholly sympathetic to adding the cognitive aspects of black studies to the curriculum but draw back from what they see as the subversive implications of the context in which that change is embedded. In addition, importunate demands for black studies have sometimes antagonized faculty by forcing them to be negotiators, if not policemen, rather than scholars and teachers. That students frequently take the lead in calling for change in the character of college education strikes many faculty members as an intolerable confusion of roles.

PART FOUR

THE PUBLIC INTEREST

Higher Education and Community Services

HAROLD L. ENARSON

JUST POSSIBLY some institution of the higher learning in this nation is indifferent to its community obligations and only vaguely aware of demands that colleges and universities unleash their immense intellectual resources in an all-out assault on the problems of urban America. It seems unlikely. Stung by the goading of critics, the conscience of the academic community has been aroused, and in small towns and big cities our institutions are searching for ways to be "part of the action." And action there is—restless action that walks and runs and marches, sometimes timidly and sometimes recklessly, in all directions. It is action that reaches out to the great burdens of the cities and, for that reason, almost inescapably touches the raw nerve of racial tension, racial discord, racial aspiration.

The efforts to help are typically American—a composite of compassion and condescension; of professionalism and amateurism; of caution and boldness. But the dominant mood is "Let's try . . . let's take the risk . . . we will learn as we go." It appears we are awakened from a long sleep, that we are ready to embark on an academic New Deal on behalf of the neglected in urban America and commit our intellectual resources to the battle for the cities.

No inventory of the new community services can be fully complete,[1] for too much is happening. The Ivy League schools and the state universities compete in admitting blacks, Chicanos, Indians. The professional schools— law, medicine, nursing, social work, and the like—claim the inner city and

---

[1] The variety of efforts to save the city defies brief description. Samples suggest their reach: Rutgers has experimented with an urban extension program, with aid (initially) from the Ford Foundation. Columbia, again with Ford Foundation aid, has discovered Harlem and committed $10 million or more to action programs. Federal City College has begun, as one project, neighborhood instruction in nutrition, budgeting, public speaking, and similar subjects for housewives and working men. Cleveland State University sponsors workshops for black entrepreneurs starting small businesses, organizes leadership training for staff in voluntary agencies, and offers short courses for supervisory personnel at City Hall. New York City adventures with storefront colleges, and public higher education in the District of Columbia offers college-level instruction in the graduate training schools of the ghetto, the prisons.

241

the nearby neighborhood as their laboratory and the beneficiary of new initiatives in service as well as training. The urban universities, newly sensitive to being "walled cities" within the city, discover concern for the slums that threaten their growth and even their survival. Many of the multiversities, long indifferent to the small towns they are accustomed to dominate, affirm a concern for improved community relations. Universities that have trained national police forces overseas now turn to training local police in community relations. Hardly a college or university cannot point to new community service programs, in housing and health, job training, leadership training, community relations. And we are giving new interpretations to the old categories: adult education, continuing education, general extension.

But is there not something a bit disconcerting, even disturbing, in all this? We all seem to be in a big fret about "community services," which it has become fashionable to place in the context of the black-white crisis. (The news media practically compel such concentration of attention.) Harvard, Columbia, Berkeley, City College in New York, Rutgers, and so on—is it not obvious that virtually every major urban university is uneasy as it rubs against the black or brown ghetto?

But surely the complex interactions of higher education and its communities go far beyond the concerns dictated by the instant melodrama of the news media. It is not escapism from the flame and gunpowder of an agonizing present to insist that issues of "community service" embrace more than the relocation of fugitives from urban renewal, rescue efforts in the nearby ghetto, or academic onslaughts on the problems of urban decay and decline. It is not simply old-fashioned innocence which insists that the resonance from the community includes much other than the now-now-now voices of militant minorities. And commentary that fails to deal with Boise, Albuquerque, and Chattanooga along with New York, Los Angeles, and Chicago will do little to illuminate interactions that transcend the immediate, the urgent, and the dramatic.

Traditional Services

The colleges and universities are not latecomers to community service. It is a premise of publicly supported institutions, especially land-grant institutions, that community service is natural, inevitable, and right. As for the private institutions, they wear bifocals; even as they proclaim their national role, they seek to be good neighbors.

Let's acknowledge first that in entertainment activities the American college and university provides a major community service: football and basketball, theater and dance—the culture low and the culture high. The entertainment role of higher education may be footnoted in the literature of education, but its functions are headlined in local newspapers and constitute a substantial, continuing service to the community.

The adult education programs are only vaguely familiar to most faculty and students, who tend to be largely unaware of the magnitude and variety of the activities of a division of continuing education. (The range is so great as to suggest an unstated commitment of the higher learning to instruction in any topic not clearly immoral or patently illegal.) Yet these extraordinarily large and ambitious efforts undoubtedly are designed "to serve the community."

Continuing education has long been genuinely innovative and flexible in the delivery of instructional services. Part-time teachers are employed; competence as well as professional credentials may be given weight. Instruction is tailored to the educational requirements of clients; customer satisfaction is thought important; the fifty-minute lecture and the quarter or semester unit are often abandoned for the short course, the workshop, the conference. In adult extension programs, our large universities—especially the land-grant universities—have truly extended their intellectual resources beyond the campus in service to the community. The history of the land-grant institutions is rich with example of concern with community so strong as to seem (to some) obsessive. Much the same can be said for urban universities about their new community services, especially to the ghetto. Urban universities have developed literally hundreds of new programs seeking to reach groups that have gone unattended.[2]

The Troubles on the Doorstep

If the reader twitches impatiently at this outline of the sweep and magnitude of our intimate engagement with community service, it is because in

---

[2] These and other visible commitments to community service obscure the massive, historic, taken-for-granted commitments. The academic landscape is littered with schools of mining and metallurgy serving dying industries. Our business colleges, engineering colleges, and schools of pharmacy are established, designed, and perpetuated in service to the requirements of local industry. In practically every state there are small, uneconomic, academically weak community colleges or university branches and centers catering to local pride and statehouse politics. (A campus provides construction contracts, dependable payrolls, a white-collar labor force, and markets for the service industries. Higher education is the new smokeless industry, only slightly less coveted than an electronics plant. Surely this is all-out service to the community.)

these frenzied and anxious days we are obsessed with current definitions of crises (nowadays the word seldom comes in the singular). The SDS, the blacks, and the Establishments are at one with City Hall and liberal academic types in asking urgently what the university is prepared to do, *right now,* about racial warfare, about black capitalism, about community disintegration, about urban renewal and human renewal. Is the university prepared to take responsibility for the relocation of people uprooted by campus expansion; to provide urban extension agents to tackle directly the complex pile-up of human problems; to extend its treasure trove of intellectual resources to the poor, and the sick, and the blacks; to roll up its gowned sleeves and take the measure of urban crises—congested transportation, decaying houses, vanishing neighborhoods, disintegrating social systems?

You will remember a game we played as children that begins with the cry, "Here I come, *ready or not.*" That phrase captures the human reality of the community demand for help. For in our deeply troubled major cities, there are angry men and women who are saying, "Here we are; we want your help, ready or not." The message is increasingly clear and emphatic: "We will not let you stand aloof and apart; you will serve us or you will burn."

What is our response? What should it be? It is a rare major college or university that does not eagerly present a laundry list testifying to its deepening involvement in the urban crisis. One large public urban university, stung by criticism of noninvolvement, issued a special report listing a potpourri of activities presumably responsive to the crisis of that community. What may be lacking in precise targeting of objectives is made up in exuberant effort. Our services to the crisis city have us in what John Gardner described as "a good kind of trouble."

> The good kind of trouble [he writes] comes from being on the move, from being acutely aware of problems, from the confusion of too many people trying to solve the problem in too many ways all at once, too many critics talking too loudly, too many things changing too rapidly.[3]

We bring to the task of community uplift Boy Scout eagerness, secular zeal, and liberal compassion. As True Believers in the Baconian notion of Knowledge as Social Power, we are not afraid to dream the impossible dream of social salvation in race relations, political salvation in community relations, and economic salvation in development. We bring as well the

---

[3] Quoted in *Stanford Alumni Almanac,* April 1969.

intolerable weight of a guilty conscience, for have we not rejected blacks in the name of high standards, trained Peace Corps workers in the arts of community development for Brazil but not Harlem, and done research in Calcutta and Pakistan to the neglect of Watts and Hough. It *is* a "good kind of trouble." It feels good to try, to be at work.

Which Part of the Action?

But are we on the right track? Should the inner city or even the city be the new sharp focus of our commitments to better service to the community? And do direct action programs represent the best contribution that colleges and universities can make? Have we the administrative capacity, the intellectual resources, and the dollars to make a difference in the grey wastelands we call the inner cities? Surely these questions are basic for colleges and universities everywhere, especially those whose campus boundaries touch the ghetto or whose aspirations are intimately bound up with the renewal of the city.

There are strong arguments for extreme caution on the part of institutions seeking to be "part of the action." These include the thinness of academic resources, the absence of regular dollar support, the frailty of existing strategies for direct intervention.

Thinness of Resources. It is folly to assume that even the large urban universities have significant numbers of faculty members both qualified and eager to divert their energies to the problems of the cities. Although many faculty share a sense of social concern, few have scholarly skills relevant to the city. Even fewer have a flair for operational programs in the ghetto. And still fewer are willing to turn aside from the academic career ladder and reorient their skills as well as their priorities. Unleashing the intellectual resources of the scholarly community may be a bit like unleashing Chiang Kai-shek; it is best talked about but not done. This is not to denigrate the talents of academic man; it is simply to say that with rare exceptions these talents are strictly academic. For the most part the scholars with a taste and talent for direct action already are where the action is—in the many and diverse programs that government at all levels has mounted on the problems of the cities.

The Absence of Regular Dollar Support. It is tempting, but fatal, to disregard the sources of educational dollars. Neither in publicly nor privately supported institutions is there predictable funding of good works done in the name of community service. With few exceptions, all community service programs for the inner city are funded by "soft dollars" from foundations and governmental agencies. Such dollars are small, unpredictable, and temporary—hardly the base upon which to build strong, continuing programs with maximum, long-range impact. We should not be mesmerized by ritual incantations about the great triumvirate of Teaching, Research, and Public Service. With the exception of subsidies for sports and agricultural extension, the "public service" dimension is largely without direct, continuing dollar support. The great bulk of the dollars go, as they must, to operate the instructional program and to underwrite research. Regardless of how sympathetic individual academic administrators may be to the ideal of community service, the intense competition for funds leaves them little choice. Given the budget crunch, the amounts available for community service must be relatively trifling—now and in the foreseeable future.[4]

Frailty of Existing Strategies for Direct Intervention. Our colleges and universities are now the primary source of the trained manpower at work on the problems of the city. They prepare the experts and specialists who man the dozens of public and private agencies already at work on every front—health, housing, jobs, transportation, community development. But it is now alleged that contributions to education and training are not investment enough, nor is the involvement that accompanies field work or research in urban affairs enough. We are now invited into the ghetto to engage in a variety of "community development projects"—to upgrade leadership skills in neighborhood organizations, to prepare the inexperienced to launch small businesses, to advise on delicate matters of community control of the public schools, to bring the gospel of good nutrition to the poor and uninformed, to plan job clinics, family planning clinics, and new patterns of health services.

In short, we are invited to create imaginative programs, primarily of a self-help nature, that will succeed in doing what dozens of well-established public and private agencies have failed to do—reverse the downward spiral of physical and human decay in the ghetto. It is not too much to suggest that the university is asked to become a kind of general-purpose social action agency. There is one big hitch in all this. There is little evidence that

[4] For example, in the past decade, the best of the major universities have developed an international dimension. Note that they have done so with Federal AID funds and foundation grants. So far state legislatures are not persuaded that "foreign affairs" are here to stay and that the international dimension is a proper investment in strengthened education and a brighter national future.

our colleges and universities have mastered the strategies for intervening skillfully and with good results in the life of the ghetto.[5]

The Ghetto—Human Emergency Disaster Area

The long and short of it is that the universities, laboring under severe shortages of manpower and dollars and without effective strategies of intervention, are now being summoned to take upon themselves the burden of the ghetto. Now we should be perfectly clear, within the limitations of our intellectual perception and our capacity for empathy, what the ghetto is all about. It is the place where you live or work because there is no escape—no escape to better housing, better schools, better police protection. It is the place where every failure of society and the individual is cruelly magnified, where the odds are most heavily stacked against the integrity or even the safety of person. And finally, it is the place where the despair of the afflicted is rivaled only by the despair of the outsiders who try to help.

Admittedly the ghetto is a fascinating laboratory for the inquisitive researcher. The targets for study are boundless: landlord-tenant relationships, patterns of income distribution, the anatomy of both legal and illegal violence, forms of political expression, and so on. The life style of the ADC mother, the hustler, the mortician, the landlord, the ward politician, the Black Nationalist deserves the kind of sympathetic exposure that only an Oscar Lewis has been able to provide, and that for a foreign culture. (The historian of the future will puzzle over the antics of a generation of Americans who sent their young to live and study in overseas foreign cultures, yet was blind to the distinctive and essentially foreign cultures only a few miles from the affluent suburbs.)

Surely the university ought not to accept as a working principle the in-

[5] Community development caught fire as an export commodity. We trained cadres of Peace Corps in the art of community development for rescue efforts in the *barrios* and *favellas* of Brazil and Costa Rica, the slums of Monrovia, and the isolated mountain villages of Peru. Our limited successes were widely publicized; the Peace Corps *had* to succeed. Americans themselves indulged in the willing suspension of disbelief. The failures were concealed from us—and even from the Peace Corps trainees themselves. (They were taught that frustration and a sense of failure was a predictable personal problem, which may have diverted attention from the *reality* of failure.) In short, we exported a skill that we had never really perfected in the dingy, dirty, dismal backyards of our own cities. We are now long overdue in being honest with ourselves.

No one doubts that eager and dedicated Americans of all ages can make a slight, temporary difference in the life of a few persons. But there is no hard evidence in support of the gospel of community development. For our programs of community development rest, at bottom, not on intellectual constructs and verified proof but rather on mushy social gospel: on *faith*. To repeat—the university lacks what is most required—skill that produces results.

definite continuation of ghetto living for ever larger numbers of minority groups in the big cities. Are we to be only clinicians fumbling with the human debris of social disaster areas? Are we prepared only to study the malfunctioning of schools and job markets, the deterioration of families and social systems, the growing triumph of violence as a way of life, the steady erosion of any sense of community? One fervently hopes not. For if this is to be the primary response of our universities to the agonies of ghetto America, we shall indeed deserve the very fate that we most fear: to be irrelevant in a time of revolutionary change and accelerating crisis. Bringing snippets of knowledge and fragments of rescue programs to the ghetto is less relevant than the load of coal provided in an earlier day by the ward politicians. At least the coal warmed bodies; few of the "action programs" of the universities warm either body or soul.

The charge to America is not to extend token programs of assistance to the ghetto, nor to do tiny and timorous things to make life a wee bit more bearable for a few persons. *The ghetto is a human emergency disaster area.* Tokenism won't do, whether in slight reductions of the rat population or slight increases in the clothing allowance for the children of ADC mothers. We have long since passed the point where the ghetto "community" can bootstrap itself into jobs, city services, decent homes, and dignity with the aid of technical assistance services, whether by public agencies or by university extension services.

Our colleges and universities do a disservice to the residents of the ghetto, to the society at large, and to themselves by pretending that "community development" and other rescue efforts can make more than a slight difference in the accelerating deterioration of life in the ghetto. The ghetto needs help, but the help must come through massive organized programs funded by government: to rebuild housing, to provide jobs as well as training for jobs, to provide an array of human renewal services.

Renewal in Instruction and Research

In this great task of renewal, the colleges and universities can play an important role. But it is not that of a free-wheeling social service agency or a staging ground for revolutionary politics.[6] The distinctive role of the

[6] In the long run, support from the public treasury must correlate rather closely with what the public wants to buy. In this connection, see the excellent essay by Karl Kaysen, *The Higher Learning, the Universities, and the Public* (Princeton, N.J.: Princeton University Press, 1969), in which he argues that "Some readjustment in the relation between the universities and their public sources of support which brings the purposes of donors and recipients together is inevitable, whether in the direction of finding new bases of support, or new uses for funds, or both" (p. 4).

university, perhaps never more important in our history, is to prepare the "action intellectuals" with the courage and competence to operate sophisticated renewal programs of every conceivable kind. The greatest service that the university can render to the community—and to state and nation as well—is to reaffirm in new and creative ways its primary and priority tasks: instruction and research. These are the tasks for which the colleges and universities are uniquely equipped and which are beyond the competence of any other institution in our society.

For academic man, the reform and renewal of the city and the society begins with the reform and the renewal of the university. The university will truly serve the community in the most effective way only as it clarifies its purposes and drastically reorders its priorities. It is one of the great ironies of the age that our finest universities have brought the gospel of institution-building to the underdeveloped societies, yet have failed to remold their own programs and priorities so as to serve better a society which itself struggles with massive problems of development. It compounds irony that the institution which is the prime source of the new knowledge that alone permits intelligent response to rapid and often disastrous change is itself least capable of quick and flexible response to new conditions. We struggle, Gulliver-like, against countless constraints that inhibit responsiveness and slow down change to the pace of the snail. The academic guild system—reinforced by faculty control, doubly reinforced by departmental organization, and triply reinforced by the accrediting agencies—makes for a sluggish conservatism. The upshot is a tragic lack of responsiveness.

The best-kept secret of higher learning is that much of the curriculum is badly out of focus and out of date. Much of our instruction is not tailored either to the talents and interests of our students or to the changing requirements of our society. All too often the profile of class offerings and requirements reflects for the most part the tastes and preferences of the faculty. It is hardly surprising that a growing number of frustrated students cry for "relevance."

Our desire to mobilize our intellectual resources in service to the city provides us with the opportunity to reorder our priorities and to renew our institutions. What the city most needs from us is knowledge and understanding, not action initiatives. And with all our efforts, both vigorous and feeble, at community service programs and the like, we are not bringing knowledge and understanding to bear on the life of the city. The most productive, most prestigious scholars—along with the best minds—of the regular departments are not yet truly engaged. With exceptions that are too rare, the best minds tend to be prisoners of their craft, their tradition, and the current intellectual fashions of their craft. Perhaps in exhaustion or frustration, we have come to accept—sometimes reluctantly—the accelerating fragmentation of the intellectual enterprise. The cult of the expert and the specialist reigns triumphant. The intellectual vice of insularity is transmuted into pragmatic virtue. Only the students are prepared to declare that "the King has no trousers," that the fragments and shards of a deepening specialization fail to provide anything approximating intellectual coherence.

The State of Three New Services

It is not unfair to say that we have provided only the appearance of bringing our intellectual resources to the battle for the survival of the cities. The sham is apparent in the three most common academic responses to the urban crisis: black studies programs, centers and institutes for urban studies, and rescue efforts for the academically disadvantaged. They share the common characteristics of being rooted in a passionate desire to "do something," and they tend to stress immediate service to "the community." But to date they have required only minimal involvement and an infinitesimal investment on the part of the overwhelming majority of faculty members.

Bluntly, too much is made of much too little. The black experience *is* neglected in the university curriculum and the winds of change are long overdue. But black studies programs may easily become a new kind of tokenism and a new and dangerous form of academic and racial separatism —separate *and* unequal. It would be madness for hundreds of colleges and universities suddenly to offer ancient Chinese literature if (*a*) the field were not reasonably well developed and (*b*) enough qualified faculty were not available. Yet the collective commitments of our universities to black studies programs exhaust many times over the extremely limited pool of persons qualified to teach in these programs. The short-term effect of the intensive raiding has been to force salaries up and redistribute scarcity. And it is the weakest and most needy sector, the predominantly Negro institutions of the South, that suffer the greatest losses.

Urban phenomena have also been neglected, but the mere creation of a center or institute in urban studies (too often as a result of administration edict rather than faculty initiative) creates much appearance and little reality.

As for the academically disadvantaged, the marginal students (choose your own euphemism to describe poorly prepared minority-group students), it is painfully evident that the college doors have been effectively barred to many who, through no fault of their own, are educational cripples. But to lower admission standards without at the same time making significant changes in academic requirements, along with generous provision for tutorial and remedial work and financial aid, is double deception. It tricks the disadvantaged into believing they can make it, when in fact many cannot, and it tricks the institution into the belief that it does good by doing bad.

In each of the three new "services"—black studies, institutes for urban studies, and open doors for the disadvantaged—the universities essentially graft on programs without connecting the programs into the vital energies of the university. This process is hardly a new phenomenon. Programs of international service have long suffered the same fate. All these become "added activities" that are never quite absorbed into the mainstream of university activities. Thus we hide, even from ourselves, the continuing failure to commit our intellectual resources in new and vital ways to new and vital tasks.

Is the task beyond our reach? Do we confront what one cynic, parodying American optimism, called "insurmountable opportunities"? Absolutely not! The American university responds slowly, but it *does* respond. Over the years, the university has either generated or absorbed important new program elements: the land-grant idea, continuing education, new professions such as nursing and social work, new cross-discipline fields such as labor and industrial relations, materials science, and the like. Moreover, new disciplines and subdisciplines are constantly created and are absorbed into the lifestream of the university. The Federal and foundation dollar has been a prime power source for new program initiatives. In medicine, for example, the major Federal commitments of the 1950s have created a large cadre of medical scientists and made possible a major thrust in health research. Surely the curriculum need not be a grab bag, a product of logrolling by vested interests. It can and must respond to the emerging needs of society. The developing societies believe this to be true of their new universities; we should determine that it be true for our universities.

No Time for Dangerous Distraction

The university's task is nothing less than to think anew across the whole spectrum of the social process. Definitional squabbles need not detain us; the "urban crisis" is essentially shorthand for the crisis in human affairs, for increasingly men live in an urban culture. But the revival of hope is as much dependent on the control of DDT on the factory farms as upon pollution control in the city, as much dependent upon the control of the migration from the farms to the city as upon the migration from the city to the suburbs. On this small spacecraft earth, where the Apollo spacemen viewed the first "earthrise" in human history, no process, no discovery, no weapon, no crop, no fear, no process of politics or economics or life itself is cut off from anything else. Everything connects and relates—if only we have the wit to perceive it.

The challenge of the city must not be the exclusive domain of the social scientists and the engineers. The systems approach may provide for more economical and efficient mechanisms for moving traffic, for processing the business of the city, and even for constructing mass housing more cheaply. But until the deeper disorders of the human spirit are attended, we simply move further toward what Lewis Mumford calls the "mega-machine," where the goal is "the constant increase of order, power, predictability, and above all, control," [7] and at the price of shrinking freedom of the individual.

The Roman candles of technology that light the skies (and the astronauts' heaven) are the triumph of the fading past. The young, who "have the future in their bones," know that the new life they seek lies somewhere beyond technology. It was a philosopher-president, Mason Gross of Rutgers University, who asked that we discard the deceptive metaphors that lead us to think of the city as a machine (obviously malfunctioning) or as a biological organism (obviously sick). He has suggested that we consider the city as "a psychical entity" as "the outward expression of the thoughts, sensations, emotions and values of its inhabitants, past and present." And he asks the question that philosophers and poets, along with city planners and assorted experts must ask, "What is it that is rendering the city a less and less satisfactory outward manifestation and expression of the thoughts, sensations, emotions, and values of man?" [8]

The modern predicament is communicated in many ways: in the life style of the hippies, in the sagging faith of the liberal, in the hardening anger of the put-upon lower middle class (cops and taxi drivers and George Wallace fans), in the crudely inarticulate protests of the Living Theatre, in the mingled and muddled love-hate of the radical students and the militant blacks. There is the sense of spreading chaos all about us—in the escalating violence of the cities, in the anger that lurks close beneath the surface,

---

[7] *Christian Science Monitor,* March 4, 1969, col. 1.

[8] "Urbanism and Human Values" (Address at National Conference on Urban Life, Washington, D.C., March 28, 1962), pp. 5, 8.

in the deepening cynicism of old as well as young, in the creeping collapse of faith in self as well as in system, in the challenge to legitimacy of all our institutions.

Here is raw stuff—the hot drama that underlies the cold data—which awaits the necessary renaissance of intellectual curiosity and scholarly concern. It also happens to provide the elements for an agenda, perhaps the only agenda, that will bring faculty and students genuinely together in the joint pursuit of understanding. For the best of young Americans, inarticulate in their cry for "relevance," suffer hunger for discussion and analysis that probe deeply into the human condition and the contemporary predicament.

It was not an SDS fanatic but the distinguished biologist Barry Commoner who asserted that the sciences "need to learn the lesson of *relevance,*" if we are to operate the complex systems (electrical power systems, ecological systems, and the like) on which survival depends. He wrote,

> It appears that despite frequent praise for the principle of "interdisciplinary programs" in our universities, we have not yet learned how to practice what we praise. . . . Life, as we live it, is rarely encompassed by a single academic discipline. Real problems that affect our lives and impinge on what we value rarely fit into the neat categories that appear in the college catalogue: medieval history, nuclear physics, or molecular biology. For example, to encompass in our minds the terrifying deterioration of our cities we need to know not only the principles of economics, architecture, and social planning, but also the chemistry of airsheds, the biology of water systems, and the ecology of the domestic rat and the cockroach. In a word, we need to understand science and technology that is *relevant* to the human condition.[9]

We come full circle: To be "part of the action" is not to imitate the tired ways of social service agencies already at work in the city. It is to renew the ancient partnership in learning which alone justifies the existence and the public support of the colleges and universities. Until the modern university re-establishes its credibility by relevant performance, all else—however well intentioned—is dangerous distraction.

Only as the university performs well its primary mission, the instruction of the young, can it with good conscience release fresh energies for research and for the high priority of upgrading the skills of the amateur "urbanolo-

[9] "Science, Technology and Human Values" (Address at National Conference on Emerging Universities and National Concerns, Ball State University, Feb. 7, 1968), pp. 14–15.

gists" now at work in the multiplicity of private and public agencies. In the University of Utopia, all this fits together.

Faculty and students alike must escape the formalism of the classroom and share in the fumbling, halting, groping search for deeper understanding of man and the city. And as new knowledge is created, it can be put to work.

Continuing education, targeted to upgrade the skills of those on the firing line, can grow in strength and stature.

A genuine working partnership between scholars and public officials can reinvigorate teaching even as it adds to the sophistication of public policy.

In sum, the greatest service that colleges and universities can render to the community is to deny themselves the tempting distraction of direct action and concentrate on producing the next generation of leaders. In the words of Alexander Meiklejohn, "Our final responsibility as scholars and teachers is not to the truth. It is to the people who need the truth." Do this and do it well and all else we so desperately covet has a chance of coming true.

Commentaries on

Higher Education and Community Services

BARBARA FISLER, GERARD J. MANGONE
JOSEPH F. KAUFFMAN, JOSEPH P. COSAND

Assessing Aims in Community Services

BARBARA FISLER

CRISES generally elicit rather sudden, irrational, hastily conceived, haphazardly effected, uncoordinated, and disorganized responses. The variety and multiplicity of programs, plans, and projects currently being initiated by colleges and universities seem an incontestable indication that urban problems are indeed being recognized as "critical."

Dr. Enarson has criticized the inadequacy of these responses. He has questioned the worth of such limited programs, so eagerly begun, so scantily provided for, so easily discouraging, so often unsuccessful. While attacking these token efforts, he attributes them, not to lack of sincerity of intentions, but rather to the very limited resources of our universities in terms of money, faculty, other advisory personnel, time, and *relevant* skills and knowledge. He suggests, quite validly, that the ghetto and its numerous associated ills are too complex to be combated or solved by universities and that, to quote him.

> the help must come through massive organized programs funded by government: to rebuild housing, to provide jobs as well as training for jobs, to provide an array of human renewal services.

So far, I agree with all his criticisms and conclusions. But I find some of his further comments somewhat inconsistent, or at least not well clarified. For he has proceeded to say,

> In this great task of renewal, the colleges and universities can play an important role. But it is not that of a free-wheeling social service agency. . . . The distinctive role of the university is to prepare the "action intellectuals"

255

with the courage and competence to operate sophisticated renewal programs of every conceivable kind. The greatest service that the university can render to the community and state and nation as well is to reaffirm in new and creative ways its primary and priority tasks: instruction and research. These are the tasks for which the colleges and universities are uniquely equipped. . . . What the city most needs from us is knowledge and understanding, not action initiatives.

These statements, it appears to me, contain a number of contradictory sentiments. In another section of his paper, Dr. Enarson has accused faculty and universities of being "fumbling clinicians with strictly academic talents, constrained, conservative, insular, and systems-oriented in their approach." If the faculty is accurately described in this way, how can they possibly prepare "action intellectuals"? How can they instruct in *new* and *creative* ways? Agreed that the city needs knowledge and understanding; yet without action initiatives, without direct contact with and exposure to the areas which are posing such grave problems, I fail to see how they are going to be able to change their focus and tactics either comprehensively or relevantly.

Dr. Enarson and I are agreed on the need for relevant education and research. It is simply that demanding it and practicing it are two different things. I don't see how our colleges and universities are going to make their education meaningful if they do not cope directly with meaningful realities, or at least utilize them to illustrate the complexity of finding practicable solutions. For, if nothing else, action-involvement programs do quickly awaken people to the mammoth proportions of the problems and their interdependencies.

In reviewing Dr. Enarson's criticisms of the action programs, I find that our disagreements are not on the immediate results of the programs (admittedly debatable), but rather are on what our aims should be in the first place. In other words, I agree with him when he says that tokenism won't do and that university efforts cannot possibly have the needed effect on the ghetto. But he seems to be evaluating action programs on their immediate local results. Perhaps a better and more honest approach would be to revise our goals with the realization that although current experiments cannot and will not have widespread remedial effects, they have a very real value in other ways. They do provide faculty and students alike the opportunity to escape from "the formalism of the classroom [so that they can] share in the fumbling, halting, groping search for deeper understanding of man and the city." Moreover, even if efforts are not totally successful, they do indicate involvement. Those who need help will, I'm sure, find direct action, no matter how awkward, more suitable than extended, remote research committees and statistical analyses, and the like. Involvement can mean exposure, communication, understanding.

My own experience at the American University may be valuable in illustrating this. In its College of Continuing Education, a new program involves about ten AU students (all of whom are white) and about fifty inner-city PRIDE employees. PRIDE is a black-established, independent business enterprise which trains and employs the hard-core unemployable —high school dropouts, ex-convicts, etc. PRIDE encourages and aids its employees in continuing their education in addition to maintaining their jobs. Our class is an experiment, a successful one I think. Titled "Fabric of the Social Structure," it attempts to correlate and coordinate economics, sociology, and psychology. It meets twice a week, once for a lecture, once for discussion groups. Independent of the informal aspects, the course material is solid, though at times radical according to traditional terms. The real value, particularly for the AU students, most of whom have already taken courses in the subject areas mentioned, is the contact it affords with inner-city blacks and a culture that is foreign and misunderstood. Many universities, I think, feel that remedial tutoring, special admissions, and black studies projects are benevolent acts, unselfishly offered at great sacrifice, to the disadvantaged who need them. I disagree. The whites need them too. Many, so many students want to do something for and about the disadvantaged of this country. They study politics, or sociology, or prepare for teaching. They graduate, and they realize with despair and frustration that they don't even know how to *talk* with those they want to help! They can't even communicate! Such a simple thing, yet so easily and often overlooked. My PRIDE course, as I call it, has given me a new perspective. For even as I was well acquainted with elementary economic, social, and psychological principles before taking the course, I had never *faced* head on their obvious implications. I still do not agree with all the theories or sentiments expressed in my class, but that is not important. It *is* important that I understand *why* those theories or sentiments are expressed. More and more I do.

In summary, Dr. Enarson seems to have challenged our right to intervene in the ghetto crisis when we haven't the means to achieve our desired ends; I really think the problem is one of properly and honestly identifying our aims and expectations within the framework of our capabilities and resources. And I think it is a mistake to judge action programs, and criticize them, solely on the basis of their immediate, visible local effects. Dr. Enarson has called for deeper understanding. Action programs provide contact, communication, good will, coordination, understanding, and experimental ground for more concretely successful future works.

Responding to the Needs of a Populist Society

GERARD J. MANGONE

IN A TIME when American colleges and universities have had their names plastered on the front pages of newspapers for student riots, tempestuous faculty meetings, neighborhood confrontations, and presidential resignations, rather than for their academic achievements, Harold Enarson has written a sobering, sensitive essay on the service that higher education ought to render to its community. The message, briefly, is to "cool it."

He skillfully describes the big rush of universities to get in on the action and pander to the unruly, irrational demands for total and instant reform of urban society by making a minimal investment of its intellectual and financial resources. Either blatant hypocrisy or sheer ignorance must be at work to expect that black studies programs, institutes for urban studies, or special admissions programs for marginal students can be significant responses to the urgencies of ghetto blight and the despairing spirit of American cities. Beyond this window dressing—which is like having a black man in the front office to demonstrate rectitude and relieve guilt— Dr. Enarson asks and answers the key question, "Is the university a kind of general-purpose social action agency?" He rightly points out that higher education has always embraced "community aspirations" and he cites entertainment through football, theater, and dance; the development of new practical disciplines in business and industrial technology, as well as services to agriculture through the land-grant colleges; and programs for the adult and the fully employed through continuing education. Yet I think Dr. Enarson would agree that the "community" both within and without the university gates has changed radically in recent years. Therein lies the problem.

As late as 1946 only 22 percent of young people between the ages of eighteen and twenty-one were enrolled in institutions of higher education; within twenty years the percentage had more than doubled, to 45 percent.

These students came from an ever-widening socioeconomic background and intellectual range, and virtually none had ever experienced mass warfare or mass unemployment either personally or vicariously. Even without the problem of integrating a large and deprived black population into the myths and goals of white American society, there would have been questions about the relevance of university curricula, the methods of instruction, and the organization of the university. And the very infusion of vast public monies into higher education was bound to start questions about the composition, motives, and effectiveness of universities with respect to the public concerns of a highly taxed electorate. In 1946, for every student in a privately supported institution of higher education there was one in a publicly supported institution; by 1966, for every student in a private institution there were *two* in a public institution.

Meanwhile, the community outside the gates of the university had changed radically. As the large cities attracted more and more black Americans with jobs and urban freedom, the more affluent white middle class moved to newer and suburban neighborhoods. The city universities remained, rock-rooted in their expensive buildings, their playing fields, and their traditions of educational discrimination. Contrasts between the physical, intellectual, and social components of the urban university with its immediate neighborhood became bizarre.

In my view Dr. Enarson is eminently correct and sage in his observation that bringing "snippets of knowledge and fragments of rescue programs to the ghetto" will not address the fundamental reordering of American society that is required. In fact, such breathless, hastily constructed, and uneasily funded programs may divert institutions of higher education from a candid re-examination of their own first claims to existence, namely, teaching and research. The task of higher education should be to make undergraduate and graduate teaching ever more relevant to a growing student body of diverse ages and social origins, all of whom have more access to communications and far less conviction about prevailing value systems than the faculty or the officers of a university a generation ago. The further challenge to higher education, amid all the clamor for community service, is to bring research away from stultifying, scholastic exercises, so that a substantial part of the findings may be woven into policy choices for the betterment of our cities. The genius of the scientific method is not the manipulation of sterile data, but the vibrant capacity for identifying problems, natural or social, and to propose hypotheses or solutions that can be empirically tested.

It may be unfashionable to say today, as Disraeli did in 1873, that a university is a place of light, of liberty, and of learning. The admonition of Dr. Enarson that a modern university should not try to duplicate the social agency, but rather make its ancient partnership in learning viable is good sense. No higher educational system can long escape the culture that creates and nourishes it. Training the theologian, the physician, the lawyer, and later the engineer, the teacher, artist, or businessman, has been a response to a perceived economic-social need. The preparation of undergraduates in general education about arts and sciences has always reflected norms of the "educated" man and the responsibilities of leadership in American life. On October 25, 1902, the title of Woodrow Wilson's inaugural address was "Princeton for the Nation's Service," and he, like other leading presidents of the day, saw the university, above all, as an instrument for developing the social understanding of the students, quickening their conscience, and making them eager to serve their fellow man.

The sluggishness of universities in responding to the effervescent needs of a populist society has been nicely shown in Dr. Enarson's paper. Here the entrenched structures, so admirable for another age—such as boards of trustees, the president, deans, faculty tenure, departmental organization, dormitories, endowments, student government, and so forth—must all be reviewed for their efficacy in peacefully maintaining a large, specialized cluster of scholars with a costly network of supporting services in our troubled cities. And the apparatus must also be reviewed for its capacity to maintain the confidence of the students within the gates to determine whether the structure is appropriate for the cultivation and diffusion of knowledge that is relevant to them in this distressed society of America.

Whether Dr. Enarson's conclusion—that the greatest service colleges and universities can render to the communities is a concentration upon producing the next generation of leaders—will satisfy anyone may be doubtful. The intention is clear and the spirit laudable. One might ask in a day when more than half of all young people in America will be going to college whether the word "leadership" may not be overdone. Perhaps a modern society requires a larger educated "followership": college graduates sensitive to community problems, capable of perceiving the broad issues that confront our government; college graduates rational enough to choose the men and agencies through which policy must be articulated, and confident enough to entrust political leadership with the resources to cure the diseases of the cities that sicken American life,

An operative social agency, no; a place to enlighten men about the issues of social injustice, a place to speak freely and boldly about the means for reform, a place to learn by listening, reading, exploring, and experimenting, yes, that is the role of higher education in community services.

Upgrading the Role of Instruction and Training

JOSEPH F. KAUFFMAN

HAROLD ENARSON'S PAPER holds the thesis that colleges and universities must avoid the temptation and distraction of direct action and restore their credibility in their areas of top priority—instruction of the young, and vital research. I am in sympathy with this thesis as long as it does not mean a retreat to isolation, insulation, and exclusion and I want to make clear my own reasoning in arriving at a similar conclusion.

Colleges and universities should and will serve the community in countless ways beyond classroom instruction of college-age youth. Upward Bound programs, inservice training for teachers, short courses to update various professionals, and the like, are part of the service orientation of institutions. My own view is that we have not put forth fully enough our own natural talents in upgrading the instructional and training roles we could play in the community. Part of the racial crisis is the immediate need for creating educational adequacy in all our schools, including those which seem most formidable—inner-city schools.

Let us take for granted then that all educators of good will now assume this responsibility as properly theirs. Without further exhortation I am then able to come to a clear line separating those community services which are essentially instructional and those which require an institutional involvement in the management of applied programs or even in direct action commitments to a particular point of view. It is at this point that I arrive at a viewpoint similar to that of Harold Enarson.

Dr. Enarson's conclusion is a courageous one for it was not so long ago that contrary positions were stated with unequivocal zeal. (They were in fact the vogue.) For example, the 1967 annual meeting of the Council included a section on "Public Service and Education," and the author of the major paper, John J. Corson, and some of the commentators took positions advocating that universities become instruments of direct social action. They would assume the responsibility of "applying the new knowledge that will shape the society in which our grandchildren live." [1]

To be sure, there are Federal programs that call for institutional involvement in all kinds of efforts at solving our many social problems. Yet I sense a new countervailing force which sees the government's exploitation of faculty talent as potentially counterproductive. After all, the government is also legitimately interested in student unrest and in creating viable institutions of higher learning.

It has been reliably reported that President Nixon is enamored of the views of a Professor S. J. Tonsor of the University of Michigan, as they were elaborated in a speech given in April 1969. The President circulated copies of the speech to the senior members of his administration with a memorandum indicating his full support for Professor Tonsor's analysis of the problems of higher education.[2] That analysis states, among other things, that

> Both big government and big education face a crisis of confidence and they face this crisis for basically the same reason; they have done a good many things they should never have attempted, things for which they were totally unequipped.

Professor Tonsor goes on to say:

> If the institutional aspirations of education are once more to become credible, universities must regain a sense of modesty and a selectivity in the formulation of their objectives. They cannot be all things to all men . . . to compound the problem now by expecting the university to become a court of last resort for the solution of the major social problems of our time will only deepen the crisis which the university faces. Until there is a restoration of genuine educational purpose, there will be no restoration of confidence by society in its institutions of higher education.

I find myself moved by calls for a new sense of modesty for higher education and this is one reason for my support of Dr. Enarson's statement.

Two models are constantly used by advocates of university intervention in the resolution of social problems. One is the technical or scientific model, which has produced innumerable accomplishments of university

---

[1] John J. Corson, "Public Service and Higher Education: Compatibility or Conflict?" in *Whose Goals for American Higher Education?*, ed. Dobbins and Lee (Washington: American Council on Education, 1968), pp. 90 ff.

[2] See *Higher Education and National Affairs,* April 25, 1969.

faculty and laboratory that have revolutionized our technology *and* our society. From DDT to the atomic bomb, from solid-state, transistorized electronics to space science, universities have created and applied knowledge to transform both our *way* and our understanding of life.

But we can all too easily forget that such developments support our industry, our armed forces, and the policies of our government. They are seen as increasing the power of our established order, not threatening it. Kenneth Clark has pointed out that attempts to develop a precise form of "social technology," based on the physical science model, would be difficult indeed. Rather than enhance the power and prestige of an educational institution, an effective social technology could be expected to elicit controversy and conflict as it threatened the *status quo*.[3] (This presumes that a social technology can be created with the same degree of objectivity and allegiance to rationality as the technology of physical phenomena.) Further, I must add my own apprehensions about institutions of higher learning aligning themselves with specific political or ideological positions. The *critical* function is crucial to colleges and universities: as an organization, the university must foster the critical spirit including self-criticism, and allegiance to official positions or approaches is impossible in a truly free institutional environment.[4]

The second model that is often used (and Dr. Enarson is no exception) is that of the land-grant institutions. With special emphasis on agriculture and the rural extension agent, the model is held up as thoroughly applicable for urban problems along with its corollary—urban extension agents. I too admire the contributions of the Morrill Act and the land-grant idea of service. But we all too often gloss over the egregious human errors and failures as we praise technical accomplishments. I believe the record will show that the land-grant agricultural colleges and their community services were uniquely successful in introducing scientific methods to agriculture, vastly increasing crop yields, and industrializing agriculture.

Yet, paradoxically, in the process of "improving" farming, the human problems and the human fallout were virtually ignored or unpredicted. In the process of becoming a unit of surplus production, the family farm— based on subsistence and the preservation of the extended family—was doomed! Richard Hofstader[5] notes that at least half the nation's sub-

---

[3] Clark, "Toward a Defense of Non-Relevant Education." Commencement address, Amherst College, June 1969.

[4] For an excellent discussion of this subject, see Kenneth Keniston, "Criticism and Social Change" in *Whose Goals for American Higher Education?*, pp. 145 ff.

[5] Hofstader, *The Age of Reform* (New York: Alfred Knopf, 1966), pp. 123 ff.

sistence farmers failed to prosper with the advent of scientific agriculture. The competition for cash crops and surplus production was won by those most able to enlarge their operations and make them more efficient. The losers were bought out by the larger units, and they became tenants, share-croppers, migrants, and, finally, flooded our unprepared cities where we now regard them as "social dynamite." (And we ask those same universities to "do something.")

When Harold Enarson expresses doubt about whether we have mastered the strategies for intervening skillfully, I share his doubt—profoundly.

The context here is higher education and the racial crisis. Obviously, the discussion is not whether to engage in community services, for at least most of us who head public institutions regard our functions as being in the public service. Within the context of this discussion, how can we be of greater service?

We can improve our community relationships to the end that all races and economic groups see our public institutions as also theirs. Making the inner-city residents familiar with a campus and its resources should be one goal. Working to make strangers welcome and comfortable on our campuses is a corollary. No citizen should be a stranger to our campus.

We can reassess our admissions policies and our academic support services for those who require assistance to start college. And we can do this without lessening what we have come to call "standards." A substantial increase in the number of black students may heighten the "racial crisis" for a while, but until the value of higher education is experienced for a generation, there can be no substantial amelioration of the basic resentment which exists.

We can reform our teaching and our curriculum as a community service. Our undergraduate, general education programs in particular should have as their thrust an emphasis on compassion for the human condition; an emphasis on developing in students the capacity and desire to understand and resolve social and human conflict *peacefully;* an emphasis on the responsibility of implementing egalitarian principles. If we cannot do this in our instruction of the young, how can we do it in the community? And we can insist that the majority of our students confront the racism that is within them, as a part of learning about themselves.

Finally, we can recommit ourselves to the noble purposes for which we were created: to develop in the young the talent, conscience, self-respect, and courage to be responsible adults. The racial crisis is a human crisis.

I know of no greater contribution than the effective development of better men and women. And if our students are not improved by their having been our students, then that is where *our* crisis really must be confronted.

The Community College and Community Services

JOSEPH P. COSAND

PRESIDENT ENARSON subscribes enthusiastically and with dedication to that philosophy of education which includes the application of knowledge as well as the acquisition and transmission of knowledge. Stated another way, he endorses the inclusion of public service along with teaching and research as the explicit responsibilities of institutions of higher education. I am in complete agreement with this philosophy of education and believe that all institutions of higher education—universities, colleges, and community junior colleges—must reflect this philosophy with varying emphases according to the specific objectives of the particular institution.

All those in higher education are, or certainly should be, aware that the philosophy and objectives stated do not truly represent the present action of far too many institutions, perhaps even a majority. Much is being written in brochures, catalogs, and public relations articles in newspapers and magazines, but the actualities don't measure up to statements by administrators and public relations officers. This "credibility gap" can't and won't be sanctioned by the students and taxpayers much longer. There is already considerable evidence that the "open" pocketbook of parents and taxpayers is closing at an accelerated rate, and that many colleges and universities, both private and public, are in financial difficulty. This situation is no accident but grows out of an increasing disenchantment with the existing climate in far too many of our institutions. The complaints stem from the following generalities, which could be broken down into specifics. (1) Professors prefer and are engaged in research and consultation assignments, rather than teaching responsibilities. Most of the teaching is left to graduate students and those in the lower academic ranks. Most of these "teachers" are teaching only as a means to an end, the end being research and consultation. (2) Collegiate research has been taken over by the Federal government, in particular by the military, and therefore the colleges are suspected of supporting war or at least the preparations for war. The integrity of the colleges as centers of scholarship for the enrichment of mankind has been shaken and this integrity replaced, in the minds of students and citizens, with a form of "Say it isn't so" hopefulness bordering on cynicism. The professor becomes a caricature of a materialistic opportunist rather than a scholar who seeks the truth in order to transmit it so that he and his students may apply it. (3) The colleges' professed statements concerning the importance of the "town and gown" relationship are only palaver to keep the town quiet while the gown is permitted to live in its ivory tower, protected by tenure, and continues to act in a unilateral manner, oblivious of those areas of the town "where the action is."

Whether institutions like it or not, and whether they are guilty or not, these generalized statements are being made and are increasingly believed about them. There are far too many instances when the accusations are true, and each such case becomes a small fire. A few such fires aren't noticed by many people, but large numbers of fires can become a conflagration seen by the entire citizenry. We need and must have the fires of positive action in teaching, research, and public service in order to combat the cynicism among students and growing numbers of citizens concerning the self-seeking opportunism and impotency of our colleges and universities as reflected by the actions of administrators and faculty.

The first third of President Enarson's paper bothered me because he built a case that most, if not all, colleges are engaged in community service and are anxiously searching out new areas of service in which they could become involved. This may be so, but I haven't seen the evidence. In fact, there are prestigious educators professing just the opposite, and many faculty members and administrators would support them for they prefer by far the cloisters to the hot action of the city or even that of the rural countryside. Teaching and research, either singly or together, are far safer and more comfortable, and after all, isn't the college a place for scholarship for the scholars? I am afraid the evidence noted by President Enarson is much too limited and then often only for show. The "lip service" action in public relations articles is really worse than no action, for the well-publicized "for show" action must cause one to question the very integrity of the institutions.

In many colleges where vital community service action is taking place, the effort and success are due primarily to an active, dedicated administrator who, for the most part, seeks his support and teachers from the community. There is little, if any, budgetary support; in fact, it is quite often the opposite —the revenue from the community service programs helps pay for the upper-division and graduate programs of the universities. This is truly a sad commentary and a prostitution of the public service objective of a college. The lack of interest on the part of the other administrators and faculty is probably natural and to be expected. The content to be taught is different, the people to be helped or taught are different, their world is different, communicating with them is difficult and in many cases almost impossible for the professional staff of a collegiate institution. The struggle, then, if public service or the application of knowledge is to be an objective of higher education, is either to educate present professionals, or to build a college within a college which has budgetary support and which is considered to be an integral part of the institution.

Colleges and universities are being supported in the United States with a truly amazing generosity. To do the job that needs to be done, however, the support must be even greater. This increased support, be it from tuition or taxes, will not be forthcoming unless the productivity of the colleges is relevant to the interests and needs of the students and the community. Today's media are educating the people, and we in higher education must be just as astute about the newer methods of instruction—and content—as are the media. The cloistered college, separate and apart from a community, is an anachronism.

The last two-thirds of President Enarson's paper must be applauded, and certainly I support his comments. As a community college president, I wish to emphasize the importance of this type of institution as a center of community service. The college must be of the community and must, therefore, serve the needs of the youth and adults who might profit from its services. In order to do this, the professional staff has the responsibility for being aware of all aspects of the community, and for being able to seek out the interests and needs of those who make up the community. Observation from a distance won't suffice. Professional decision making without participant discussion and advice won't provide the answers to group needs. Isolated research surveys by detached research scholars are increasingly suspect. The answer is involvement, complete immersion, of all concerned so that the real expertise of the professionals and of the community leadership can jointly be brought to bear on solutions to the present and future problems of our complex society. Belief in this type of action is not enough—there must be funds to implement the action, and there must be effective leadership, respected by all concerned, to carry through the programs to acceptable conclusions.

Colleges and universities can no longer refuse to accept public service through the application of knowledge as one of the three responsibilities of higher education—and to place it alongside teaching and research as part of an inseparable triad. This, as President Enarson states in his conclusion, is our mandate. Failure on our part will result in a decline in the reputation and hence in the effectiveness of higher education. Answers sought from us, if not forthcoming, will and must be sought elsewhere. If we, through research, seek and believe in the truth; if we, through teaching, transmit the knowledge of the centuries, why then can't we through our acquired knowledge, apply it as a service to mankind?

University Governance and the Public Interest

LINCOLN GORDON

UNIVERSITY GOVERNANCE is a topic with dimensions differing from those of the central theme "The Campus and the Racial Crisis." The difference is evidenced by the fundamental review of university purposes, methods, and structure that is under way in many nations whose peoples are racially homogeneous. The discussion here will give attention to areas of intersection between the two topics, but will extend it where necessary to wider aspects of governance irrespective of racial issues.

Governance and the University Mission

Governance of any institution is—or should be—a function of its purpose. It may seem laboring the obvious to restate the purposes of American universities, but the conventional definitions are currently under challenge from so many fronts that anyone launching a discussion of governance ought to make clear his own concept of the university mission.

The central mission is the advancement of learning through the transmission and enlargement of knowledge. This undertaking is an intellectual task. Its fulfillment has a profound effect on policy making, but that fact does not give the university a political mission. On the contrary, the politicization of the university can only destroy it as a free intellectual institution.

Is this a call to return to some mythical (and historically nonexistent) "ivory tower"? Certainly not. The university is one of the major institutions of the wider society and has active links to it as one custodian of its cultural heritage, as a supplier of new knowledge, as a training ground for professional and other highly qualified manpower, as a direct agent in the application of many kinds of knowledge, and as a recipient of resources essential to the university's own functioning. The university must also have special and active relationships with the local community of which it is a physical part. But its primary mission of high-level teaching and research is the major determinant of the forms of governance appropriate to it.

In the current mood of questioning, especially among younger people, of personal and community values, of national and international political

269

goals, and of the organization of society in all its aspects, this basic concept of the university is challenged on many counts. There is the quixotic notion of the extreme New Left that, despite the institution's dependence on the wider society and their condemnation of it as an integral part of a loathsome "system," somehow the university can be captured and organized as an instrument for the total overthrow of that system.

For peculiar historical reasons, something approaching this anomaly has happened in recent years in some Latin American universities. Until late 1966, the democratic and liberal government of Venezuela was so anxious to avoid the kind of interference which had characterized previous dictatorial and military regimes that it permitted the University of Caracas to become a focus for armed guerilla warfare against the regime, as well as an asylum for common criminals. The initial result was the destruction of the university as an intellectual institution. The sequence was its occupation by the army and an effort at a fresh start. It would appear to be a gross underestimate of the resilience of American society to assume that such an effort can succeed here. But we should be under no illusion that the effort is not being made.

The Mission Challenged

The more serious challenges are subtle, although some of them merge at the edges into the extreme position just described. One of them decries the role of universities in preparing specialized manpower, contending that their exclusive purpose should be to help develop the critical faculties of a rounded human being. In historical terms, this challenge rejects not only one major contemporary function of the university but its entire traditional function. Harvard College was established to provide a clergy for the new Massachusetts Bay Colony, just as its European predecessors had been engaged for centuries in training professionals for the church, the ancient disciplines of medicine and law, and the higher reaches of the national civil administrations.

If one took this challenge literally, separate institutions of higher education would be needed to prepare for society its doctors, engineers, administrators, lawyers, architects, diplomats, scholars, and scientists. In the European pattern, general liberal and cultural education is the function of the senior high school, the university being reserved for professional training. Our own contrary tradition comes partly from the superposition a century ago of graduate and professional training on colleges which were scarcely more than advanced high schools, coupled with our pioneering of higher education on a mass scale instead of for a very small elite.

This challenge also implies a false differentiation among the various roles of adults, for all of which the university experience may help prepare the student. There is man as worker in an inevitably highly specialized economic structure (regardless of its political goals or ideology); man as citizen, of special importance in a society open to broad political participation; and man as human being, exposed to the miseries and grandeurs of the human condition. If universities were concerned exclusively with man as worker, they could be legitimately challenged, but to exclude that function entirely is an absurdity.

Then there is the challenge, often asserted as a reason for establishing dominant student power in university governance, which states the interests of the student as the sole purpose of the university and decries the diversion of professorial attention from teaching to research. There is ample room for argument over the correct balance between teaching and research activities, and good reason for believing that undergraduate education has been unduly slighted by senior professors in our leading universities. It can also be argued that the natural sciences have grown beyond their proper proportion, so that of the classic triad, too little attention is being given to the study of the Beautiful and the Good, as compared with the True. Much more effective thought is urgently needed on the nature and content of undergraduate programs, and serious students have a lot to contribute to it. But the principle of enlargement of knowledge as a top priority in the true university, along with graduate and professional training, should be beyond question.

Here again, the United States is peculiar in the proportion of basic research carried on in universities rather than specialized research institutes. It is precisely this peculiarity, however, which helps account for our present undisputed leadership in scientific and technological and administrative capacity—the essence of what is so enthusiastically (and somewhat enviously) described in Servan-Schreiber's *The American Challenge*. If the researchers are willing to teach, there is no doubt that their teaching is fertilized by their scholarship. There is also good reason to believe that scholarship is fertilized by exposure to critical undergraduate students as well as to research apprentices.

Perhaps the most curious challenge questions the whole premise of intellectual development as the basic purpose of the university. It is usually disguised by the plea for "relevance," meaning activities which satisfy the immediate emotional needs of students. Obviously the academic program is not intended to occupy the whole time and attention of the student, like a medieval religious apprentice in a monastery. The diversity of extracurricular activities in American universities has been so great as to evoke the sometime contempt of intellectuals at home and abroad. For many students, their most intense personal experiences in college are athletic, musical, or dramatic, and—nowadays in increasing numbers—social service or political.

There should be time and opportunity for all of these according to taste. But they should not be confused with the central purpose of the institution. It becomes a mockery of that purpose when a leading university gives *academic* credit for "courses" which are merely latter-day meetings of the John Reed Society or for off-campus activity not directly connected with the systematic enlargement and transmission of learning. By contrast, clinical work in a school of medicine and other similar work experiences are so connected and are quite appropriate subjects for academic credit.

Legitimate Institutional Commitments

A fifth challenge seeks institutional commitment by the university to particular moral objectives or public policies, beyond the pursuit of truth through rational inquiry and discourse. Note the emphasis on *institutional* commitment, in contrast with personal commitments which are open to individual professors as one cardinal element of academic freedom. This challenge is argued on two grounds: a pseudo-philosophical rationale that in the humanities and social sciences true "neutrality" or "objectivity" is inherently impossible; and a more activist rationale that certain causes are so self-evidently just that the university has an obligation to use its institutional influence in their support. In its more extreme form, this challenge would forbid certain types of research which might have evil applications and would deny the classroom to professors holding beliefs at variance with the challengers.

At its extremes, this challenge is not difficult to rebut. Without entering the difficult terrain of alleged inherent distinctions between natural and social science, the validity of Weber's concept of *Wertfreiheit* in any intellectual discipline, or the application of the Bohr-Heisenberg uncertainty principle outside subatomic physics, one can say with confidence that many humanists and social scientists believe that a posture of neutrality and objectivity is not only possible but is essential to true scholarship. As long as this remains so, institutional stands on disputed questions of morality or policy imply a departure from the basic conception of the university and an implicit, if not explicit, denial of academic freedom. As to the second rationale, the certainty of his moral position lies only subjectively in the eye of the advocate. An institutional commitment for or against antiballistic missiles, or the war in Vietnam, or a political candidacy, or a particular approach to the elimination of poverty would impose unwarranted constraints upon members of the institution who hold differing views.

It is one of the glories of a liberal society that the university can at the same time be a part of it, serving some of its most important functions, and yet be apart from it, sheltering and fostering active analysis and criticism of its structure and its public policies. As the main location of basic research, the university is an important prime mover of technological change. The applied research and policy proposals of its competent faculty members may also be great forces for social change. But academic freedom is a privilege accorded by a liberal society because of the general belief that the free search for truth and free competition in the marketplace of ideas are assets to the wider society, however unpopular some of the particular policies supported by individual professors at any given time. Institutional commitments on public policies would jeopardize this whole framework, since it is scarcely likely that the wider society would long tolerate any such stands if they differed from prevailing public attitudes.

In this matter, however, there are some very difficult borderline areas. During the second world war, all universities accepted institutional obligations to participate in the national defense through both research and training programs. Many consider this a legitimate institutional commitment in times of so-called "peace" as well. Within the local framework, there is an inescapable requirement for institutional commitments as a corporate "good citizen" of the community, with implications for various types of service and for fairness as an employer and a user of real estate. A university could hardly avoid an institutional commitment against the use of its premises as a base for organized crime. And in relation to the general theme of the racial crisis and the campus, there must clearly be an institutional commitment against the racial segregation forbidden by the Constitution and in favor of some form of effort toward racial harmony. Finally, the university should certainly be institutionally committed in defense of the academic enterprise against internal or external attack.

No simple guidelines can be set to determine the precise range of legitimate institutional commitments. They require thoughtful judgment and should not be undertaken lightly. Where they are undertaken, special precaution is in order to ensure the freedom of opposing views within the academic community.

Still another challenge conceives of the university as a microcosm of society. From this premise it is argued that university governance must be democratically organized, either through "participatory democracy" or by a one-man, one-vote system for all its full-time members. Here a fundamental misconception permits wrong conclusions to flow readily from faulty assumptions.

This discussion has focused on the university as the paradigm of institutions of higher education. Some of its points, notably those concerned with research, are not fully applicable to liberal arts colleges or community colleges. But the main points apply to all institutions of higher education, which should be considered as parts of a system rather than independently. Indeed, institutional governance in coming years will have to become more responsive to the need to give this whole system coherence, with flexible interpenetration among its various parts. This task is especially relevant to the racial crisis.

Governance and Community Responsibility

Some of the most difficult problems of governance arise from the ill-defined role of universities in community responsibility. That there is a substantial role of this type is implicit in the structure of formal governing bodies, whether regents appointed by public officials or lay trustees of private institutions. However selected, these boards have a special concern with the university's external relations: its sources of financial support, and its activities in relation to the wider society.

The most important such relationship is the training of skilled manpower, a central function of the university. The problems arise, however, in other areas: community services; community impact through real estate and other operations; and admissions policy and practice. In all these fields, the critical issue is how to discharge affirmative responsibilities—some undertaken at the university's own initiative and others in response to outside pressures— consistently with the fundamental purposes already described.

Services to the local community

It is fashionable nowadays to decry the "multiversity." One might indeed wish that Clark Kerr had never coined this inelegant term. The central criticism is against the use of the university as a "service station." diverting attention from its teaching duties and from basic research. Against this view is the argument that the great social problems of our time—peace, population, poverty, economic development, urban reconstruction, physical and mental health, the humanization of public and private bureaucracy, and racial harmony—are all so complex that they need the best minds applied to them. A good share of these best minds cluster in the universities. Moreover, by historical tradition, many of our greatest universities were founded as service institutions, not only to train young people in "agriculture and the mechanic arts," but also to take direct responsibility for agricultural research and extension services.

In the earlier discussion, "service" or the "application of knowledge" was deliberately omitted from the definition of primary university purposes, even though it is commonly listed along with the transmission and enlargement of knowledge. Service is essentially a subordinate function of the university, and it should be engaged in only when the service functions also contribute in good measure to the primary purposes.

That principle may reach quite far in practice. In the field of medicine, for example, clinical experience has long been recognized as indispensable to both teaching and biomedical research. Now we see the great teaching hospitals, many directly operated by universities, extending their work into comprehensive health care in inner-city and other environments. This is no departure from principle once it is recognized that health care delivery systems are themselves a legitimate subject of intellectual inquiry and specialized professional training. But it would be a departure if universities sought to operate a whole metropolitan system of community hospitals simply as a service. Demonstration, consultation, evaluation, research, and training of specialized manpower all fall within the principle; mere service detached from these functions should be organized outside and apart from the universities.

The value of clinical experience is becoming increasingly recognized in fields other than medicine. Legal-aid and legislative-assistant work by law students; field work by budding architects and business administrators; and applied research in urban problems by apprentice sociologists, economists, and environmental engineers—all help to bring together the world of reality and the world of ideas. University urban centers can become valuable aids to policy formulation and execution. But if they seek or accept direct administrative or policy-making responsibility, they are escaping the proper bounds of the university.

Responsibilities to the local community

Corporate responsibilities of the university as a local "good citizen" are harder to define. With student bodies in the tens of thousands and employees in the thousands, with large payrolls and construction budgets, the university is the dominant presence in many communities and an important one wherever it has its home. Charges of "racist expansionism," both from student groups and from outsiders, have become part of the stock in trade of activist attacks on many universities.

In these circumstances, the university must be a good citizen in appearance as well as action. It needs active communication with all significant elements in the community, some form of structural relation (probably through the composition of the governing board), and a sensitivity to community concerns often lacking in the past. On the other hand, the university is not a substitute for official local authorities, and its community responsibilities should always be designed to serve its primary mission. Participation in urban planning is wholly appropriate, and no wise administration today would embark on land acquisition without assurance against undue ill effects on its neighbors. But it is difficult to accept the claim that university resources should go directly to subsidize housing for local citizens displaced by new buildings. This is typically a governmental responsibility, and not one for which resources have been entrusted to the university. It is hard enough to find adequate resources for its true purposes, and efforts at omnicompetence are likely to be self-defeating.

Admissions

Admissions policy is another major facet of community relationships, and one deeply involved in the racial crisis. "Open admission" is a popular slogan of the day, backed by arguments that universities have no right to continue as "elitist" institutions. But in a broad sense, higher education is elitist by definition. Even if open to everyone and joined by everyone, the university would still be creating elites of professional and scholarly competence. No human society, least of all a technologically advanced one, can function without many such elites. The question is whether they are elites of birth and fortune or elites of talent, merit, and dedication. The whole thrust of American universities for decades has been toward "meritocracy," and there is no need to be defensive about that kind of elitism.

To be sure, the results so far of this thrust leave much to be desired. Genuine equality of opportunity, although closer than in any other society or any earlier age, may be within reach but has not yet been grasped. Its achievement, however, is beyond the capacity of any single institution acting alone. It can only be achieved by the educational system as an integrated and coherent whole. Much of it—probably most—depends on earlier phases of education, from preschool through high school. Much depends on new kinds of linkages between high schools, community colleges, four-year colleges, and universities.

Here is a new problem for university governance, so far faced in only a few of the most progressive states. Almost all private universities, and many of the public ones, have been much too inward looking, ready to leave the humdrum higher education of less apt students to their less-favored sister institutions. But if there is one type of community service for which the university should be especially fitted, it is precisely in the development of the educational system as a whole. This requires a more active commitment to cooperation with community colleges and four-year colleges, greater flexibility in transfers, and serious applied research on problems of remedial and compensatory education at all levels and by all types of institutions. With so much ground to make up, there is ample room for upgrading efforts, provided that they do not jeopardize the basic standards of the institution concerned. But if these programs lead to second-class enclaves within first-class institutions, they are likely to frustrate the ultimate aims of the very disadvantaged groups which seek their creation.

Internal Governance and External Authority

In the heat of recent campus disturbances, much confusion has arisen about the relation between internal university governance and external authority. Many students and professors have denied not only the wisdom but also the right of police and other local authority intrusion in any and all circumstances. Some congressmen have sought the withholding of Federal funds so as to "strengthen the spine" of the administrators in ensuring order on campus. Some student sea lawyers have invented bizarre theories of double jeopardy in order to escape discipline by either civil or university authority. And some universities have worked out extraordinarily complex rules and procedures to define "respective jurisdictions," as if they were sovereign states within the state.

Some of the confusion derives from an erroneous assumption that European medieval traditions (also generally followed in Latin America) have been sanctioned in the United States. Under this tradition, the university does have sanctuary from intrusion by civil authority and autonomy in disciplining its own members, even for many common crimes if committed on university premises. Legally such a concept has never been accepted in the United States, although by informal arrangement in many cases, local authorities have yielded de facto disciplinary authority to universities for minor infractions. In return, the university was prepared to act in loco parentis and to use its own sanctions by way of reprimand, probation, suspension, or expulsion to see that the local community was not adversely affected. Many universities also employ a substantial security force of their own, whose members are sometimes deputized as local policemen.

For many reasons, the practice of acting in loco parentis has been disappearing apace. Some vestiges remain in residential universities, but the trend is against them. The change results partly from the weakening of parental authority within the family, but mainly from the active desire of students themselves to be treated as responsible adults.

The change inevitably cuts both ways. If the university ceases to watch over the private lives of its students and some of their actions violate the general law, the students must face the expectation of legal sanctions. In such matters as illegal possession and sale of drugs, the student cannot rightly expect sanctuary from police action on campus no matter how irrational many of the state laws may be. The university may choose to assist or not in this kind of law enforcement, but it is not exempt from a valid search warrant.

Organized disruption of university activities is a somewhat different case if it is nonviolent in character. The institution has great latitude in deciding whether it wants to treat a building occupation as a civil or criminal trespass and to request outside assistance in removing the occupiers. That it has a right to such assistance is beyond question. The operational question is whether it is wise in particular circumstances to invoke that right.

While the university enjoys no sovereignty, it does have substantial disciplinary authority as a specialized community, extending to suspension or expulsion from its membership. To preserve the sense of community, and in public institutions perhaps to meet legal requirements, the university will want to avoid arbitrary use of that authority, providing for some form of hearing and review before imposing the more drastic or long-lasting sanctions, although not extending full "due process of law" in the technical sense applied to public criminal proceedings. The choice between university discipline and resort to outside authority is a matter of policy, and it must depend upon the particular circumstances, including the effectiveness of the internal disciplinary machinery and the responsiveness of the offenders to such discipline.

As organized disruption has escalated, amnesty has become a priority "nonnegotiable demand," and has been granted in a dismaying number of cases. Traditional disciplinary machinery, adequate for individual wayward students, has often proved ineffectual against organized disruption. Hence there has been increasing resort to judicial restraining orders as a means of avoiding violent confrontation while evoking an outside authority against which disruptive students have no leverage.

It should be recognized, however, that a court order is just as much an intrusion on the campus by civil authority as is action by the local police. If the disruption escalates to the point of disregarding court orders, physical enforcement must follow. After the experiences at Columbia and Harvard and many others, abroad as well as at home, the danger of mass radicalization as a reflex to police action is obvious enough. The deliberate provocation of police confrontation is an ancient tactic of extremist disrupters. For a university to forswear the invocation of external force under any conditions, however, is to abandon its control to any sufficiently obstinate and reckless minority.

The alleged issue of "double jeopardy" is a mystification. The wider community has its own code of behavior written into the civil and criminal law. Specialized communities, whether universities or clubs or trade unions or business firms, have their own norms of behavior appropriate to their purposes. A particular act may violate both sets of standards and may be subject to sanction by both institutions.

This exposure to overlapping penalties has nothing to do with the constitutional provision forbidding that "any person be subject for the same offense to be twice put in jeopardy of life or limb." Universities cannot jeopardize life or limb, and they have no obligation to maintain membership in good standing by an offender against their own standards merely because the same offense violates public law. There may be technical questions whether a university hearing prejudices subsequent criminal proceedings, and the university may choose to refrain from acting or await the outcome of a public trial. How it will choose should depend, not on supposititious theories of double jeopardy, but upon the seriousness of the offense in relation to the functioning of the university as a community.

In practice, the relationship between external authority and internal governance will depend on the effectiveness of internal governance itself. University authorities should take some heart from the hopes expressed on all sides that they can find within themselves the means for effective self-government. Tolerance in some quarters may be running low, but these widespread hopes reflect continuing respect for the university as an institution and recognition of how unappealing the alternatives might be.

The Components of Internal Governance

"Restructuring" is the order of the day in the university world, as trustees, administrations, faculties, and students seek to grapple with internal tensions and external pressures. The storms have blown up so quickly that institutions which seemed to be functioning satisfactorily have discovered that they do not even know how decisions were made in the past, much less how best to make them now.

The university is in fact a unique organism. It is highly decentralized, with many different loci of decision, with loose articulation among the parts, accustomed more to informal than formal communication, relying on consensus rather than vote, and heavily dependent on a shared sense of community. For this organism, other institutional models offer only limited guidance. The hierarchical patterns of armies and business concerns are inappropriate to the authority and freedoms of faculty members. Nor are governmental models, based on the differentiation of legislative, executive, and judicial functions, fully applicable.

An effective university structure must take proper account of its three full-time components: administration, faculty, and students. Under present organization, great residual power, usually exercised very sparingly, rests with governing boards as the closest part-time component. But there must also be linkage to the more remote part-time components, such as alumni and parents, public and private sources of financial support, and the organized local and national communities.

Among the full-time components, the most vocal current pressures for reform arise from the student search for power. But there is no monolithic student viewpoint. A very large group—probably still a majority—is concerned with studies and extracurricular activities rather than institutional power. Among the seekers for power are a small extremist group which would destroy the institution; some larger groups which would like to politicize it; and still larger groups interested in participating in university policy within the proper bounds of the academic mission. Of these three, some means must be found to isolate and resist the first—if possible, to remove it by expulsion. The second must be contained and fully exposed to the arguments against politicization. The third should be recognized and given its proper role.

What that role shall be depends upon the area of decision making. Once the notion is abandoned of a single, all-purpose hierarchy, the structure can be organized into a number of decision-making bodies, with degrees of participation by respective groups appropriate to the various categories of decisions. Thus in extracurricular affairs, student representatives might well have the principal voice, helped by administrative associates—for financial and space and other practical reasons—and perhaps with faculty advisers. On curriculum, students are in a position to make substantial contributions through their current view of "how it really works," their interdepartmental perspective, and their felt complaints and needs. Controlling voice in curricular determination, however, ought to remain a faculty prerogative. Disciplinary boards may appropriately be composed on a tripartite basis, representing student, faculty, and administration components.

When it comes to faculty appointment and promotion, student participation is inappropriate, since students lack the scholarly competence to judge alternative candidates and the long-term stake in the character and quality of the institution which are uniquely influenced by the critical power of professional recruitment. Students may well have valid opinions on teaching ability as it is felt in the classroom, and there should be ample opportunity for systematic canvassing and communication of such opinion. But this is only one of many issues on which a sound university structure will provide for inputs and communication from various sources without necessarily extending to participation with power.

Whether students should be represented on governing boards depends upon one's conception of the de facto jurisdiction of boards, in contrast to their extensive formal power. In most institutions, authority in matters of legitimate concern to students has long since been delegated to administrations and faculties. It would be a retrograde step to draw these back into the hands of governing boards by virtue of student representation. Here again, however, there is room for new devices for communication between governing boards and student representatives, both for its positive merits and to assist in removing unwarranted mutual suspicion and mistrust.

All devices for student participation depend upon an effective system of representation. "Representation" means not only appropriate electoral machinery, with the usual safeguards for freedom of nomination and campaigning, but also continuous communication between the representative and his constituency. The development and maintenance of such a system are no easy tasks, but otherwise the voice is merely of an individual student and not of the student body.

With respect to the components of faculty and administration, one of the stranger aspects of recent discussions of university governance has been the notion of antagonistic interests between these two groups. If the purpose of the university is properly conceived, this notion becomes incomprehensible. Faculties are the heart of a university; on their competence and performance the whole enterprise stands or falls. Administrators are both their servants and their leaders, with complementary functions but scarcely opposing interests. Of course administrations must frequently turn down specific faculty requests, sometimes for reasons of institutional policy and more often for lack of resources. But the collective interest of the faculty is identical with the administrative interest: it is the well-being of the institution as a whole. Where conflicts seem to exist, they must reflect faulty communication between administration and faculty, a harbinger of disaster for any university.

Administrative structures have been greatly enlarged in recent decades and all the signs point toward further enlargement. The need for administration is inherent in the American effort toward higher education on a mass scale. There are also many external pressures pointing toward more elaborate administration, some arising from the handling of governmental funds and others from the need for interinstitutional cooperation, already mentioned. It is sometimes facetiously suggested that administration should be relegated to a Quonset hut on the edge of the campus, to deal with money and buildings and grounds and custodial personnel. If this were attempted, faculties would soon discover that more powerful administration would have to be invented. In fact, a period of rapid change creates a special need for administrative leadership, not against the faculty but of the faculty in its collective interest. Faculties decentralized into schools and departments, with great and precious freedom for the individual professor within that framework, are inherently resistant to change. Without some effective centralized leadership, any university is likely to wither on the vine.

This is why, despite their relative loss of power to faculties, university presidents are subjected to heavier pressures than ever before. It is often suggested—and some universities are experimenting with the idea—that the position of president be divided into two: one for external relations and one for internal leadership and management. In the larger institutions, this may well become a necessity. As the history of Roman consulates makes clear, however, its workability requires exceptional harmony between the two coequals.

In many institutions today, the weakest structural link appears to be in the organization of the faculties themselves. They are made up, after all, of highly individualistic scholars who customarily carry on their professional activities alone or in small groups. Most of them are interested only marginally, if at all, in the broader problems confronting the institution and they have little time to spare for such concerns. To expect rational decisions from a plenary faculty meeting of several hundred professors, suddenly convened in the face of some emergency and often acting under intense emotional pressures, is to expect the impossible. In the governmental sphere, large legislative bodies are able to function only because their members work full time, they are controlled by time-tested procedures, and they are equipped with effective committees and specialized staff.

What appears to be needed for the effective exercise of faculty power is comprehensive delegation to small numbers willing to devote substantial time to broad institutional problems—in effect, bridges between the faculty at large and full-time administrators. The price to the professor of this function in diversion from teaching and research is substantial. Like student representatives, such faculty members have an obligation to maintain contact with their wider constituency. With institutional survival at stake, however, it should not be impossible to find qualified faculty members able and willing to pay that price.

A final word is in order on the growing trend to establish large senates or councils with carefully apportioned representation from senior faculty, junior faculty, administration, students of various categories, the various schools within an institution, and sometimes alumni and trustees as well. As a deliberative and consultative assembly on an occasional issue of very wide interest, such as the introduction of coeducation or the establishment of a new professional school, such a body may be useful. It may also be useful as a sounding board in crises of campus disorder. Most university decisions, however, are not of a broad general character and are far better handled in smaller, specialized bodies composed in accordance with the issue at hand. This is where communication and representation can really count. Much of the energy being devoted to the constitution of these large senates is likely to prove futile, as the scarcity of topics of universal interest becomes clear and the vast number of man hours spent in inconclusive debate takes its toll in boredom and frustration.

The Crisis of the Free University

Whatever the new arrangements for university governance, they will meet the needs only if they have a clear view of their critical function: the enhancement and protection of the basic mission of the academic enterprise.

If American society as a whole is in crisis, the free university is in a more acute stage of crisis. It is caught in a financial squeeze between inexorably rising costs and the demand of society for true equality of opportunity in higher education. At the same time, its very essence is under attack from militant white anarchism, militant black separatism, and external reaction against internal disorder.

More insidious than any of these external challenges is a weakness within the ranks of the university, among those professors and students ready to abandon truth, reason, and objectivity as their standards. If the universities are destroyed, the cause will lie more in this new *trahison des clercs* than in the headline-creating tumult of these times. Against this danger there is only one remedy: a shaking loose from their apathy and complacency by the vast majority of true scholars who compose our faculties.

They must learn again that the battle for academic freedom and for the unfettered cultivation of the intellect is never permanently won, and that only an active defense will conserve the American university for the greater challenges which lie ahead. There are many hopeful signs that recent academic tragedies on some of our greatest campuses are driving this lesson home. It is not quite too late.

Commentaries on

University Governance and the Public Interest

W. BRADFORD WILEY, A. LEROY WILLIS, JOHN J. BUDDS

The Public Interest Must Have a Greater Voice

W. BRADFORD WILEY

THE SHORTCOMINGS of university governance in the public interest undoubtedly contribute to unrest in the higher academic community, especially among those being governed almost without representation. College and university students throughout the world are dissatisfied and protesting. We are pleased when students elsewhere in the world resist authoritarian governments, and indignant when our students oppose the inertia of their institutions.

Students in Japan, India, Australia, East Africa, Czechoslovakia, West Germany, and Canada, for example, have not joined our students in an international conspiracy; they are trying to tell us something and we must listen. Their common dissatisfactions are addressed to the cost of creating, staffing, maintaining, and using military establishments (now euphemistically called defense departments). All of them agree that there must be something wrong with a worldwide economy which permits starvation and other forms of poverty to exist even in the richest countries. They further agree that social injustice must be eliminated. Most especially they are determined to improve the academic programs of their institutions of higher education.

If universities are to serve the public interest, their governance must be in keeping with their avowed purpose, size, and complexity. A third of a century ago in a depression economy a "large university" enrolled from three to five thousand students, and a very few were larger, usually because of an urban location. The problem for the director of admissions was simply to find enough high school graduates to fill each incoming class; overt or covert segregation took care of *that* problem. Faculty appointments despite low salaries were eagerly sought, teaching and research were compatible, consulting was mostly done off premises, and the Department of Defense was represented on campus only by ROTC units. The inhabitants of the university community were a fairly homogeneous society, and the spectrum of political views broad and tolerant. Alumni and the general public were relatively benign.

A third of a century later, after a World War and two undeclared wars and in a period of unprecedented affluence, nothing is the same. When the universities undertook the necessary obligation to train technical manpower under war conditions they had to forego intellectual freedom for the duration. Retraining in the postwar period was a proper and inevitable sequel. Higher education is no longer a privilege, public funds are essential even to private institutions with the largest resources, and the public must be served. The institutions of higher education are sensitive to their different responsibilities and are trying to carry them out.

It is not difficult to identify the groups in and around the community whose needs and interests must be served and who can reasonably expect to share in the governance of the university. They are students, faculty, alumni, and the general public. To serve those groups there are trustees, administrators, and the nonacademic staff.

Those who make up the student clientele of universities are increasingly heterogeneous in their ethnic, social, economic, political, and occupational origins. Some gladly participate in training programs, others pursue programs chosen in early youth, many drift for a year or two before choosing or leaving, but a growing minority of superior intelligence is questioning the Establishment, and their questions all too frequently cannot be addressed to a responsive communication channel. And computer consoles just won't do.

The faculties and students share many problems and are beginning to exchange views toward their solution. Mutual tolerance is emerging but real progress is probably at best minimal.

Alumni and the general public are as prone to emotional response as are more youthful and impetuous students. Alumni threaten to reduce or discontinue financial support and they demand wholesale dismissals starting with presidents on through the faculty and, of course, the students. The general public is clamoring for legislative action to "control" and it neither understands nor cares about the consequences. Trustees have become frustrated, administrators disenchanted, faculties demoralized, and students sullen or, in the extreme, violently mutinous.

Physical violence and obstruction have no place in the universities. The spectrum of political-social views does belong, and there must be a forum equally available to right, center, and left. A university should be a place for ferment and not be expected to conduct its affairs in an idealistic, academic vacuum when the rest of the world is engaged with doubts and turmoil.

The size and complexity of our universities have far outstripped traditional methods of governance. The American Council should accept the challenge of designing models around which this basic problem can be solved. Universities can and must serve the public interest, but the total public interest must have a voice beyond anything yet achieved. If this is not accomplished, small pressure groups will prevail and their interests will be served.

Greater Influence by the Black Community

A. LEROY WILLIS

LINCOLN GORDON has demonstrated the difficulty of relating university governance and the public interest to the theme of the campus and the racial crisis. A closer approach is through thinking about university governance and the interests of the black community. Here, the black community may be broadly interpreted to include both the black people who inhabit the ghettos of American and all other black people who are vitally concerned with alleviating the undesirable forces affecting those ghettos.

University governance, as a system, is complex and varies from institution to institution, but essential groups can be identified. At the policy-making level, the board of trustees—usually made up of wealthy businessmen, lawyers, and public figures—stands out. A more amorphous group consists of large contributors who may try to influence policy directly or indirectly and who have to be considered by university decision-makers in light of their ability to contribute or not to contribute in the future. A third group is the alumni, whatever the degree of its organization. Additionally, some university people hold membership in more than one of these categories.

Traditionally, the operations of a university have been administered by the president, his administrative staff, and various faculty committees. The balance of power between administrators and faculty may shift, depending on the actors, historical developments, the nature and gravity of conflicts and crises, and so on.

Two other prominent groups should be considered part of the university community—the students and the residents who live in the vicinity, especially of the large urban institutions. Both have been largely excluded from governance bodies. Why? The university is an elitist institution more intent on controlling members of the society than assisting them to understand and cope with the dynamics of the society. The rules (never mentioned in the catalogs) are very simple and include: (1) Recognize that presidents and trustees have achieved their status positions by serving apprenticeships in the university or other Establishment institutions; by not commenting too strongly or too loudly on the problems in the society which could and should have been solved long ago; and, in effect, by protecting the status quo (and notice how people admire them). (2) Recognize that positions of power within the university are reserved for those who have either attended the university and successfully obeyed its dubious rules and regulations or have somehow shown that their support for the educational status quo is strong through their contributions (no youngsters or street folk please, even if their lives are vitally affected). (3) Recognize that those who do not threaten the equilibrium of the university's power structures may be admitted to the elitist club one day. And (4) recognize that those who push too hard for redistribution of university governing powers will be isolated and neutralized (race notwithstanding).

A glance at the history of race relations in America and the composition of the boards of trustees of major American universities reveals to black students that the probability of their being admitted to the club is nil under any circumstances, and certainly nil if they follow the traditional peaceful route.

The issue on the minds of a majority of the black students today is how they can use their talents and energy to control the awesome forces at work against people in the ghettos and black people in general. Black students want to know how to come to grips with those forces and with themselves in order to counteract the negative forces and to move in a positive, aggressive manner to end the miserable conditions that blacks are forced to endure.

Consciously or unconsciously, black students reach the conclusion that many of the problems faced by the black community have their roots in the major institutions of America, including the universities, which have from their beginnings spread damaging, racist attitudes that have poisoned the minds of blacks and whites alike. Therefore, since so many of the decisions affecting members of the black communities are made by predominantly white institutions, part of the solution to the race question lies in gaining access to decision-making bodies of these institutions. (The other part concerns strengthening existing institutions and creating new ones within the black community.)

Many students come to this realization while attending predominantly white universities and decide that they have the responsibility to change the white institutions they are closest to. Unfortunately, university decision-makers have not appreciated the students' idealism, insights, determination, goals, or the programs that the students have believed are necessary to bring about meaningful change for the black community.

This competition—and outright strife—between the white symbols of the status quo and black students for drastic changes may be termed "the campus and the racial crisis."

In getting at the matter of governance and race, we should try to keep our minds fixed on problems of the low quality of life for many people in America today and the need to upgrade it. The things that clearly disturb black students are the existence of the ghettos in an affluent society and the absence of blacks in the decision-making roles in the institutions that created and maintain the ghettos. In most cases, it is very difficult for black students to gain access to the higher-up, residual decision-makers.

Black students want to see these problems solved now and are beginning to see themselves as the last hope for really bringing about progress in the ghettos. In order to achieve progress, however, the students see the importance of increasing the number of like-minded students, adjusting the curricula, and assisting in the selection of faculty to help them prepare for the tasks that *the students have decided are necessary and important.* If white university decision-makers ever had a right to suggest the curricula and a set of values that would best prepare black students to deal with the urban problems, then they should clearly relinquish that right, on the basis of their miserable failures in urban affairs. And still the Lincoln Gordons would suggest that "When it comes to faculty appointment and promotion, student participation is inappropriate, since students lack the scholarly competence to judge alternative candidates. . ."

When it comes to the governance of a university, do black students have a basis for trusting that the existing university power structure will act in the best interests of the black community, when most of their records would show a history of indifference and outright opposition to the aspirations and interests of the black community? The answer is no. In order to establish good faith with the black students on this issue, the university will have to appoint black students and other representatives of the black community who intimately understand legitimate concerns of the black community.

I wish now to set out some recommendations that would forward the interests of black students and the black community.

First, the universities, especially those in urban areas, should admit to their governing bodies a significant number (10-15 percent) of blacks to represent that community so that their views and interests can be considered *before* decisions that affect their lives are made.

Second, the governors of the university should practice what they preach: open their minds to the new thoughts needed to deal with the complex problems facing both blacks and whites today. Students easily see the hypocrisy of invitations to participate in a university of free ideas when in fact they are rewarded for espousing the ideas of the Establishment and punished for espousing really different and sometimes revolutionary ideas.

Finally, the university Establishment must recognize that black students today are in the vanguard of a movement that began the day the first black man landed on these shores. There is a proud legacy of resistance and struggle for liberation that will not be crushed by brute force. The black student movement will subside only after the needs and interests of the black community have been met.

The next move is up to the Establishment, including the educational Establishment.

Building on Inherent Values

JOHN J. BUDDS

Dr. Gordon objectively examines the university system and its relationships to our society. He recognizes the weaknesses and deficiencies that have caused unrest and dissent and also clearly establishes the strengths and values that have contributed so much to higher education and to the development and well-being of our society. He concludes by rejecting the defeatism and pessimism expressed by so many and embraces the hopeful signs for greater development and progress in the years ahead. I shall comment briefly on each of the five areas of his paper.

In dealing with governance and mission, he affirms the central mission of the university as the advancement of learning through the transmission and enlargement of knowledge. Several common challenges to this basic concept are identified: the criticism that too much emphasis is placed on the role of preparing specialized manpower instead of developing the critical faculties of a well-rounded human; the challenge of the heavy emphasis on research; the challenges that the emotional needs of the student are not adequately satisfied; and the challenge of the lack of sufficient commitment to particular moral objectives or public policies. These functions, it is shown, have their rightful places as long as they do not seriously conflict with the central purpose of the university.

In treating governance and community responsibility, he makes the point that, among the university's external relations, the most important is the training of skilled manpower, which is considered a central function. However, the corporate responsibilities in the community—good citizenship and the service functions—are also recognized. While not referred to, the responsibilities of tax-supported institutions seem greater in these areas than those of the private universities. In discussing the highly controversial question of admissions, he defends the policy of selectivity. It seems to me that all possible assistance must be given to the disadvantaged as early in their educational experience as possible, but to deviate substantially from admission standards would tend to invite the eventual disillusionment and bitterness of those students who cannot make the grade in the university setting. Dr. Gordon here points out the importance of university aid and support for the educational system as a whole, especially support to the four-year and community colleges in accommodating qualified transfer students. In Connecticut we have been working cooperatively to assist a rapidly developing system of state-supported community colleges.

Matters of internal governance and external authority have, in the past year, caused confusion over the relations between university governance and external authority. With the disappearance of the exercise of in loco parentis, it is logical that students, like other citizens, must be subject to civil legal sanctions. However, reasonably effective internal discipline and control must be exercised to avoid disruptive conflicts.

In dealing with the components of internal governance, agreement is widespread that students must have opportunity for a greater voice in institutional policy making. It is important, in this context, to dismiss that small group of extremists who would destroy our institutions. On the other hand, the large percentage of students who are sincerely concerned and serious in their efforts to change and improve the educational processes must be listened to. At the University of Connecticut we have had a committee of faculty members, administrative officers, and trustees which has met periodically to discuss university policy. More than a year ago we invited student representation on the committee; we now include four students—the elected officers of the established student organization. The committee has functioned effectively, and we have found it highly advantageous for representatives of the academic family to meet and discuss freely all phases of institutional policy. The student participation has been most beneficial.

We must recognize the need for change and be ready and willing to take required action. We should not relate today's problems to our own academic experiences—they are, for most of us, too far in the past. Yet we should not overreact to the extent of impairing the great traditions and values inherent in the American system of higher education. Let us involve the entire community in a rededication of efforts to meet the challenges at hand so as to guide our institutions to nobler goals in the years ahead.

For the past twelve years, I have served as a trustee of a public university and for ten of those years have been board chairman. It has been an honor and a privilege for me to have had this opportunity, and the exposure to academic life has been most rewarding. I have devoted much time and effort to the duties of trusteeship and have been glad to do so. At times I have been subjected to pressures and criticisms, but this has not greatly concerned me since my shoulders are sufficiently broad. Our university has grown substantially over these years both in size and quality. I have seen the rapid development of the graduate programs and the recent opening of a school of medicine and dental medicine. All of this has been tremendously rewarding.

I do have some fears and apprehensions about the present and future position of higher education, especially because it is being attacked from so many sides. My fervent hope is that there will continue to be sufficient people in the educational domain—faculty, administrators, trustees, and students—who are loyal and dedicated to the noblest principles and who are willing to give the devoted service and support needed to carry us into a brighter future.

The Black Revolt and the Student Revolt in Perspective

T. E. McKINNEY, JR.

ONE OF THE DICTIONARIES defines *revolution* as, among other things, an extensive or drastic change in a condition, method, or idea. In this same sense both American students and black Americans have been in a state of revolt for some time. Today these revolts can be viewed clearly enough to see that they involve drastic changes in traditionally accepted methods and ideas concerning well-established patterns of college and university organization and educational leadership. For both students and black Americans, the revolt has arisen from circumstances that have led the protesters to decide that the last traces of evil must be eliminated.

Among students, the revolt is against the institutional structures of present-day society, especially the patterns of university and collegiate organization. For black Americans, revolt emanates from unwillingness to accept the remnants of a segregated society and its implications. In both cases, protesters have embraced new methodology and have armed themselves with new weapons in combating previously accepted patterns of institutional organization and leadership. The revolts have been directed against established institutions and leadership, including those of higher education, as part of the status quo. The protests themselves constitute weapons that, though they accomplish some gains, have proved incapable of dealing with basic problems of contemporary society including racism, segregation, and violence.

To suggest that the revolt among students and among blacks is directed against certain methods and the institutions that have sponsored them in the past does not say that the two groups of protesters have completely abandoned or turned against the institutions. It means rather that both blacks and students have demanded practical changes that conventional leadership and institutions have debated rather than acted on. While established leaders and Negro leaders were still locked in methodological debates, rank-and-file protesters moved on their own, employing new tactics and achieving incomparable results. Consequently, established leadership in higher education as well as established leadership among Negroes stands in the position of the oddly dressed man who said to a bystander, "Please tell me which way the parade went; after all, I'm leading it."

Both the American student revolt and the American Negro revolt constitute part of worldwide uprisings that hold significant domestic implications. In each case the protester holds grievances against the conventional leadership and the established institutions of society. The grievances have received recent and bitter expression in the form of open and bloody conflicts on university campuses, around the world, and in the form of riots and other violence in major urban and metropolitan areas. In a very real sense, the present generations of college and university students and of young black people hold the key to a strikingly different and newly emerging world order. It is only to the degree that the question of popular participation in solving the problems of modern society is admitted to and resolved in terms posed by both black and student protesters that the likelihood—and even probability—of a world free from conflict and violence will be increased. The sit-in demonstrations of almost ten years ago illustrate a significant convergence of the student revolt and the Negro revolt. On February 1, 1960, four black freshmen from the Agricultural and Technical College at Greensboro, North Carolina, walked into the local Woolworth store and sat down at the lunch counter reserved exclusively for the use of whites. When they were told to move, they refused. When the manager closed down the counter, the students opened their textbooks and began to study their lessons. When the local radio station interrupted its program to flash the news, scores of other students from A&T College poured into town and joined the demonstration. This incident was a historic occasion in American higher education as a revolt against segregation and entrenched leadership.

Although the sit-in demonstrations at Greensboro were spontaneous, students succeeded in rallying the support of adult assistance including aid from well-established civil rights organizations. As a result of the sit-ins, which spread to every state in the Deep South and to several border states during the spring of 1960, more and more people became convinced that direct mass action was a shorter and more effective route to the goal of desegregation than the previous legalistic approaches through cases submitted to the Supreme Court. The increasingly popular view became that any and all kinds of demonstrations and direct action by youth, adults, and everybody else in this grave discrimination were badly needed and ought to be supported by all Americans. The sit-ins were a major and decisive victory for college students. They constituted a rousing triumph over segregation and a victory for direct and clear-cut action. The sit-in demonstrations marked, perhaps, the end of an era of traditional leadership and the beginning of a period of expanded popular participation by students and blacks in every aspect of American life. Two immediate and unexpected results of the sit-in movement were the organization of the Student Nonviolent Coordinating Committee as a protest organization formed by students, and the development of sophisticated approaches to promote adult support of student activities through such mechanisms as economic boycotts. These developments have also helped bring about a shift in leadership from hand-picked institutional leaders such as university and college presidents to leaders more representative of a wider community—in this particular case, representatives of the wider Negro community.

The most severe pains created by the Negro revolt and the student revolt stem from cleavages that have developed within society at large, involving institutions that have served their time well but have now fallen into disfavor because they are inexplicably tied to the status quo. Among these institutions must be counted the colleges and universities, along with mass media, political structures, and churches. A key factor for the future of all organizations and people is whether they can change and develop new goals and plans to meet rapidly changing conditions. Colleges and universities have a vital role to perform in instructing masses of people in the art of first-class citizenship. Only when Negroes and students accept their responsibilities along with their rights can the victory of these two simultaneous revolts be enjoyed.

Life is process, and in the process of correcting and restructuring our colleges and universities, we activate the forces that will preserve humanity and modern civilization. The crisis of modern man is spiritual. The surface conflicts of black versus white, East versus West, students versus administration, are only symptoms of an illness that afflict all the world. The basic disease is man's continuing inhumanity to man, the perpetual assault upon the dignity of some individuals by other more powerful individuals and institutions. The powerful political, economic, and social forces that have combined to produce inhuman treatment must now be restructured to stop it. They must now be manipulated to bar such evils as racism and political domination in the contemporary world.

PART FIVE

FROM THE FEDERAL VIEW

Challenge and Response
in the American Educational Environment

ROBERT H. FINCH

To come to grips with one urgent problem, the campus and the racial crisis, is to range outward over the totality of our concerns as a nation. All groups within our society—every minority, every race, and ever-greater numbers of the preponderant Middle Americans—are demanding of our schools that they do better with their traditional assignments and, at the same time, that they take on new ones. Our schools are at the spear-point in the thrust toward equal justice, broader opportunities, more diverse life styles—toward the fulfillment of a new American Dream.

The problems of the campus are, then, deeply linked with the nation's quest for racial justice and with all the other unresolved problems that constitute the nation's agenda of unfinished business. This is, as it always has been, the dimension of the burdens we impose on our educational institutions. In light of the challenges, it is wise to move directly to consideration of *how* change can occur. Whether we like it or not, change *will* occur. We can influence only how orderly and how thoughtful it will be.

I set as my task here an attempt to define the parameters of the social environment in which the institutional response will take place. I want to help articulate the problems—to ask what tasks our educational institutions can and should undertake. And, equally, the question must be considered of the tasks our educational institutions cannot and should *not* undertake. Tough-mindedness is an exquisite virtue, and sometimes it counsels us against indulging the luxury of raising expectations that cannot be fulfilled.

Let me note three key factors that I see currently affecting our institutions of higher education.

The first is the state of preparation of the entering student. Through such studies as the Coleman Report and its many subsequent critiques, we are beginning to learn a good deal about the strengths and weaknesses of the nation's elementary and secondary school systems. Much of the record—particularly in the area of compensatory education for the disadvantaged—

is dismaying or, at the least, one of lack of success. But the problem is not alone that of the disadvantaged. Children now mature faster; they pile up thousands of hours of TV; they live in a totally new social environment. Yet the structure of elementary and secondary instruction is substantially the same today as it was for their parents and even their grandparents. We sense, with some evidence, that the system works badly. Even worse, we do not really know *how* it works or even how to *measure* its level of performance. We operate in ignorance.

The second factor is the growing acceptance of the proposition that all qualified young Americans have a positive right to some form of higher education. This development is astounding, even in a nation always noted for its egalitarianism. American colleges and universities always have opened their doors wider than their counterparts in other countries. But we talk increasingly as if selectivity should end altogether—as if our institutions of higher education should be the great equalizers of opportunity for all Americans.

The implications of this trend are enormous. We will have to find new ways for young people to finance their education—at a time when educational costs are rising. We may require new standards for academic admission—and perhaps new standards for graduation, as well. Beyond this we will have to provide each entering student with something like an equal chance to profit from his educational experience, and this involves more than making higher education meaningful to members of racial minorities. We also must educate increasing numbers of students—of all ages—whose cultural backgrounds are in some sense alien to the ivied walls.

To do so, we will have to commit ourselves to increasing the variety and diversity of educational experience and bettering the quality of every form. In precisely this spirit, the Nixon administration in 1970 will offer major legislative initiatives for the rapid evolution of the community college. These will be multifaceted institutions, with a strong career orientation and with a built-in capability of responding to the differing needs of many different constituencies. The community college will add substance to our commitment to broader educational opportunity.

In 1975, there will be six college students for every five at present. If all we have to offer the Class of '79 is today's program only in larger classes, we will have failed our responsibilities. Worse, we will have jeopardized the order and structure of all our campuses, and nourished the view of some young people that they should receive their education in gypsy encampments of their own making.

A third key factor, equally momentous, is the growing extent to which we look to our colleges and universities to control access to full participation in our society. In part, to be sure, a college education *is* necessary in order to live the full and good life in a sophisticated "postindustrial" society. It is hard to be a consumer, let alone a participant in civic life, without the attitudes and the information that higher education provides.

But college education has also become mandatory simply because we have come to depend on college degrees as indices of an individual's potential, status, and even his personal worth. A student knows the grave risks he will run throughout the rest of his life if he leaves the campus and drops out. The working man outside college knows all too well the ties between academic credentials and upward mobility.

In a real sense, then, we are assigning to our colleges and universities the license of playing Providence over the lives of us all. I do not think it is in the interests of either our schools or our nation to let this simply happen as a result of social pressures. Is it not possible for higher education to enter the span of human life at many points and on a much more "elective" basis? Might not our young people be better off if we could discourage the notion that schooling *is* education, rather than one *form* of education?

If we do not have answers to this range of questions, then perhaps we must find them—must, ultimately, redesign our institutions to accommodate these trends. In all likelihood, the trends will not cease running, and the alternative would be an intolerably polarized society. H. G. Wells once prophesied that "Human history becomes more and more a race between education and catastrophe." How terribly ironic it would be if education, or the gap between the educated and the uneducated, were to become the focal point of catastrophe.

Even as I state these concerns, I realize how immense are the demands on all our social institutions, and how limited are the Federal resources for meeting these expectations. We are turning the corner in the President's dedicated search for peace in Vietnam, but the post-Vietnam bonus on whatever scale will not be available tomorrow. Thus the increasing sense of urgency about all our unresolved problems—poverty, crime, environmental abuse, to name just a few—creates agonizing pressure in the competition for Federal dollars.

It is a truism in politics that where one sits conditions what one sees and believes. And thus, as we look forward to the time when our social energies can be focused mainly on our internal problems, leading groups are requesting that space be provided for them on the next Federal vehicle for a trip to the moon. But who shall go first, and who second, and how are we to take care of the crowds? Having spent the past several months trying to arrange trips for a few of these groups—including college and university administrators and their future students—I am impressed with how distant the goal is, and how difficult it is going to be for the Federal government to increase its share of the fare.

The issues I have described add up thus: Our colleges and universities are being subjected to expectations that they should serve as great equalizers of opportunity, that they should exercise a sort of providential influence over people's lives. Indeed, educators themselves have created expectations that they can tackle the most intractable problems of our society. These expectations imply enormous new responsibilities. And I see some of our educational leaders gradually attempting to assume these responsibilities, without much protest, and perhaps without being fully candid with the American people about the limits—as well as the potentialities—of the institutions they represent.

I am not a college president, but let me pretend for a moment that I am in order to relate my thoughts to your problems.

If I were a college president, before I took on something altogether new, I would reexamine how well my campus was doing the old things. I would ask what the new things implied for the already difficult tasks we have. I would ask whether the money and organizational ingenuity involved might not be better spent doing the old things better. And I would take on only those new things I could do well.

Facing up to racial problems in this mood, I would be careful not to confuse commitment with immodesty. Putting it another way, I would not assume that intensive efforts need imply extensive goals. If my institution were especially well equipped to teach auto mechanics, I would do everything possible to improve courses and expand opportunities in this field.

I would think of admission as a promise, and would regard the recruitment of black students and members of other minorities as the beginning, not the end, of special concern with these students. I would not assume that they could be taught traditional subjects by traditional methods. Rather, I would search for new ways to help them seek their own special relationship with their history and their aspirations.

If I were a college president, I might hope for more Federal aid, but I would hedge my bets. I would attempt to enlist private sources of support, and do a better job with whatever resources I had. I would even dare to ask whether it might be possible to reduce the costs while upgrading the quality of higher education. I would explore ways to arrange faculty and students in different patterns.

I would hope that I would be big enough to take a large view of the problems of meeting the educational needs of black America. Does it make sense for our prestigious universities to raid the small Negro colleges for their best teachers and scholars? These, after all, are the institutions that struggled for so long, alone, to bring the dream of higher education to black America. The problems are complex, but my feeling is that this sort of competition among our colleges and universities may be weakening rather than strengthening the capacities of our whole system to serve the needs of black Americans. I have made a strong personal appeal to the private foundations to support "return incentives," to make studying and teaching at the traditional Negro colleges an attractive, viable alternative.

If I were a college president, I would be deeply concerned about questions of university governance, about the campus as a political and legal community. I would be concerned to know who, on a continuing basis, is running the shop—administration or faculty. I would inquire—again without suggesting that I have even isolated the range of potential answers—whether or not a faculty elite is entitled to ask both for tenure and for teachers unions. And based on my personal experience as a trustee and a regent, I would also ask whether faculties, as collective entities, have always behaved responsibly in urging their students toward precipitous courses of action, only to "opt out" themselves when consequences that should have been anticipated begin to appear.

Finally, if I were a college president, I would challenge the notion that higher education should be allowed to determine the fate of our youth. I would ponder how growing up might be made more tolerable and productive for young people not attending college, and I would want society to strengthen other institutions as viable alternatives to higher education. And I would try to do this even if it goes against the grain of habit, against the persuasions of flattery, even against the boast that someone—the academic community, one supposes—must save the nation. For the fact is that we all must save the nation.

The questions concerned with the campus and the racial crisis also are questions with which our society must grapple—as they were, indeed, long before they exploded on the campus. The challenges are infinitely greater than before, and the time-frame within which they must be confronted, and accommodated, is dangerously short.

It may be that depending merely on the traditional processes of problem resolution, merely on the good will of narrow elites, will no longer produce acceptable solutions. But one thing is clear—if history imparts any lessons: we cannot allow these questions to be settled in the streets.

We all must save the nation—with burning dedication and commitment —through institutions truly open to all who would participate in good faith.

Higher Education—A View from Washington

JAMES E. ALLEN, JR.

IN ADDRESSING my subject, I should note that my position in New York State, before I came to Washington, included responsibility for higher education, and so the problems of administrators of institutions of higher education have long been my concern also. Here, however, I shall view higher education from the new perspective afforded by my position in Washington.

The most significant dimension of this new perspective has been the confirmation of my feeling of optimism concerning the future of higher education. Despite uncertainties and formidable problems that abound in both the present and future of higher education, this *is* a time of opportunity. In the present situation there are constraints—particularly financial ones—that must influence immediate operations, but the long-range picture encourages the hope that the needs we foresee for higher education can be met. We *are* searching for new patterns of financial support to enable all who can profit from postsecondary school education to have it, whatever their economic or social circumstances. Developing exactly the right pattern for sharing the financial responsibility for higher education between the private citizen and his government and among the various levels of government will, however, undoubtedly involve a considerable period of trial and error.

The important thing, in my view, is the strength and clarity of the national commitment to higher education—a commitment transcending partisanship, a commitment expressed by the last administration and reaffirmed by President Nixon. It has been evidenced in many other ways as well: Section 508 of the Higher Education Amendments of 1968 required the President to submit to the Congress by the end of 1969 "proposals relative to the feasibility of making available a postsecondary education to all young Americans who qualify and seek it"; in October 1969 a Presidential Task Force on Higher Education, headed by President James Hester of New York University, was appointed; and plans are under way in the Department of Health,

Education, and Welfare for the development of a "comprehensive Community College Career Education Act of 1970."

Of perhaps greater significance to the character and quality of future higher education opportunities is the atmosphere of change that is pervading the campuses of our nation. In justification of many college administrators and faculty, it should be noted that many of the reforms being advocated have long been proposed and sought. This period of widespread dissatisfaction and unrest is providing the possibility to achieve a fundamental restructuring and revitalization of our postsecondary school programs and institutions.

Yet the perspective that affirmed my optimism also brings into sharper focus certain hazards that could frustrate our hopes for making the most of this time of opportunity. These hazards will lie in our failure (1) to plan for change, and (2) to prepare the way for change, that is, to decide where we want to go and how to make it possible to get there.

Planning is, of course, always necessary to orderly development, and never has it been more essential or more difficult than now. The kind of objectivity required in planning is hard to come by when much of the time and energy of those responsible is being consumed with reacting to and dealing with the immediate pressure and the far-reaching results of campus unrest. In addition, uncertainty about financial support is raising questions not only of the adequacy of support but also of the effects of changing patterns on sources of support. Underlying all these difficulties of planning is the knowledge that the future we are attempting to chart will see change to the extent that our system of higher education may be totally transformed.

Rather than serving as any justification for either timidity or delay in planning, the very nature of these difficulties emphasizes its importance and the imperative need to be objective, judicious, selective, and—most of all—unpanicked.

The Department of Health, Education, and Welfare, particularly the Office of Education, has, I believe, a definite responsibility in helping to chart the future of higher education. In the past few months we have moved both to strengthen our general capability for this function and to initiate a number of studies and programs. A brief sampling will help indicate the range.

A new Office of Deputy Assistant Secretary/Commissioner for Planning, Research, and Evaluation has been created to improve the coordination of these essential functions. This office will give increased attention to higher education, concentrating not only on research and development, but also on better means of making the results of research and development available to the policy-makers and administrators in the field. This office will foster the development of a variety of experimental models as new approaches to reform and change in higher education.

The Bureau of Higher Education will be strengthened by the creation of the position of Deputy Commissioner for Higher Education, whose primary function will be to assist in the formulation of plans and policies in this field.

The increasing importance of the community and junior colleges in the total American educational enterprise is to be recognized by the establishment of a special high-level unit in the Office of Education to serve this area.

A Committee on Campus Unrest has been appointed for the purpose of examining all ways in which the Department of Health, Education, and Welfare can respond constructively and promptly when the need arises for Federal assistance.

An Office of Students and Youth has been established in the Office of Education, staffed by students and youth, whose assignment is to maintain an open channel to young people across the nation and to see that HEW policies and programs reflect the needs and views of students and youth.

Also contemplated is the setting aside of a modest amount of research funds for financing student-sponsored projects, administered by youth and students.

These activities of the Office of Education provide some indication of the directions in which higher education is moving. They also reflect principles and needs which must be guideposts for higher education's future course:

- Increasing access to higher education opportunities for all qualified youth.
- Developing realistic means for the involvement of all parts of the academic community in the formulation and administration of programs and activities.
- Removing all vestiges of injustice, discrimination, and prejudice in the treatment of disadvantaged groups.
- Actively involving the higher education community in the special problems of society, particularly urban problems.
- Preserving academic freedom and institutional autonomy.
- Retaining and encouraging the diversity and innovation provided by our system of dual control in higher education.
- Reinforcing the continuing need for support from all sectors of society, public and private.

To consider these principles and needs is to realize the enormity of the task of melding such variety and scope into a coordinated, clear plan for the future of postsecondary education. We must, however, address ourselves to the task, for the day is past when noble sentiments and generalized statements of need will engender the necessary support. The realization of the potential of this time of opportunity depends in large measure on our ability to translate our decisions about the future of higher education into definite plans of action.

The preparation and presentation of plans will remove only one of the hazards that could thwart our hopes. The magnitude and novelty of plans that foresee a really new day in higher education preclude easy or automatic approval, and the forces of education must accept the necessity for a more concentrated effort to marshal support. This effort itself will face formidable obstacles. First to be overcome will be a pervasive and debilitating lack of confidence in the efficacy of much of our present system which, justified or not, has crept into public thinking. Financial support sought amidst an ever-greater competition for both public and private funds will be won only by the most cogent, well-reasoned, and persuasive case. Also to be overcome is the natural resistance to change. The extent of resistance is determined by the degree of change, and change of the magnitude contemplated for higher education can thus be expected to generate resistance of massive proportions.

Our success in overcoming the obstacles will depend on finding an answer to how the forces of education can best use their power to achieve their goals. Indeed my experience convinces me that this is one of the most important challenges we face.

The forces of education have the potential of enormous power, stemming from the nature of education itself, from an inherent respect for the educator, and from the vast numbers of individuals associated with the education enterprise. In my opinion, however, this potential has not been realized. Power has been underused, diffused, dissipated, and too often diverted from fundamental considerations to special interests and relatively minor matters.

If the forces of higher education are to prepare the way for an acceptance of their plans for the future, every bit of power at their command must be put to use. The concentration of their power on the achievement of goals cannot be left to chance but must be systematically programed into the overall thrust of their efforts. So many needs, ideas, and goals are competing for support in these turbulent times of social change that it can no longer be assumed that education will have its rightful place or be allotted its rightful share of support. Our voices must be heard, not just at times of special crisis, but steadily in a way that will keep educational considerations in the forefront of both public and governmental thinking and be an ever-present, continuing influence on the course of the development of education.

In conclusion, then, may I state once more the feeling of optimism that my Washington perspective gives on the future of higher education in our nation. The hazards of failure to plan with sufficient conciseness and clarity or to take those actions which will prepare the way for fulfillment of plans are very real.

Very real also, however, is the recognition among the members of the higher education community that this is indeed a time of opportunity—a recognition that has generated a growing openness to change and a spirit of determination to overcome whatever hazards or obstacles lie in the way of honoring our responsibility to provide postsecondary educational opportunity for all those who qualify and seek it.

From those frantic postwar days of accommodating a flood of GI students, through a period of unprecedented building and expansion of facilities, into these days of efforts to adapt to a period of fundamental social change, higher education has a remarkable record of success in meeting its obligations to the youth of our nation and to society. With even greater demands ahead, I am confident that we shall not now fail to continue this record of success that has contributed so much to the progress of our nation.

AMERICAN COUNCIL ON EDUCATION

LOGAN WILSON, *President*

The American Council on Education, founded in 1918, is a *council* of educational organizations and institutions. Its purpose is to advance education and educational methods through comprehensive voluntary and cooperative action on the part of American educational associations, organizations, and institutions.